Educational Cooperation between Developed and Developing Countries

H. M. Phillips

Educational Cooperation between Developed and Developing Countries

with a chapter by Francis J. Method

Praeger Publishers   New York   Washington   London

PRAEGER SPECIAL STUDIES IN INTERNATIONAL ECONOMICS AND DEVELOPMENT

Library of Congress Cataloging in Publication Data

Phillips, Herbert Moore, 1908-
    Educational cooperation between developed and
developing countries.

    (Praeger special studies in international economics
and development)
    Bibliography: p.
    1. Underdeveloped areas—Education.   2. Educational
exchanges.   3. Educational assistance.   I. Title.
LC2605.P45   370.19'6   75-19807
ISBN 0-275-55900-9

PRAEGER PUBLISHERS
111 Fourth Avenue, New York, N.Y. 10003, U.S.A.

Published in the United States of America in 1976
by Praeger Publishers, Inc.

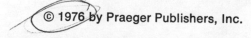

FOREWORD
F. Champion Ward

The prevailing spirit of the "Second Development Decade" unites operational persistence with growing self-criticism on the part of the "development community." Second efforts are matched by second thoughts in the face of second-generation problems not anticipated in the period of uncomplicated striving with which the age of development began. At more or less the same time, programs of industrialization, population control, and agricultural production have all reached their moments of self-doubt.

Nor has education been spared this chastening. Meeting in 1972 at Bellagio, Italy, principal officers of some 15 "agencies assisting education" and a number of individual educators from the developing countries initiated a series of meetings and other activities designed to explore and clarify a number of "areas of uncertainty" concerning education and its relationship to the social and economic development of third-world nations. Papers prepared for these meetings have since been published under the title Education and Development Reconsidered (New York: Praeger Publishers, 1974). Prominent among these areas of uncertainty is the question of the "redeployment" of assistance to education by assistance agencies, and it was the author of the present volume who provided the seminal paper for the Bellagio discussions of this subject.

One of Mr. Phillips's theses is that the actual redeployment of resources and the actual revision of procedures by complex agencies follow only slowly and painfully after the verbal proclamation of new priorities and reformed methods. No one is better placed to describe this lag with accuracy and to help reduce its length than Mr. Phillips. An inveterate agency-watcher, he is not content with mere watching. Rather, he is best seen as an analyst whose criticisms are directed to the thoroughgoing adaptation of practice to policy, and of both to the real state of education.

Following the first meeting at Bellagio, a number of participating agencies encouraged the Ford Foundation to make it possible for Mr. Phillips to give his time and attention to the writing of a book on external assistance to education. The Foundation was happy to do so, for the years since 1972 have made it clear that changes in actual practice not only take time but will not occur at all unless the case for them is persistently put forward by sympathetic, semi-detached analysts, and counselors like the author of this book.

F. Champion Ward is Program Advisor in Education for The Ford Foundation.

ACKNOWLEDGMENTS

The author expresses his appreciation to the Ford Foundation and especially to Mr. F. Champion Ward, who kindly wrote the Foreword, for their sponsorship and support given to the book, though the views expressed are not necessarily theirs. He is also very grateful to Mr. Francis J. Method, at the time a member of the Foundation staff, with whom much of the book was discussed in detail and whose valuable comments were drawn upon at various points. He has contributed the results of a study made in Indonesia, and these appear as Chapter 11. Much appreciation is also due to many officials and commentators from both ends of the cooperation network whose views and information contributed to the study. Thanks are also due to Elena Giglioli, who helped in the collection of the material and typed the manuscript.

CONTENTS

LIST OF TABLES

ACRONYMS AND ABBREVIATIONS OF AGENCIES CONCERNED

AAEA   African Adult Education Association

AAU   Association of African Universities

ACC   Administrative Committee on Coordination (UN)

ADB   African Development Bank

ADB   Asian Development Bank

ADC   Asian Development Centre

ADETOM   Association pour le Developpement de l'Enseignement
Technique Outre Mer

AEDF   Asian Economic Development Fund

AEOM   Association pour l'Etude des Problemes d'Outre Mer

AESTE   International Association for Exchange of Students for
Technical Experience (U.K.)

AFSC   American Friends Service Committee

AID   Agency for International Development (U.S.), formerly
ICA

AIDE   Association Interamericano de Educacion

AIR-Rand   American Institute for Research-Rand Corporation

ALESCO   Arab League Educational, Cultural, and Scientific
Organization

ALFIN   Program of Integral Literacy (Peru)

APEID   Asian Program for Educational Innovation for Development

APO   Asian Productivity Organization

ASFEC   Arab States Fundamental Education Centre (Egypt)

ASMIC   Association pour l'Organisation des Missions de
Cooperation Technique

ASTEF	Association pour l'Organisation des Stagees en France
AUCAM	Association Universitaire Catholique d'Amitie Mondiale
AUDECAM	Association Universitaire pour le Developpement de l'Enseignement et de la Culture an Afrique et a Madagascar
AUPELF	Association des Universites Partiellement ou Entierement de Langue Francaise
BTAO	Bureau of Technical Assistance Operations (UN)
BVP	British Volunteer Programme
CAD	Comite d'Aide au Developpement (of OECD)
CAEM	Conseil d'Assistance Economique Mutuelle
CAFRAD	Centre Africain de Formation et de Recherches Administratives pour le Developpement
CAMES	Conseil Africain et Malgache pour l'Enseignement Superieur
CAT	Comite de l'Assistance Technique de l'ONU (UN)
CCCET	Catholic Coordinating Committee for the Sending of Technicians
CCIA	Commission of the Churches on International Affairs
CCIC	Comite Catholique International de Coordination aupres de l'Unesco
CEC	Commonwealth Education Cooperation
CEC	Commission of European Communities
CEDEU	Centre d'Etude des Problemes des Pays en Developpement
CEDO	Centre for Educational Development Overseas (U.K.)
CEIA	Centre d'Entr'aide Intellectuelle Africaine
CENATRA	Centre National d'Assistance Technique et de Recherche Appliquee (Belgium)

CEPIA	Coordination Etudiante des Programmes Inter-Americains (Coordination of Inter-American Student Programmes, CIASP)
CESD	Centre Europeen pour la Formation de Statisticiens-Economistes pour les Pays en voie de Developpement (France)
CFAM	Centre de formation pour Africaines at Malgaches
CFECTI	Centre de Formation des Experts de la Cooperation Technique Internationale
CFEI	Centre de Formation et d'Echanges Internationaux
CFL	Centre Chretien de Formation pour Laics au Service des Pays en voie de Developpement
CFTC	Commonwealth Fund for Technical Cooperation
CIDA	Canadian International Development Agency
CIEO	Catholic International Education Office
CIMADE	Service Oecumenique d'Entr'aide
CMEA	Council for Mutual Economic Assistance
COMECON	Council for Mutual Economic Aid (USSR)
CONUP	Peruvian National University Council
CRSVI	Conference Regionale du Service Voluntaire International
CTETOC	Council for Technical Education and Training for Over-seas Countries (U.K.)
CWS	Church World Service (National Council of Churches)
DAAD	Deutscher Akademischer Austrauscholienst (German Academic Exchange Service)
DAC	Development Assistance Committee (OECD)
DED	Deutscher Entwicklungsdienst, Gemeinnutzige Gesell-schaft (German Volunteer Service)

DEG	Deutsche Gesellschaft fur Wirtschaftliche Zusammen-arbeit (Entwichlungs gesellschaft)
DESAL	Centro para el Desarrollo Economico
DSE	Deutsche Stiftung fur Entwicklungslander (German Foundation for Developing Countries)
DTC	Department of Technical Cooperation (U.K.)
ECA	Economic Commission for Africa
ECAFE	Economic Commission for Asia and the Far East (UN-Thailand)
ECLA	Economic Commission for Latin America (UN) Commission Economique pour l'Amerique Latin Comision Economica para America Latina (Santiago, Chile)
ECME	Economic Commission for the Middle East (UN)
ECOSOC	Economic and Social Council (UN)
EDI	Economic Development Institute of IBRD
EEC	European Economic Community Communaute Economique Europeen Europaische Wirtschaftsgemeinschaft
EPTA	Expanded Program of Technical Assistance (UN, now UNDP)
ESAN	Escuela Superior de Administracion y Negocios
ESEP	Higher Schools of Professional Education (Peru)
FAC	Fonds d'Aide et de Cooperation
FAO	Food and Agriculture Organization
FNDC	Fonds National pour la Cooperation au Developpement
FSC	Friends Service Council

FUNDWI	Fund of the United Nations for the Development of West Irian
GATT	General Agreement on Tariffs and Trade
GUE	Grandes Unidades Escalores
IABE	Ibero-American Bureau of Education
IAEVI	International Association for Educational and Vocational Information
IASTE	International Association for the Exchange of Students for Technical Experience
IAU	International Association of Universities
IBE	International Bureau of Education
IBRD	International Bank for Reconstruction and Development
ICA	International Cooperative Alliance
ICAP	Inter-American Committee on the Alliance for Progress
ICED	International Council for Educational Development
ICFTU	International Confederation of Free Trade Unions
IDA	International Development Association Association Internationale pour le Developpement Asociacion Internacional de Forrento
IDB	Inter-American Development Bank Banque Inter-americaine de Developpement
IDRC	International Development Research Centre (Canada)
IEA	International Association for the Evaluations of Educational Achievement
IEDES	Institut d'Etudes du Developpement Economique et Social
IFC	International Finance Corporation

IFCT	Institut Francais de Cooperation Technique
IFCTU	International Federation of Christian Trade Unions
IFCU	International Federation of Catholic Universities
IFFTU	International Federation of Free Teachers Unions
IFWEA	International Federation of Workers' Educational Associations
IGGI	Inter-Governmental Group for Indonesia
IIEP	International Institute for Educational Planning
ILO	International Labour Organisation
ILPES	Instituto Latinoamericana de Planificacion Economica y Social
IMF	International Monetary Fund
INACAP	Instituto Nacional de Capacitacion Profesional (Chile)
INADES	Institut Africain pour le Developpement Economique et Social
INIDE	National Institute of Research and Educational Development
INNOTECH	Regional Center for Educational Innovation and Technology (Saigon)
IPPF	International Planned Parenthood Federation
ISA	International Schools Association
ISVS	International Secretariat for Volunteer Service
IUC	Inter-University Council for Higher Education Overseas
IVS	International Voluntary Service (Switzerland)
IVS	International Voluntary Services (Washington, D.C.)

LWR	Lutheran World Relief
NESBIC	Netherlands Students' Bureau for International Cooperation
NIER	Japanese National Institute of Education Research
OAS	Organization of American States
ODA	Overseas Development Administration
OECD	Organisation for Economic Cooperation and Development
RECSAM	Regional Center for Education in Science and Mathematics (Penang)
RELC	Regional English Language Center (Singapore)
SCAAP	Special Commonwealth African Assistance Program
SEAMEC	Southeast Asian Ministers of Education Council
SEAMEO	Southeast Asian Ministers of Education Organisation
SEAMES	Southeast Asian Ministers of Education Secretariat
SEARCA	Regional Center for Graduate Study and Research in Agriculture (Los Bamos)
SECPANE	Servicio Cooperativo Peruano Norte-Americano de Educacion (Peru)
SENA	Servicio Nacional de Aprendizage (Colombia)
SGBT	Indonesian Teacher Training Institute
SID	Society for International Development
SIDA	Swedish International Development Authority
SIL	Summer Institute of Linguistics
TAICH	Technical Assistance Information Clearing House

TANCA	Technical Assistance to Non-Commonwealth Countries in Africa
TETOC	Organisation for Technical Education and Training in Overseas Countries
TSP	Total Systems Programing
TROPMED	Regional Project for Tropical Medicine and Public Health (Bangkok)
TUFEC	Thai-UNESCO Fundamental Education Center
UNCTAD	United Nations Conference on Trade and Development
UNDP	United Nations Development Programme
UNESCO	United Nations Educational, Scientific, and Cultural Organization
UNICEF	United Nations Children's Fund
USAID	United States Agency for International Development
WCOTP	World Confederation of Organizations of the Teaching Profession
WFP	World Food Program
WFTU	World Federation of Teachers' Unions
WHO	World Health Organization

PART

I

THE OVERALL SCENE:
TRENDS, NEEDS,
AND POLICIES

Educational cooperation in the form of assistance from the more to the less developed countries has been an important feature of development policy for the last 20 years. It has shared in the problems and difficulties of overall development aid and those of other individual sectors. But it has also shown a considerable degree of independence from them, growing at times when overall aid and the other sectors have declined and progressing steadily to become, after 20 years, by a slight margin over agriculture the largest single sector[1] of bilateral official aid.

In what follows the words "educational cooperation for development" are used to describe the flow of educational resources (such as teachers, expertise, equipment, loans, fellowships, and grants) between the developed and the developing countries. The word "cooperation" implies equal partnership, mutual responsibility, and common interest and rightly has replaced for some years* old expressions based on conceptions of tutelage and the notion of aid as charity.

On the other hand, it is not possible to drop entirely the expression "donor and recipient countries" because we are analyzing a flow or transfer of resources and discussing the problems that arise at each end of the flow, as well as the process as a whole.

---

*A number of bilateral agencies have used the term "cooperation" for their activities for several years, and the Pearson Commission set up by the World Bank titled its report Partners in Development in 1969. The Development Assistance Committee changed the title of its annual report from Development Assistance to Development Cooperation in 1972, though its own name remains the same.

It would conceivably be possible instead of "donors" to say each time "countries and agencies at the supply end of the cooperation network," and "countries at the receiving end of the cooperation network." This would lead to a very clumsy text, and we prefer to make it clear at the outset that the process should be cooperation and to use for convenience the expression "suppliers of aid" or "donor agencies," on the one hand, and "receivers of aid" or "recipient countries," on the other.

Moreover the word "aid," though not liked at the recipient end, has value at the supply end of the network. Many people are prepared to subscribe to the education of children in other countries without necessarily wanting to cooperate with the policies of governments with which they may be in strong disagreement.

This is illustrated by the case of Unicef (United Nations Children's Fund), the largest single provider of grants for the education of children, which has continued to receive contributions from and assist countries which are at war with each other. Since contributions to Unicef's general resources are not earmarked, the warring countries have, in effect, been aiding each others' children. The concept of "cooperation," with its air of negotiation and agreements between governments, should not be so used as to drive out words like "help" and "aid," necessary for the personal and humanitarian contributions,* even though the transfer of resources has to take place through governments.

The 20 years over which educational cooperation has grown have seen changes in needs, as the educational systems of the developing countries have evolved, and in methods of meeting them, as the cooperating partners, both recipient and donor, have extended their experience. Although the outlook is at present poor for cooperation for economic and social development on a world scale equal to the nature of the challenge, there is no reason to suppose that educational cooperation will not continue to play an important role and to continue to change.

In what follows we attempt to delineate and evaluate the experience hitherto and to trace the perspective for future needs and new methods. But there are some preliminary remarks that may seem obvious but that need to be made, since unless they are taken into account, there are risks of misunderstandings.

---

*A clear case of the distinction between cooperation with governments and humanitarian aid occurred under the government of Haile Selassie in Ethiopia, which for internal policy reasons of its own failed to report famine in certain provinces that international agencies were ready to assist.

It is quite common to read comments and criticisms about educational cooperation that envisage it as a homogeneous development instrument or process that is being used in a certain way and ought to be used differently. Actually, educational cooperation consists of a mass of individual transactions between a large number of countries, each with their own individual educational systems and educational needs, and many donor agencies (governmental and nongovernmental, bilateral and multilateral) with their own sources of finance and individual objectives and practices. There are at present 204 countries and territories in the world, according to the 1973 Unesco* Statistical Yearbook, each with its own system of education; and a widespread network of educational cooperation exists, covering both relatively simple lines of action such as language teaching and the promotion of cultural exchanges, and also more complex activities such as assistance in setting up new universities and technical institutes and the supply of foreign teachers, in order to fill gaps in the educational system.

Further, to be effective, recommendations have to be of a kind that can be applied by both of the cooperating partners in a set of transactions that have political as well as technical and diplomatic aspects. There is a considerable amount of purely technical aid, such as in science or technical education, but in matters of educational structure and planning and the selection of the educational level and type of project to be assisted, educational cooperation has to fit in with the educational policies of the developing countries, which in turn usually reflect political stances on development.

Moreover, except in the case of certain aid by voluntary organizations to the private sector, educational cooperation relates to the public educational system and therefore has to pass through official channels and public accounting procedures, especially as external aid usually means additional cost to the national budget. Educational aid can be innovative and usually should encourage experimentation rather than buttress old ideas, but, since it is fundamentally a diplomatic transaction between governmental agencies, the process is not as simple as if it were a straight educator-to-educator action.

The flow of educational cooperation around 1973 may be estimated as running at about $2,350 million annually. As we show later, this is the cost to the donors rather than necessarily the value to the recipients, and even in these terms there are both offsets and onsets to be added to this sum when it is analyzed in detail. Moreover, while there have been high returns on many cooperation projects,

---

*United Nations Educational, Scientific, and Cultural Organization.

others have failed or even done more harm than good. Nevertheless,
this effort, which costed in this way represents nearly 17 percent of
the educational budgets of all the developing countries, taken together,
is an important one, which could be of much greater significance if it
could increase its efficacy and respond better to new needs.

    International development relations are taking on a new aspect
following the shocks to the world economy caused by the energy
crisis. The United Nations called a Special Session in May 1974 to
review the economic state of the world and produced a Declaration
on the establishment of a New Economic Order, which commanded a
considerable consensus, though not all of the participants could agree
to all of its clauses.

    This Declaration states,

> We, the Members of the United Nations,
> Solemnly proclaim our united determination to
> work urgently for
>
> THE ESTABLISHMENT OF A NEW
> INTERNATIONAL ECONOMIC ORDER
>
> based on equity, sovereign equality, interde-
> pendence, common interest and cooperation among
> all States, irrespective of their economic and so-
> cial systems which shall correct inequalities and
> redress existing injustices, make it possible to
> eliminate the widening gap between the developed
> and the developing countries and ensure steadily
> accelerating economic and social development in
> peace and justice for present and future genera-
> tions. . . .

    It is clear that there can be no equitable economic and social
order in the world while the developing countries have large sections
of their populations living in a state of mass illiteracy and educational poverty, and do not have the necessary educational infrastructure to make use of their potential of human skills.

    The developing countries have been defined for the purposes of
aid policy by the United Nations as having less than $500 of gross na-
tional product per head of population, although it is recognized that
there are some countries with oil resources that have higher per-
capita product but are developing countries in the sense of having incomplete social infrastructures. This is a rough criterion by any
standard, and the concept of gross national product (GNP) as a measure of progress is subject to many qualifications, and notably as to
how national income is distributed, as the United Nations realizes

TABLE 1.1

School Enrollment Ratios

Per Capita[a] GNP	Number of Countries	Total Population in 1970 (millions)	Enrollment Ratios[b]								
			First Level			Second Level			Third Level		
			1960	1965	1970	1960	1965	1970	1960	1965	1970
I--Up to $120 (excluding India, Indonesia, Pakistan, Bangladesh)	25	168	34	39	43 (31)	4	5	5	0.3	0.3	0.4
India, Indonesia, Pakistan, Bangladesh	4	802	43	56	71 (63)	9	11	18	1.7	2.6	4.3
II--$121-250	23	287	67	79	83 (68)	9	14	19	2.1	3.0	5.6
III--$251-750	38	433	73	83	97 (77)	11	17	25	1.9	3.3	5.3
IV--$751-1,500	9	112	90	93	97 (80)	33	44	49	6.2	8.4	10.5
V--Over $1,500	24	625	100	100	100	58	65	83	17.0	23.7	30.2

[a]Countries in each group are as follows:

I--Afghanistan, Bangladesh, Botswana, Burma, Burundi, Chad, Dahomey, Ethiopia, the Gambia, Guinea, Haiti, India, Indonesia, Lesotho, Malawi, Mali, Nepal, Niger, Nigeria, Pakistan, Rwanda, Somalia, Sri Lanka, Sudan, Tanzania, Upper Volta, Yemen Arab Republic, People's Democratic Republic of Yemen, Zaire;

II--Bolivia, Central African Republic, Cameroon, Equatorial Guinea, Egypt, Ghana, Kenya, Khmer Republic, Republic of Korea, Liberia, Malagasy, Mauritania, Mauritius, Morocco, Philippines, Senegal, Sierra Leone, Swaziland, Thailand, Togo, Tunisia, Uganda, Republic of Vietnam;

III--Algeria, Bahrain, Brazil, Republic of China, People's Republic of Congo, Colombia, Costa Rica, Dominican Republic, Ecuador, El Salvador, Fiji, Gabon, Guatemala, Guyana, Honduras, Iran, Iraq, Ivory Coast, Jamaica, Jordan, Lebanon, Malaysia, Mexico, Nicaragua, Oman, Panama, Papua New Guinea, Paraguay, Peru, Portugal, Romania, Saudi Arabia, Syria, Turkey, Uruguay, Yugoslavia, Zambia;

IV--Argentina, Chile, Cyprus, Greece, Singapore, South Africa, Spain, Trinidad and Tobago, Venezuela;

V--Australia, Austria, Belgium, Canada, Denmark, Finland, France, Federal Republic of Germany, Iceland, Ireland, Israel, Italy, Japan, Kuwait, Libya, Luxembourg, Netherlands, New Zealand, Norway, Qatar, Sweden, United Arab Emirates, United Kingdom, United States.

[b]The enrollment ratios have been obtained by dividing the total enrollment at each level with the appropriate age group. These "gross" enrollment ratios are inflated by over-age students. For 1970, it has been possible to exclude the over-age students and estimate "net" enrollment ratios at the first level. The net ratios are indicated in parentheses and show that the over-age students form 10-20 percent of the total student body at the first level.

Source: Education Sector Working Paper, World Bank, December 1974, p. 17.

very well. In educational terms, this standard has a certain validity,
since there is a link between national income and degree of educational development, but there is no exact parallelism to be traced,
and considerable variations exist in educational development among
countries at similar income levels. These variations reflect differences of culture and types of economic and social systems with different histories.

The World Bank groups together, for the purpose of the world
picture, countries having up to $120 per capita income, divided in
turn into a group excluding India, Indonesia, Pakistan, and Bangladesh,
and another group including those four countries.

The school enrollment situation on this basis is shown in Table
1.1. Public expenditure on education per student is shown in Table
1.2. Illiteracy rates are shown in Table 1.3 for the population over
14 years of age.

TABLE 1.2

Public Expenditure in Education per Student
(U.S. dollars, current prices)

Countries Grouped by per Capita GNP	1960	1965	1970	Net Change 1960-70
I--Up to $120	16	21	18	+13%
II--$121-250	33	40	49	+49%
III--$251-750	43	58	57	+33%
IV--$751-1,500	114	165	179	+57%
V--Over $1,500	338	504	749	+121%
Group V amount as a multiple of Group I	21	24	42	--

Source: Education Sector Working Paper, World Bank, December 1974, p. 20.

TABLE 1.3

Estimated Number and Ratio of Illiterates in the
Developing World Around 1960 and 1970
(in millions)

	Developing Countries		Africa		Asia		Latin America	
Around 1960								
Males	295	50%	56	73%	224	45%	17	28%
Females	406	69%	68	88%	318	63%	23	37%
Total	701	59%	124	81%	542	55%	40	33%
Around 1970								
Males	306	40%	61	63%	231	37%	16	20%
Females	450	60%	82	84%	348	57%	23	27%
Total	756	50%	143	74%	579	47%	39	24%

Source: Education Sector Working Paper, World Bank, December 1974, p. 29.

The latest figures for educational progress in the developing countries at the time of writing in early 1975 are those for 1971, as shown in Tables 1.4 through 1.6. They show a decline in enrollments and a reduction of the proportion of GNP going to education, with a particularly acute situation as regards primary education.

It would seem that a crisis of educational imbalance is looming, which, by producing masses of young illiterates of marriageable age in the 1980s, may reverse the decline in population growth the UN has projected for the late 1980s and 1990s and touch off another population explosion.

The main sources of educational cooperation for development are official aid from government to government (bilateral aid), aid from intergovernmental agencies (for example, Unesco and the World Bank Group), and that given by nongovernmental organizations and philanthropic sources such as foundations. The sources and estimated amount of educational aid are shown in Table 1.7. Purely commercial arrangements (for instance, Ethiopia recruits Indians to teach English under private contracts) are not regarded as aid, though they imply a measure of cooperation. Voluntary assistance between universities and institutions without a grant element attached also are excluded.

TABLE 1.4

First-Level Enrollments

	1970	1971	Increase	Annual Percentage Increase	
	(thousands)			1971	Average 1965–71
Africa (excluding Arab states)	23,776	24,169	383	1.6	4.4
Asia (excluding Arab states)	135,314	137,450	2,136	1.6	4.6
Arab states	12,088	13,159	1,071	8.9	3.6
Latin America	43,314	45,343	2,029	4.7	4.6
Developing countries	201,453	207,002	5,549	2.8	4.4

Source: Unesco Statistical Yearbook, 1973.

TABLE 1.5

Annual Percentage Increase in Enrollments 1970–71 by Level

	First	Second	Third
Africa (excluding Arab states)	1.6	3.4	19.8
Asia (excluding Arab states)	1.6	4.6	17.7
Latin America	4.7	7.6	17.3
Arab states	8.9	7.2	17.5
Developing countries	2.8	7.1	19.5

Source: Unesco Statistical Yearbook, 1973.

TABLE 1.6

Estimated Population Growth Rates
1970-75--5-9 Age Group

Africa	3.0
Asia	3.1
Developing countries	3.0

Source: Unesco Statistical Yearbook, 1973.

The largest source of educational cooperation is the bilateral
flow from government to government, which accounted in 1973 for
60 percent of the total. France is the largest donor, followed by the
Federal Republic of Germany, the United States, the United Kingdom,
Belgium, Canada, the Scandinavian countries, the Netherlands, Australia, and the other members of the OECD (Organisation for Economic Cooperation and Development) Development Assistance Committee.* About $2.5 million of bilateral aid was channeled through
Unesco under Funds-in-Trust agreements.

The next largest source is nongovernmental organizations and
various nonprofitmaking and philanthropic foundations. No precise
figures are available, but drawing on estimates made earlier by the
OECD, it would seem likely that this source covers nearly a quarter
of annual educational assistance. Church and philanthropic societies
of various kinds make up most of the total. The Ford, Rockefeller,
and Carnegie Foundations have large programs of educational assistance.

The greater part of multilateral aid, which constituted in 1973
about a quarter of the total, consists of loans and long-term credits
from the World Bank Group (the International Bank for Reconstruction and Development and the International Development Association),
and the Inter-American Development Bank (see Table 1.7). The
other regional banks for Asia and Africa have not yet embarked on
educational assistance on any scale. the UNDP and Unicef also have
important programs undertaken in cooperation with Unesco, though
the amounts are only a small fraction of the bilateral and nongovernmental aid and of the loans and credits from the World Bank Group.

---

*Australia, Austria, Belgium, Canada, Denmark, France,
Germany, Italy, Japan, the Netherlands, Norway, Portugal, Sweden,
Switzerland, the United Kingdom, the United States, and the Com-
mission of the European Economic Community.

TABLE 1.7

Educational Assistance from Developed to
Developing Countries, 1973
(in millions of dollars)

Bilateral official	
Member countries of the Development Assistance Committee of the OECD	1,142
Centrally planned socialist economies	200 (estimate)[a]
Total bilateral official	1,342
Multilateral	
Unesco regular budget	14
United Nations Development Programme (UNDP) around	25[b]
World Bank Group	293.5
Inter-American Development Bank (IDB)	91
Unicef	22.1
World Food Programme (WFP)	50
UN Relief and Works Agency (UNWRA) for Palestine refugees in the Near East	29.7
Other international agencies (European Development Fund, Organization of American States, Southeast Asian Ministers of Education Organization, Asian Development Bank, ILO/Unesco, and FAO/Unesco projects)	50 (estimate)[a]
Total multilateral aid approximately	600
Nongovernmental	400 (estimate)[a]
Approximate grand total	2,350 (estimate)[a]

[a]Estimates made by the author.

[b]Projects allocated to Unesco of a more strictly educational kind, excluding about $10 million for projects in science and technology.

Unesco, through its own regular though small program, and by acting as the cooperating agency with the World Bank, Unicef, and
UNDP programs, exercises a major normative role.

As regards the scope and direction of official bilateral educational assistance, about a fifth of the total effort was directed to
spreading the language and culture of the donor country. The other
four-fifths went mostly to higher education, technical education, and
general secondary education; relatively little went to the primary
level or to literacy programs. Eighty-two thousand students and
trainees were financed in 1973, and 60,000 to 70,000 foreign teachers and educational experts were in developing countries under educational assistance programs. Some $150 million of capital aid was
given from this source.

The methods used by both multilateral and bilateral agencies
have mostly been the supplying of teachers and experts, institution-
building, study grants, and help in the development of curricula,
educational techniques, and administration, the production of textbooks, and so on. About a quarter of the total was capital aid in the
form of loans and long-term credits to governments for specific
projects. Assistance for recurrent expenditures, in which educational expenditure figured, was limited to certain dependent or near
dependent countries whose national budgets as a whole were supported.

Africa obtained about three-fifths of the total, Asia was next,
followed by Latin America. South Asia, with its massive population
size, received only about one-twentieth per capita of what Africa received, and Latin America about one-sixth per capita. The overall
average was just short of $1 per capita.

Up to some 25 years ago, official educational assistance was
almost entirely between metropolitan powers and dependent countries, except for some mutual exchanges taking place between common cultures. It was with the process of decolonialization and the
initiatives taken to promote development on a worldwide scale (especially the Truman Point Four Doctrine, followed by the setting up
of the United Nations Expanded Programme of Technical Assistance)
that a major change occurred.

This change was of a threefold nature. In the first place, the
ex-colonial powers were called upon to help to expand as rapidly as
possible, but under a new relationship the existing educational systems of the newly independent countries. Secondly, funds were provided by their Member States to enable the multilateral agencies to
create educational assistance programs. Thirdly, new donors, in
the form of countries that had not had dependent territories, also
set up programs of their own and provided resources for international action.

More than 70 countries obtained independence in the late 1950s
and the 1960s and have continued yearly to build up their national
status. As this process has progressed, international assistance
has been affected. Independence has led to a diversification of contacts and relationships among countries and thus to a diversification
of assistance relationships. It has increased the pressures for
rapid expansion of education, and it has fostered an increased role
for intergovernmental assistance agencies, in which the new nations
themselves had an increasing influence on policy. As a result, from
the early 1950s to the late 1960s, a growing flow of educational assistance took a prominent place in the aid given by the more developed
to the less developed or developing countries, and its steady quantitative progress seemed to be largely independent of the fluctuations
that took place from year to year in the overall growth of aid.

As the 1960s progressed, educational assistance was influenced
by two different situations to which the word "crisis" was applied.
The first was the situation as regards aid as a whole; the second was
widespread dissatisfaction with the current functioning of educational
systems.

In his Annual Review for 1968 of aid from the developed to the
less developed countries, the Chairman of the Development Assistance Committee of the Organisation for Economic Cooperation and
Development, Edwin Martin, wrote,

> There is no question that the economic and
> social progress of the developing countries,
> which contain most of the desperately poor
> majority of mankind, is entering a critical
> and decisive phase. . . . Far too little sense
> of urgency exists either in the majority of aid-
> providing countries or in many developing
> countries about taking practical steps to meet
> obvious and pressing development needs. . . .
> The needs of development continue to be too
> often relegated to a second level of priority
> in spite of all the efforts made in the Devel-
> opment Assistance Committee, in the United
> Nations family of organisations, in regional
> organisations, and in voluntary agencies. . . .
> It is tempting, therefore, to paint a uniformly
> black picture to past achievements and future
> prospects. But this would neither correspond
> to the facts nor would it constitute sound tac-
> tics. Good progress has been, and is being
> made--but its rate is still, with a few

exceptions, too slow to make a morally and
politically acceptable difference to the economic and social situation of the developing
countries, is well within their capacities--
and is, indeed, vital if the progress already
made is not to be thrown away.

About the same time, the Committee appointed by the World
Bank to review the aid situation under the Chairmanship of Lester
Pearson, reported, "The climate surrounding foreign aid programmes
is heavy with disillusion and distrust. This is not true everywhere.
Indeed there are countries where the opposite is true. Nevertheless,
we have reached a point of crisis."[2]

At the same time, the same Report points out that "international cooperation for development over the last twenty years has
been of a nature and on a scale new to history."[3] This crisis in development aid as a whole did not have an especially marked effect on
the volume of educational assistance, which continued to be popular
with both recipients and donors.

In the 1974 Review of Development Cooperation made by the
Chairman of the OECD Development Committee, Ambassador Maurice
Williams writes,

For some this "slow crisis of development"
has become a fatalistically accepted aspect of
relations between rich and poor countries; for
others, it is cause for despair and disillusion.
Yet the material and technical means for dealing with it exist. We could, if we chose to do
so in a cooperative international effort, substantially reduce mass hunger and unemployment in the Third World. . . . The situation
of the poor countries has not received the attention from the world's leaders and governments which its seriousness warrants. Hundreds of millions of people live so close to the
margin of subsistence that sudden changes in
their physical and economic environment can
create a desperate crisis for them.

Educational cooperation does not have behind it the same
threat of a "desperate crisis" as does the specter of hunger and unemployment, which international cooperation could help to prevent.
But in the regions where there are 800 million of the population illiterate, it has an urgency of its own because education is a normally

slow process, and yet, combined with other measures, it can contribute greatly to the economic and social progress necessary to raise food production and achieve reasonable levels of development and employment in the low-income countries, as well as act as a restraining influence on excessive population growth.

The Director General of Unesco in 1973 summed up the situation as follows in his address to the Economic and Social Council of the United Nations, "Talk of an aid crisis was certainly exaggerated and defeatist. . . . A new phase was opening with needs, possibilities, and responsibilities which required new attitudes."[4]

What hit educational aid hardest was the appreciation that became widespread that the educational systems that the newly independent countries had inherited did not fit their needs. This produced a crisis in the form of questioning the utility of educational aid in its present form as a contributor to development.

Criticism of the modes and content of education was not limited to the developing countries but was part of a general dissatisfaction spread throughout the world. Studies such as the Coleman Report in the United States, the Plowden Report in the United Kingdom, and the OECD studies of education in Europe drew attention to needed reforms in the developed countries. In 1971, an international commission of seven members, chaired by Edgar Faure, was commissioned by Unesco to study and make recommendations on educational development, especially in the developing countries. The report of this commission, published under the title of Learning to Be, contained many radical suggestions, most of which have met with widespread interest, though there has been as yet little implementation.

There was, and still is, considerable overlap and sometimes confusion in the various debates on educational cooperation between arguments about the weaknesses of current educational systems and practices for which educational cooperation is not necessarily responsible and those about the failings of educational aid as such—some authorities stressing the responsibility of external influences for the disabilities of education in the developing countries and others the responsibilities of the countries themselves.

Educational cooperation, like cooperation for development in general, has undoubtedly suffered from the despondency about attaining overall aid targets and the continuation of certain attitudes inherited from the days when educational assistance was associated with dependency. But the sector was relatively free from the acute political tensions that surrounded more financial and commercial subjects, such as the terms of trade and grants of capital required for industrial development.

Moreover, in quantitative terms, educational cooperation was probably not much below the absorptive capacity of a number of the

most needy countries. In some African states the aid contribution
amounted to some 40 percent of the second level teaching force; and
when higher and technical education were added, it was a major factor in the whole system of such countries. Dissatisfaction was not
predominantly quantitative--in terms of what assistance had traditionally supplied in the form of educational resources--it was more
a criticism of the traditional types of aid and how they were carried
out.

This criticism was often more vocal in the progressive circles
of the international educational profession itself, and in the various
aid-supplying agencies, than in the developing countries themselves.
Most leaders in those countries and the sources of power in the educational profession and the community had themselves been educated,
if not abroad, at least under systems of foreign extraction. These
forms of education had helped to create both their own and their fel-
low countrymen's capacity to build an independent nation, and initially there were far too many gaps in the administrative and technical
cadres to permit the delays associated with educational reform.
Moreover, despite some uneasy talk of neocolonialism and continuing
cultural dependency, it had suited their general purposes to encourage bilateral activities with their ex-colonial powers, while the ex-
colonial powers, whether by way of amend for past neglect or as a
matter of continuing cultural and economic interest, or both, regarded this as their natural opportunity to respond to the growing
pressures for greater contributions to international development.
There were thus many attitudes and forces in the developing countries supporting the existing types and methods of cooperation.

Support for the existing type of educational cooperation, either
for the above reasons or because it is in fact the most effective form
of assistance, continues to be strong. The flow of education assistance grows annually with little change in its character, despite the
criticisms made. There appears to be a "silent majority" that finds
the system effective. The "crisis" view of the situation seems to
have been mostly in the minds of statesmen, educators, and social
scientists, both in the developing and the developed countries, whose
range of vision extended into the longer-term needs for educational
reform. The "crisis" view was also held by some for general political rather than purely educational reasons. They wished educational
aid to assist social reforms as well as meet purely educational or
human resource requirements.

Thus, today, a double trend has emerged. On the one hand,
there is much pressure from progressive educators to use educational cooperation as an instrument of educational reform. On the
other hand, the amount of reform actually taking place is limited,
and, partly because of this and owing to built-in constraints in the

machinery of cooperation, little change has yet taken place. A major redeployment of its education aid has, however, been announced by the World Bank Group, and, as will be seen in Chapters 3 and 4, other changes of policy among donors have been declared or are on the horizon.

As regards the operational methods, educational assistance between countries today still relies mainly on the movement of persons (study abroad, expatriate teachers, visiting experts, and such), on institutional action (setting up of universities and technical institutes, for example), and on loans or grants for selected projects or programs. Relatively little aid is yet allotted to research, experimentation, and the encouragement of innovation, or to whole programs of reform.

As regards the objectives and the direction of aid, commercial and religious motivations also play a role, and particularistic non-educational factors enter in the sense that donors often seek ideological partners or countries with allied interests or cultural heritages or avoid those with which they have a conflict of interest. But broadly, since the 1950s, when educational assistance lost most of its links with dependency and aid to colonies, there has been a steadily growing stream of assistance motivated in terms of a genuine international concern for the problems of the development of the world as a whole and for the part education can play in raising the standards and levels of living (of which it is itself one) of the less developed countries. This is illustrated by the increased use being made of multilateral as compared with bilateral systems of assistance.

At the same time, while cooperation for education has been increasingly seen as a contribution to the solution of the overall development problem, the trend has been also to emphasize its role of subservience to the recipient countries' policies, which by design or inadvertence may not be development-oriented as may accord with approved international recommendations.

Thus there is an innate dualism. Aid should be designed to help development; aid should be an instrument of each country's policy. The supposition is that each country expresses through its government, with which educational aid is negotiated, a desirable development policy in terms of international norms (for example, those expressed in the resolutions and instruments of the United Nations and Unesco). It is possible, as in the case of the Union of South Africa, for governments to be publicly declared by the international community not to be following those norms and to be ostracized, but this is rare.

This dualism, as shall be seen in the discussion on the extent to which educational assistance can promote reform and innovation and the democratization of education, is not only a conceptual one;

it is also a live, practical issue to which good solutions have not yet
been found except in the very general formula, at present little in
use, that aid should be given to strengthen a country's capacity for
reform. The task of ensuring that aid does not buttress undesirable
educational situations and, at the same time, is not a pressure activity that interferes with sovereign national values and objectives is
a difficult and delicate one.

If the establishment of adequate minimum standards were to
replace the development criterion as the first aim, the task would be
less difficult. It is easier to define measures to eliminate educational poverty than measures to deal with the whole of educational development, though, as will be seen in Chapter 6 on basic education,
this safer path is not necessarily followed.

The foregoing trends in outlook, though they are only partially
reproduced in action, affect educational aid strategies and operations
as well as policy. Instead of skills, knowledge, and institutions being transferred, the idea is increasingly to build up the ability of the
countries themselves to create the national skills and institutions.
It would be wrong to say that this idea is entirely new. It was said
long ago that the purpose or end of technical assistance was the end
of technical assistance. The newer factor is in the emphasis placed
less on the country taking over from its foreign experts as soon as
possible and more on the donor supplying continuing forms of technical and financial cooperation and long-term partnerships in building
up adequate levels of educational development.

The change in conditions between the 1960s and the 1970s also
affects the nature of the donor-recipient relationship. When it was
largely a matter of transferring known skills and resources for the
linear expansion of existing systems, the flow could be based on
quantitative factors to a large extent. But now that the systems
themselves are being called into question by some and fundamental
reform is being urged by many educators in both developed and developing countries, the relationship changes from facilitating a flow
of resources to a more intensive dialogue between the two partners
as to the definition of a country's needs and of external capacities to
meet them.

The intensification of the dialogue involves the closer definition
of the dialogue itself. The basic framework for the dialogue would
seem to be as follows. At the one end is the recipient country. No
donor has the right to impose an educational policy. A developing
country may accept or reject aid as it wishes. But it cannot wholly
determine itself the nature and conditions of the contribution of any
individual provider of aid. This is because at the other end of the
dialogue there are aid agencies governed by their own regulations
and policies. These will be of an accounting or procedural nature,

or may be constitutional (for example, that Unicef should help children rather than adults, that Unesco should not aid projects in which racial discrimination was practiced, that a Commonwealth fellowship has to go to a Commonwealth member, that a bank has to make loans and not gifts with funds it raises on the commercial market).

The aid agency may also be an instrument of national policy as well as of educational cooperation, and its funds be voted as part of overall appropriations for foreign assistance to which legislators may set conditions circumscribing the type of government to which aid may be allotted. In the same way, a nongovernmental organization of a religious character may circumscribe its aid to countries and projects in which its own religion is followed. Between the one extreme consisting of agencies that simply insist on proper accounting and the other made up of those that highly circumscribe their assistance--there is a rainbow of variations not only of regulations and policies but also of what may be negotiated in each case.

On the recipient side, there are also considerable variations within the possibility the country has of simply accepting or rejecting aid. Rejection is frequently difficult for poor countries or for countries deeply involved politically with stronger partners. This may result in their accepting conditions and assuming commitments that are unduly onerous for independent countries. Here again, there are many grades of possibilities.

The plurality of aid is, on the whole, an advantage in that it increases its volume and the range of skills involved. But the intensification of the educational dialogue has to be accompanied by a greater effort than is being made at present to equalize the negotiating power of the two parties, and aid should be used for this purpose. What this means for recipient countries is that they should strengthen-- and seek aid to help them to do so--their capacities for diagnosing their aid needs and their identification and preparation of projects. This will involve not only the reinforcing of the official section involved but also the country's research and data collecting facilities related to education. Where, as so often, reform and innovation are required, research and development and experimentation will also have to be promoted. On the aid-providing side, less circumscribing of educational cooperation by noneducational factors is to be hoped for. Similarly, terms and conditions should be as flexible as possible.

Positive steps can be taken to reduce inequalities in negotiating aid by supporting the services in the recipient countries concerned with aid formulation, either by measures of the kind in the preceding paragraph, or by ad hoc assistance given to the recipient country by third-party experts from the outside, paid for by the aid-providing agency or agencies taking part in the negotiation.

The bringing-about of these changes involves not only altera-
tions in the policies and attitudes to cooperation on the part of both
sides but also technical and logistical implications for the planning
and implementation of educational assistance. These can only be
fully perceived and the necessary adjustments made by action spread
over time. Swift changes to ideal patterns cannot be foreseen, because of the deep roots of the present system. Developing countries
would still have to request and use aid for emergency stop-gap purposes and for medium-term bridging operations, but generally they
would have to regard it more than they do at present as an active in-
strumentality that can contribute especially to those aspects of their
educational policies that involve reform and innovation.

Donor agencies would have to take parallel action. Administrative and educational skills would have to be provided to fit new
types of action. The flow of information as to needs, the techniques
of negotiating aid agreements, and the back-stopping services of
documentation would all be affected.

Memory systems and evaluation processes would have to be
built into the administration on both sides of the cooperation--not
only to assist operations and improve performance but also to service analysis offices that would have the task of foreseeing new
trends in aid patterns, exchanging information with other donors,
and of being central points in the diffusion of new ideas, practices,
and procedures within the educational aid process.

The reinforcement of inspection services and the regular review of projects while they are being implemented are also important
steps to be taken both by developing countries and aid-suppliers.
The study of aid projects that fail reveals that the difficulties are
usually identified at an early stage, but that remedial action, which
often involves putting the machine into reverse and rewriting the
project description, is seldom undertaken. Commitments continue
to be made, and the project plows forward because suitable procedures and mechanisms do not operate to call for a halting and a
revision of both objectives and means before the difficulties that are
identified become endemic.

In the chapters that follow, thought is given to possible types
of change in patterns and structures that these policy changes might
require. The patterns obviously would have to vary according to the
extent of each developing country's desire to use aid as an instru-
mentality of the kind discussed and according to the extent to which
each supplier of aid was prepared to foresee continuing streams of
aid in the sense and direction indicated.

Progress on all these matters has been initiated over the last
five or six years. The Development Assistance Committee (DAC) of
the OECD, together with the suppliers of bilateral aid, had already

at a meeting in 1966 examined the role educational aid was playing
in the technical assistance programs of its members and noted that
it amounted to about half the total funds committed for technical
assistance. In 1968-70 under the chairmanship of Edwin Martin of
the United States, a series of review and meetings were undertaken
to reexamine educational aid. Later the multilateral suppliers of
aid, especially Unesco and the World Bank Group, were involved in
similar reviews.

These reviews, however, were mainly concerned with the nature and direction of aid and recommended important policy changes
rising out of the actual experience of the Member States of the Development Assistance Committee as well as a technical study of educational trends and needs. They had little to say on the problems posed
in this chapter as to the implications for both developing countries
and aid suppliers in terms of the procedures, structure, and new organizational patterns required to bring the redeployment of resources
required into actual operation. Thus, while policy has changed fairly
rapidly, implementation has not followed at the same pace.

NOTES

1. See Table 4.1. Its first position among the sectors, it
must be noted, is influenced by a particularly high proportion of
French educational aid, which makes up a quarter of total educational cooperation.

2. Lester Pearson, ed., Partners in Development (New York:
Praeger Publishers, 1969).

3. Ibid.

4. The Unesco Conference statements quoted throughout the
book are taken from the proceedings of the Unesco Executive Board
and the Economic and Social Council of the United Nations when questions of educational cooperation were discussed at the date indicated.
See especially 84 EX/INF 5, 94 EX/4, 94 EX/5, 94 EX/SR 5, 94
EX/26, 94 EX/27, 18 C/133, and 84 EX/INF 5. The text of Director
General Maheu's speech to the Economic and Social Council is in
94 EX/SR 9.

2

THE DEVELOPING
COUNTRIES: POLICIES
AND NEEDS

The recipient countries in the cooperation process are in principle in complete control of educational needs and policies, since all aid projects have to be requested by them. Nevertheless, even at the level of principle, there are limitations to that control. These arise from differences that may exist between the type of external resources available as compared with those required and from the legitimate desire of donor agencies to be assured of the proper accounting and administration of the assistance. There is also a further set of limitations due to donor agencies having assistance policies (for example, that Unicef will aid primary rather than second-level education) and to their insistence, in most cases, on participating in the process of project selection and preparation, though they do not claim to have the final say. Sometimes, too, weak recipients are unduly influenced by stronger donors because of a lack of administrative, technical, or political strength.

In practice, what is usually involved is a process of dialogue and negotiation in which both technical and policy factors are ventilated and out of which policy is formed, instance by instance, and operations set on foot.

Thus, the policies of developing countries toward educational aid have grown up as a matter of practice rather than through declared principles. Their policies have evolved mostly as a result of their dealings with previous colonial powers and other bilateral donors and from their participation in the multilateral agencies.

While most of the donor countries are grouped in the Development Assistance Committee of the OECD and meet to discuss educational aid problems regularly with technical documentation from a secretariat, the recipient countries have no similar standing machinery, although they have meetings on overall development and aid

questions, especially in the framework of the United Nations Conference on Trade and Development (UNCTAD). So far as they have
formulated general principles and declarations on educational cooperation, these have been made at Unesco's Regional Conferences
of Ministers of Education and Those Responsible for Overall Planning at or in regional organizations, such as the Organization of
American States (OAS) and the Organization for African Unity. Educational aid, however, has not been debated in depth in the UN agencies or in Unesco itself, as shall be discussed in Chapter 3, but
rather in donor agencies. One reason for this is that whereas aid is
the total preoccupation of donor agencies, for the Ministers of Education of the recipient countries it is usually a lesser and sometimes
only a marginal preoccupation.

The practices used in the negotiations between donor and recipient as to project identification and preparation are at the heart
of the problem of improving educational aid. Developing countries
usually expect that multilateral assistance, which in principle represents a more disinterested donor group than does bilateral aid,
will set standards in this matter. Much progress has been made by
both multilateral and bilateral agencies in improving these practices, but there are still substantial steps to be taken.

There is still an inheritance of poor practices of the past.
When educational aid first appeared in considerable dimensions on
the international scene in the 1950s, funds far exceeded soundly conceived projects put forward by the developing countries, most of
which were still in the early stage of decolonization.

This led to the practice of "ventriloquism." Officials from
aid agencies descended for a few days in the capital cities, and their
visits resulted in requests the broad lines of which had already been
conceived at agency headquarters. Senior officials of Unesco, for
instance, covered in an almost athletic manner most of the developing countries in a remarkably short time, and projects sprouted
overnight like mushrooms.

This practice still exists in less extreme forms but is being
progressively eliminated. In 1971 the Director General of Unesco
commented on the choice of aid projects as follows in a statement
to the Executive Board on the Country Programming Procedure:

> I now come to the third source of difficulties,
> those due to the executing agency, in this case
> Unesco. In the first place, I think that the
> Secretariat makes certain basic mistakes in
> devising projects, though less now than former-
> ly, since it should be borne in mind that we
> were carrying out projects which have frequently

been devised five or six years ago, or even
earlier. Doubtless to begin with we were
often much too optimistic. We overestimated
the capacity of countries, we did not always
study their needs in a sufficiently specific
manner, and our projects conceived by specialists in too abstract a fashion, did not al-
together fit into the general context of each
national situation. I am convinced that country programming will remedy these defects.
Lastly it should be added that, where projects
are defective from the outset due to lack of
realism, their faulty conception inevitably
shows up at the stage of execution. We must
in particular steer clear of what I would call
"Prefabricated projects," i.e., those initiated by the Organization not the Member
States. Here again country programming
should make improvements possible.

The new factor is the much greater strength of the educational
administration in most of the developing countries, especially at the
higher echelons--though one of the theses of the present book is that
this strength should be promoted still further and more aid be devoted specifically to this purpose. The problem has to be faced that
as the processes of choice and preparation of aid projects become
more improved and sophisticated, more demands are made on the
middle range of good administration and technical personnel, who
are often in short supply in the developing countries.
  Similarly, the more varied the set of criteria to be applied by
the donor, the more difficult become the choices of projects and the
evaluation of results. Much is being said currently in donor circles
about the need to introduce "equity criteria," that is, policies based
on the social justice of better distribution of education within countries. Some donors hope to see educational aid given as an instrument of social change in societies where a sharp stratification exists.
  Recipient countries, on the whole, remain reticent on these
matters. In societies where little social change is taking place, it
is not seen how foreign intervention can improve matters, especially
when in some cases the governments are themselves not dedicated to
change. In those where change is active, an opposite set of considerations arises. Fears that aid may take conventional forms and will
have the effect of "buttressing" (to use the expression of the Pearson
Commission) the status quo are often mostly a donor rather than a
recipient preoccupation. For this reason there is no common

doctrine or policy of educational aid on the recipient side. For the
recipients, the status quo is visibly there and in need of help.

Nevertheless, certain clarifications of their positions--mainly
of a quantitative nature--have been made by the developing countries.
The objectives set for Africa at the Addis Ababa Conference of 1962
included heavy provision for external assistance, but little guidance
on modalities.

Later, the African Ministers of Education at the Unesco Regional Conference, which was held in Nairobi in 1968, concluded,
"whatever steps may be taken by African Governments to make
greater resources available to education, it is clear that the desired
objectives and targets will not be met unless increased external resources are also available."

A few years later, Asian Ministers of Education at the last
Unesco Regional Conference held in Singapore in 1971, passed a
resolution (no. 13), which stated,

> The largest proportion of the educational en-
> deavour is necessarily supported and sustained
> by the financial resources of the countries
> themselves. . . . It is unlikely that future
> mobilisation of national resources will fully
> meet growing demands for educational oppor-
> tunities and qualitative improvement of educa-
> tional systems . . . invites the Member States
> outside the Regions to increase their assistance
> to Member States in Asia.

The Unesco Conference of Ministers of Education of the Arab
States held in 1971 at Marrakesh (Resolution no. 2) called upon Unesco
"to increase its efforts to assist the Arab States, severally and jointly . . . and requests the Director General . . . to continue to use his
best offices with the various international financing organisations . . .
in order that they may increase their aid." The conference further
stated (Resolution no. 5), "considering the great shortages in the resources of UNRWA [the conference] calls upon governments to contribute generously to the Agency's funds."

A more explicit but still broad statement was made by the
Director General, who, in his address to the 49th session of the
Economic and Social Council, stated,

> External aid should, of course, provide the ex-
> isting systems with additional means, which in
> some cases are indispensable. This is true,
> for instance, for the building up of the economic

and social infrastructure, or again for providing
pioneering sectors with equipped and trained
staff. . . . But the needs are so enormous that
many governments, despite all the innovations
and rationalisation, will not be able to continue
their efforts on behalf of education, while maintaining a rate of growth compatible with the
"takeoff" of their economics and the moderni-
sations of their social structures, unless they
receive more generous aid.

A clear statement on the relation of aid decisions to national
policy also was made at a conference convened in the United Kingdom in 1967 at which British and U.S. aid officials participated with
representatives of recipient countries. The report of this conference stated, "The final decisions on an area as central to public affairs as education must be made by a country's own leaders, often
on political grounds. . . . Donor countries should not therefore expect their educational aid to give them the right to a major say in the
shape of a recipient country's education system."[1]

The absence of common formulations by the developing countries of recommendations for a doctrine and practice of educational
aid may in part have been influenced by the desire of many of them
to keep the maximum liberty in their negotiations with individual
donors, and if necessary to play one off against the other. For perhaps the same reason, movements in favor of better coordination of
educational aid, both in principle and at the local level, were usually
instigated by the multilateral agencies, either Unesco or the UNDP,
though the tendency for the recipient country to take the lead, as indeed is its role, is now increasing. Nevertheless, both on the donor
and the recipient side, there is little positive planning of the coordination of educational aid, partly due to the tendencies just described
and partly inevitably, owing to the plurality of the sources of aid.

In any donor-recipient relation there is less need for a policy
at the recipient than there is at the donor end. Since the donor is
the provider of funds, the assistance process has to be justified before legislatures and conceptions have to be clarified as to the purpose and use of the funds. At the receiving end, however, the availability of the assistance is often short term and even fortuitous--
though some donor agencies are making longer-term commitments--
and cannot be made the subject of detailed policy analyses in advance.
Normally the view of the recipient is that the funds should be made
available to the largest degree possible and with the smallest number
of ties and regulations attached, so it becomes, in effect, a part of
the national budget. This is clearly not consistent with what donors

have to justify to their legislatures. Accordingly, the inclination to statements of principle and guidelines for policy comes more from the donor than the recipient end, particularly from the multilateral agencies.

This inclination, as shall be seen in the next chapter, has sometimes betrayed the multilateral agencies into a lack of realism. While the proportion of multilateral aid is and should be increasing, the practical realities have to be faced, as is recognized in the statement of Unesco's Director General to the Economic and Social Council in June 1973, quoted in Chapter 3. The policy issue that the developing countries face between using multilateral or bilateral aid is largely a pragmatic one. This is well illustrated by an article discussing the merits of the two systems written by the United States delegate to the Development Assistance Committee of the OECD.

> The debate is rather a mixture of the idealistic and the very practical problem of getting appropriations. The argument for multilateralization usually runs along the line that by this means the political content of aid can be neutralized and attention focused on the real needs of the underdeveloped, that priorities among countries and within countries will not be dictated by the special political or commercial interests of any individual donor, and that the recipients themselves will play a part in deciding the distribution and the priorities for aid funds.
>
> These virtues have an undoubted appeal to the aid theoretician, but the practical possibility exists that removal of the political content of aid may eliminate the aid as well. The French aid program, for example, is dominated by a concern for its former dependencies; it is unlikely that the French government would have provided the same level of aid to a nonpolitical, multilateral agency as it has to its former colonies. The outcome of the debate over which administrative channels to use will thus certainly affect the amount of aid made available. In this connection, it is not without interest to note that the recipients themselves have expressed no clear preference for multilateralism.

This again illustrates the pragmatic approach of the developing countries. While a country resents outside interference, it is an error to suppose that in no case does it welcome guidance on vital matters, especially when sought on its own initiative. Ministers of Education in recipient countries are incensed if aid officials from other countries try to dictate policy but are disappointed if they do not give frank advice when asked for it.

A mission sent out to help a country to identify and prepare projects for aid should start with the assumption that the government knows what it wants and that the donor is providing only the means and technical assistance. Sometimes, however, the actual situation encountered is that the Minister is anxious that the mission should have wider and more determinant functions because he needs an underpinning of prestige, owing to lack of support for education in other key Ministries. Or it may be simply that work pressures are so strong and his people so busy that they are content to let foreigners do the job.

Thus, a certain amount of dependency, which is attacked in theory, is in fact created by the developing countries themselves. This situation is sometimes complicated by a rapid turnover of Ministers so that the aid agency and its officers become the main source of continuity of purpose and design. The Director General in the statement to the Executive Board of Unesco cited above remarked, "When examining an educational project the other day I found that, since its commencement, there had been a succession of six Ministers of Education over a period of five years."

Further, counterparts to foreign experts are often career people and move on to other areas during the lifetime of a project and are not easily replaceable. A suggestion that has been made is that there should be special branches of the career service with inducements opened for counterpart staff, to provide the necessary continuity.

Sometimes there is also an underlying erosion of purposefulness and effort due to the difference between the weight of the forces that the aid agency can bring to bear, the standards it applies, and those that the country itself can muster for the average project. The recipient administration may well at the worst regard the main objective as achieved as soon as the aid has been obtained. The project is expected to be neither more nor less efficient than the run of educational projects in the country. The donor agency is less likely to take this view since the officials concerned do not have the rest of the country to look after, as do the national officials.

On the other hand, recipient countries sometimes find that their own methods of evaluation, and the cost-efficiency of their educational system as a whole, are helped by the application of high standards from outside and attempts at outside evaluation, and special administrative and research support are given. Behind the

extent to which this can be done looms the substantive problem of
how far aid projects should integrate themselves into the present
educational levels of efficiency and how far they can move ahead in
a pathfinding fashion (for a discussion see Part III of this book).
That difficulty comes to a head particularly in the case of pilot projects. Aid agencies tend to introduce pilot projects with a degree of
sophistication that makes them difficult to duplicate or to maintain
once the aid resources are removed. Recipient countries, therefore,
have grown to have a certain hesitation about pilot projects and prefer, if possible, support leaving the country itself to develop its own
dynamisms of efficiency and change. The implications of this are
also discussed in Part III.

    As will be seen in the following chapters on the policies of the
donors, there is thus inevitably an underlying confrontation between
recipients, which take the view "Give us the resources and we will
do the job," and aid agencies, which say "We are prepared to help
and to fall within your policy lines, but we cannot support dysfunctional and inefficient projects and educational methods."

    The confrontation seldom presents itself in such an acute form,
and pragmatism usually prevails. But it is the central issue in determining the policies and doctrines of educational aid. Efforts to
improve and develop the aid process must revolve round the better
clarification of the terms of this dialogue, and one of the new and
growing educational aid needs discussed later is precisely in the
area of assisting developing countries to participate in the dialogue
on more equal terms.

    In the autumn of 1973 the oil crisis occurred, which intensified
the case for aid for the developing countries and led to the Special
Assembly of the United Nations held in May 1974, which declared the
necessity for a New Economic Order. At the Executive Board session of Unesco in June 1974, the tone of the comments of the developing countries on aid problems in education became sharper and
the interest deeper. The delegate for Algeria said that many different realities were contained under the overall formula "aid to development," since there exists in fact a form of aid based on power,
that international cooperation for development was not in a good
state, and that the true remedy was that indicated by the Director
General when he underlined "the necessity of resolutely engaging international cooperation in efforts to reorganise international economic relations of which the impact would be much more direct and
radical than aid as such." Delegates did not attempt to outline the
implications of a change in international economic relations on educational aid, except that there was emphasis upon equality of negotiating power between donor and recipient when educational aid was
determined.

The delegate for Jamaica said that he found the Director General's analysis of aid very much in line with the point of view of many developing countries including his own. The Prime Minister of Jamaica had put forward similar views on the psychology of donor and recipient countries.

> The concept of aid was frequently misunderstood and aid supplied often inadequate and too late on account of the reluctance of donor countries to grasp the meaning behind the undertaking and of recipient countries to shake off the feeling that they were in an uncomfortable position. Aid was not charity but an important instrument in international cooperation having as its main objective peace in the world. While peace might be necessary for development, it was equally true that development was essential to peace.

He went on to agree that "international aid must no longer seem to be--and still less actually be--intervention by an alien will and an alien body."

A paper presented by the Mexican delegate drew attention to a statement by the President of his country that said, "We must increase our countries' capacity to devise, assimilate, and adapt technology, which is today largely concentrated in the industrialised nations." The paper stated that Unesco should see to it that these implications are given practical effect to a large extent through education, through the transmission of scientific knowledge, and through closer and more fruitful cultural relations.

The psychological tone of the debate can be seen by the suggestion of many delegations that the words "expert" and "counterpart," which were regularly used (one being an active and the other a passive term), should be replaced by terms illustrating equal cooperation. The delegate for Colombia particularly stressed this point. The point of view of one of the least developed countries (Ethiopia) was that "the only lasting solution to the problem of development was to establish and strengthen local structures in the developing countries." He also agreed with the second idea that international aid should go particularly to ventures of an innovatory nature but wished to emphasize that any approach by a developing country aimed at solving a problem directly was to be welcomed. The third point--cooperation in the preparation and adoption of policies, strategies, and plans--was also important. In Ethiopia a review had been made of the education sector, and it had been found that the assistance of

Unesco and other bodies was useful mainly for purposes of comparison. He also referred to cultural barriers, quoting the Director
General's remark regarding the purpose of development that "It is
not a question of having more, but of being more."

The delegate for Zambia attacked the attitude of certain donor
countries, which he described as opposed to the whole philosophy of
development, and spoke of "the need to dispense with considerations
of self-interest and power and to make aid a matter of real cooperation," which meant facilitating the establishment or strengthening of
structures within the beneficiary countries. He felt that radical
changes were needed also in the United Nations approach to international aid, and he hoped Unesco would set the example. In the course
of his remarks he stated that "it was not uncommon to see the maintenance of a foreign culture included as a condition in aid agreements," meaning by this that the systems of education in the developing countries that received aid tended to reflect the culture of the
former colonial power.

The comments of the developing countries as to how they understood educational aid, while taking on more force and coherence than
at earlier sessions, were still centered around the United Nations
resolution on the New Economic Order; and there was no discussion
in depth of the problems of educational cooperation apart from
Unesco's executing and advising on the funding programs of the UNDP
and other international bodies, such as Unicef and the World Bank.
Nor did the developed countries have officials from their aid agencies
present, so that bilateral aid for education became a subject of debate. At the same time, the debate on the aid given by the UNDP and
Unesco was the subject of lively discussion, and to put this in focus
it is necessary to look briefly at how the system works.

The other multilateral agencies in the United Nations family
that are major sources of finance and technical assistance for education in the developing countries are the UNDP, Unicef, and the
World Bank Group, consisting of the International Bank for Reconstruction and Development (IBRD) and the International Development
Association (IDA).

Educational aid needs vary, of course, from country to country according to their level of educational and economic and social
development. It is useful nevertheless to look at the broad types of
needs. The special cases that the different educational levels present are discussed in separate chapters in Part II. Here we are concerned with sketching out the overall categories of needs against
which the supply, present and future, of educational aid has to be set.

First, there is the massive problem of the presence in the developing countries of 800 million illiterate adults over 14 years of
age (1975 estimate) and of some 300 million children aged 5 to 14

out of school. According to the World Bank's calculations, some 140
million new pupil places would be needed to be created by 1985 to
take care of the out-of-school group on the basis of a six-year cycle.
On the basis of a four-year cycle, the number would be 60 million.

The elimination of adult illiteracy of this dimension is difficult
and can take place only as the older illiterates die and younger
school-leavers become adult. The process can be hastened by accelerating the spread of universal primary education and minimum
basic education and by functional work-oriented literacy programs
for adults. Here there is a large need for assistance, which is only
being very partially met partly because developing countries' governments have not made the necessary priority requests and partly because of the innate difficulty of this area of educational activity and
lack of experience in mobilizing aid resources for the purpose.

The heavy and persisting educational poverty among children
and youth will involve considerable assistance of a quantitative kind,
especially in the least developed countries, to build new schools and
train new teachers. But taking the developing countries as a whole,
the main issues are of an organizational nature or of an "educational
engineering" type. Most of the children who grow up illiterate do,
in fact, attend school but attend primary cycles, which are not devised to universalize basic education but to provide access for the
few to the secondary level; and then the majority drop out too early.
The greatest single contribution to reducing educational poverty
among the young is, therefore, the reorganization of educational systems to bring the teaching and learning process into closer relation
with local learning needs and possibilities of school attendance and
thereby to reduce the dropout rate.

The need is for aid in introducing new curricula and teaching
methods; training large numbers of teachers to adopt new approaches;
ensuring action at the local level to reduce the material causes of
dropout, such as lack of transport or school meals; improving the
relationship between the school and the home through methods of
health and welfare betterment; and (at the provincial and national
level) restructuring the primary cycle so that it provides complete
terminal courses for the masses who leave after six years of education, rather than give them, as so often at present, courses from
which they drop out designed for the pupil who will go to the second
level.

Even in those rural areas in which schools are entirely lacking,
the problem is not simply one of building schools and training teachers. Help for school building and teacher training for the geographical extension of the existing system has to be given because there is
no other system, and the children cannot be left without any education, however inadequate. What is needed in a number of areas is

assistance for the creation and spread of new systems more suited
to the needs of the population. This is explored further in Chapter
10, which discusses aid for research and development and innovation. The serious position at the first level can be seen by the fact
that the growth of enrollments has fallen well below population growth
in both Africa and Asia, as indicated in Tables 1.4, 1.5, and 1.6.

Assistance to help educational change is also required at the
other levels of education. At the second level the aid needs are
qualitative rather than quantitative, except in the least developed
countries. The priority allocated to the second level in the 1960s
has tended to overproduce school-leavers at that level for whom comparable employment is not available. Nevertheless, in certain vocational streams at the second level, in technical, industrial, and agricultural education, and in the aspects of the general syllabus concerned with science and technology, there remain clear aid needs in
the form of buildings, equipment, and expert consultation.

At the higher level the needs are even more qualitative and are
focused on greater emphasis on science and technology, the creation
or development of centers of excellence, and greater democratization
of access to higher education as a whole through scholarship systems,
the reorganization of entrance examinations to eliminate social bias,
the provision of fellowships and grants for study at home or abroad,
and the building up in the graduate schools of a national research and
training potential--not only in science, industry, agriculture, and
technology generally but also in the social and administrative disciplines.

Trained staff to cope with the problems of administration and
"social engineering," which the developing countries face in so many
spheres--including education, employment, family planning, urbani-
zation, pollution prevention, and health, nutrition, and welfare ser-
vices--are also much needed.

The need now is less for the establishment of traditional universities based on Western models as for the creation of new types
of institutes of higher learning and science and technology that have
a direct relation to each country's development needs, including that
of entering ever closer into the world economic community and of
participating more fully in technological progress. Within these
broad needs, as shall be seen later in this book, there are a large
number of subcategories of requirements that call for newer and
more imaginative types of aid.

In considering needs, however, a typology is helpful of roughly
three types of developing country along the lines already indicated.
The first, it will be recalled, consists of the least developed countries, defined by the United Nations.[2] These countries generally
have first-level enrollments of around 18 percent, second-level at

2 percent, and less than 0.5 percent at the third and represent 8 percent of the total population of the developing countries.

The second group has between 50 to 60 percent enrollment ratios for the first level, 12 percent for the second, and 1.5 percent for the third. Their population is about 56 percent of the total population of the developing countries. They have a per-capita income of between $100 and $200 annually.

The third group accounts for 36 percent of the population of the developing countries. Most in this group have achieved up to 90 percent of first-level enrollment over the first seven grades, and the second-level enrollment is around 25 percent for grades 8 to 12. Third-level education enrollment is around 4 percent. Per-capita income is between $200 and $500 annually.

The needs described have to be interpreted in terms of quantity and quality in order to be geared with the supply. On the quantitative side it is likely that the demand during the 1970s will be less than was the case in the 1960s for an initial period until a new equilibrium is struck between demand and supply. A large portion of the present volume of aid is made up of salaries for teachers and other forms of direct participation in the education system and for study abroad. As the developing countries achieve greater maturity in their education systems and the supply of nationally trained teachers increases, this need declines. Similarly, since most fellowships are designed to replace gaps in educational facilities in the developing countries, there is likely to be a reduction of demand for study abroad.

While these needs will decline in volume, other forms of needs that have been accumulating may increase, for example, aid for research and development and experimentation with new educational methods and structures, and for action to relate education systems more closely to development needs, or for a large-scale attack on educational poverty and illiteracy.

Such new demands would require a period of "running in." Education and Finance Ministers who request aid would have to become convinced of their need, and the donor agencies would have to reassess their own expertise and possible contribution. Although educational cooperation appears to be in a between period before a new demand replaces the old, the past has shown that educational assistance has a substantial momentum of its own under which the educational "establishments" of the donor countries cooperate in the promotion of programs with the "establishments" in the developing countries. This form of cooperation tends to be for the encouragement of traditional types of education for the most part and for scholastic rather than applied or developmental purposes, though it now includes increasing exchanges of scientific knowledge and mutual support among scholars who are advancing the thresholds of knowledge.

The tendency may well be for one of the following things to happen:
as the problem of development and the educational needs change,
there will also be needed a change in both quantity and type of aid
(the cost of different types of educational aid being different, the
financial and real resources in demand will vary as the educational
aid "mix" alters); however, even if the recipient countries reformu-
late their demands, the character of aid will not change unless the
donor agencies redeploy in time and thereby have the resources to
meet new needs.

The problems are great of achieving a redeployment that will
shift the types of requests and the resources available to meet them,
especially as no central machinery exists for such a process and, as
has been seen, the recipient countries themselves act pragmatically
case by case. Neither Unesco nor the Development Assistance Committee of the OECD could undertake alone the task of offering some
long-term planning advice to aid the redeployment of demand and supply. There seems to be a need for some central body, formal or informal, that would have the role of organizing data and analysis to
permit some forecasting of the requirements for redeployment. Such
a piece of machinery obviously could be only of an advisory nature.

The need for such machinery is seen in the popularity (among
both donors and recipients) of the series of high-level meetings on
world educational development and aid problems organized by the
Ford and Rockefeller Foundations in the Bellagio series. The value
of this exercise is the opportunity it gives for developing a common
thinking by the exchange of research results and operational experience in an atmosphere free of the administrative and political considerations that abound when such matters are considered by governments in formal decision-making organizations.

The estimates made by the International Labour Organisation
(ILO) of the future employment situation show that heavy unemployment is likely to persist in the developing countries unless specific
steps are taken to promote employment, for example, by the use of
labor-intensive rather than labor-saving techniques. This throws on
the leaders of the developing countries and their businessmen, managers, and technical staff a task of particular difficulty.

What they have to do is not only to introduce the means of production that will move the economy quickly ahead but also at the same
time to devise new means, not copied from the industrially developed
countries, that will meet the social needs of employment in their
large populations. A paradoxical feature of the ILO studies is that
they show that the greater the pace of development on the basis of the
United Nations economic model for the developing countries, the
greater the amount of unemployment. This is because the model had
geared development to the industrial sector, which is the largest
user of labor-saving methods.

To secure widespread employment the impetus of growth has
to extend into the rural areas where the masses of semiemployed or
subsistence-economy population live. This again is an area where
progress is not possible unless there is the necessary infrastructure
of basic education in the rural areas and unless there are the right
technical and managerial skills in the developing countries, which
can find their own solutions suited to their populations and local economic problems, rather than copying from abroad.

It follows that an important area of aid will remain the assistance given to education for rural development, on the one hand, and,
on the other, for national institutions for research and development
and training personnel for the organizational and technical tasks involved. This would be one of the main areas into which traditional
educational aid could usefully be switched as its current form becomes obsolete.

If this chapter on aid needs had been written in the early 1960s,
it might have contained a detailed catalogue or "shopping list" of the
shortages of educational resources in the developing countries.
Since then the emphasis has shifted to diagnosis and identification of
aid needs on the spot in the light of each country's development plan.
It follows that there is not much that can be said of a general nature
other than the broad indications that have been given. The best contribution that can be made to the discussion of aid needs is to establish adequate procedures for their diagnosis and identification at the
national level.

NOTES

1. See Aid to Education: an Anglo-American Appraisal (Over-
seas Development Institute), pp. 17, 18, containing the report of the
section of needs, the discussion of which was introduced by Dr.
Awokoya, Permanent Secretary of Education, Nigeria; Mr. Prem
Kirpal, Secretary for Education, Government of India; Dr. Sherlock,
Vice Chancellor, University of the West Indies; and Dr. Siddiqui,
Vice Chancellor, University of Islamabad, Pakistan.

2. International Development Strategy for the Second United
Nations Development Decade (New York: United Nations Center for
Economic and Social Information, 1970).

3

COOPERATION WITH
MULTILATERAL
AGENCIES

To start reviewing the donor side of changes that have recently taken place in educational assistance policy, let us look first at the United Nations and Unesco. If one examines the educational component of the United Nations International Development Strategy adopted by the UN General Assembly in October 1970, it is clear that it belonged in spirit to the 1960s. The emphasis on educational reform and innovation and on its structural change and egalitarian aspects had not yet found their way into the United Nations resolutions.
The Strategy states,

> Developing countries will formulate and implement educational programmes taking into account their development needs. Educational and training programmes will be so designed as to increase productivity substantially in the short run and to reduce waste. Particular emphasis will be placed on teacher-training programmes and on the development of curriculum materials to be used by teachers. As appropriate, curricula will be revised and new approaches initiated in order to ensure at all levels expansion of skills in line with the rising tempo of activities and the accelerating transformations brought about by technological progress.
>
> Increasing use will be made of modern equipment, mass media and new teaching methods to improve efficiency of education. Particular attention will be devoted to technical training, vocational training and retraining.

Necessary facilities will be provided for improving the literacy and technical competence
of groups that are already productively engaged as well as for adult education.

Developed countries and international institutions will assist in the task of extending
and improving the systems of education of developing countries, especially by making
available some of the educational inputs in
short supply in many developing countries and
by providing assistance to facilitate the flow
of pedagogic resources among them.

This resolution was, however, elaborated further in the Unesco
General Conference Resolution 9.1 adopted shortly afterward. The
Unesco resolution stated that the General Conference decides that
Unesco will make its full contribution to the International Develop-
ment Strategy and added references to the need for educational re-
form and renovation and an overall review of educational strategies.
On educational cooperation it calls upon Member states:

. . . particularly the economically and technically advanced countries, to increase substantially their financial and technical assistance
to developing countries, to attain at least the
recommended 1 percent of their gross national
product, particularly through multilateral channels, to help improve the operational efficiency
of such assistance, and to review their international policy in the fields of education, science,
culture and communication in order to assist in
the efforts to achieve the aims and objectives of
the Second Development Decade; . . . in view of
the need for rational and more effective programming, to make concerted efforts to carry
out country programming of international assistance for development and to promote coordination of multilateral and bilateral assistance at
the national level. . . .

Unesco's relation to the problem of educational aid during the
1960s had been a checkered one. The view was traditionally taken
on its Executive Board that Unesco would occupy itself with its own
multilateral forms of aid and with coordination with the other agencies in the United Nations system and with Funds-in-Trust, but that

it would not attempt to evaluate or coordinate the whole of educational aid. The main reason for this attitude was not only the plurality of sources but also the divergence of political and ideological motivations of the different suppliers of aid, governmental and nongovernmental.

As the 1960s wore on and the developing countries became more organized and vocal in other agencies in their expressions of needs, delegations became more inclined to raise educational aid issues in the General Assembly and the Executive Board of Unesco. Usually, however, the references were of a very general nature, and the average delegate was not well informed as to what was passing in respect of the total scene, including bilateral aid.

Indeed, there was little literature on the subject and little interchange of information and views between the multilateral organizations, led by Unesco, and the bilateral agencies grouped in the Development Assistance Committee of the OECD. The Secretariat of the DAC produced annual bilateral statistics, but these were not set out in a particularly significant form for educators, but rather as part of overall technical assistance.

At this point a setback occurred owing to an overambitious proposal being made to the Executive Board by the Unesco Secretariat, under which Unesco would assume a coordinating role that went beyond what the governments giving bilateral educational assistance were prepared to envisage. These proposals were withdrawn by the Director General when it was perceived that they would not be acceptable.

Thus, the main initiative for the study and the reviewing of educational aid continued in the late 1960s to rest with the Development Assistance Committee of the OECD. This Committee covered all the major bilateral donors of educational assistance, excepting the USSR and the other centrally planned economies. A number of policy changes were being effected by individual bilateral donors. The DAC, not being an executive body, had no means of working except by its studies and through the individual donors. These, however, were becoming increasingly influenced by the need for educational reform, which was becoming generally recognized, and by that of placing greater emphasis on social and egalitarian issues and on using aid to stimulate educational change. Accordingly, a number of policy recommendations were made by the DAC that led in the direction of the redeployment of aid to meet new needs.

A feature introduced in the DAC's work was that Unesco for the first time became a regular participant (in an observer capacity) in its various meetings concerning educational aid. Further, the Committee's Chairman, Ambassador Edwin Martin, addressed a letter to recipient countries suggesting that informal coordination could be achieved through the country itself or the principal donor (bilateral or multilateral) calling regular informal meetings for the purpose. A number of such informal mechanisms, known as educational "donors' clubs" were in fact set up. Where the step was not actually taken to hold informal meetings, the exchange of information on a more casual basis increased.

Unesco at this point felt the situation was ripe for further involvement on its part in the overall educational aid scene, and its General Conference passed a resolution asking the Director General to call a conference of governments and multilateral agencies taking part in educational aid to consider the whole problem. This resolution was passed without significant debate in the Conference, but hesitations arose on the Executive Board and in the mind of the Director General himself when the question of implementation came up. The initiative was regarded as untimely, and the resolution was quietly buried by the Executive Board without opposition from any quarter.

The doctrine accordingly remained that the best method was to let informal arrangements grow up naturally and to let action for coordination spring directly from needs rather than from abstract principles, and that a Unesco intervention in the whole aid picture was premature.

However, Mr. Maheu, Director General of Unesco, in his speech to the United Nations Economic and Social Council in July 1973, clarified his attitude on educational assistance in the following terms:

> Talk of an "aid crisis" was certainly exaggerated or defeatist. Objectively, what was needed was an admission that some concepts and practices must be revised and, to a greater or lesser extent, changed in order to move international action in favour of the developing countries into a new phase in which it would be more responsive to the realities of the present-day world. The first change that should take place related to the evaluation of the possibilities of "aid" and the results which could be expected from it. The limits of aid were now better known and all illusions must be firmly eliminated from "strategies" which were often over-optimistic. For example, it was clear that public aid would not reach the levels envisaged. . . . The situation which had existed in the 1960s no longer prevailed, and a new phase was opening with needs,

possibilities and responsibilities which required new attitudes.

Firstly, it was now better realised that
financial and technical assistance were especially useful if their aim was to facilitate
the establishment or strengthening of the recipient countries' structures and cadres for
their own development. Since it was intended
to increase their potential rather than their
present performances, such aid was necessarily medium-term or long-term and was
therefore particularly suitable for action by
the specialised agencies.

Secondly, it was becoming increasingly
evident that international assistance--though
naturally provided at the request of and in cooperation with the Governments concerned--
should not contribute to the systematic consolidation of the economic and social status
quo. . . . assistance from international or-
gans should be channelled principally towards
innovation enterprises. That was where it
would pay the greatest dividends and where
international organisations could best serve
Governments.

Thirdly, international systems should be
adapted to the new concepts and profound
changes which had emerged in the situation
and attitudes of recipient countries. The contribution of international organisations should
increasingly be seen as a means of promoting
the maximum mobilisation and optimum utilisation of national resources.

That new relationship between national
authorities and international organisations could
no longer be referred to as aid or assistance,
but constituted cooperation in the form of joint
research, in which the role of the international
organisation was primarily to encourage and
perhaps to expand that research, but not to
direct it. . . .

It was in those circumstances that the joint
research in the preparation and elaboration of
national policies and plans had begun. Governments and the Unesco secretariat both had much

to learn in that new and difficult kind of cooperation, but on the one hand, it led to the
establishment of original strategies and systems conforming as closely as possible to the
realities of each country and avoiding blind
imitation of foreign models, thus providing
education with internal and external efficiency and producing considerably better
results.

In his Report issued in 1974 on the Activities of the Organisation in 1973, Mr. Maheu, the then Director General, went further.
He stated,

The limited impact of what is done, when it is,
by its very nature, intended to exert a general
influence, the unduly high energy losses, both
human and financial, involved in the operation
of a stiff and cumbersome machinery, the costly commitments it imposes on countries receiving aid, giving rise to so many misunderstandings and clashes which spoil the atmosphere of
relations from the outset: all these things,
which are considerably more serious than the
particular shortcomings that are so often the
target of short-sighted criticism, are due to a
policy line and a psychological approach which
both require correcting at every level of action.
In short, I would say that international aid must
no longer seem to be--and still less actually be--
intervention by an alien will and an alien body.
Only then will it truly become what it alone can
be, since it alone can dispense with considerations of self-interest or power: only then can
it be real cooperation, in which mutual trust,
the free exchange of views, and the close com-
munion of joint endeavour allow of transcending
the barriers of separate identity.

This statement by Unesco's Director General, much of which
referred to overall aid rather than to the educational sector, received
widespread approval both inside and outside the Economic and Social
Council, to which it was delivered. While no formal arrangements
are in existence for Unesco to take a degree of leadership in educational assistance matters, its influence in this sphere is growing.

The other multilateral agencies in the United Nations family
that are major sources of finance and technical assistance for education in the developing countries are the UNDP, Unicef, and the
World Bank Group, consisting of the IBRD and the IDA. All of these
sources of funds use Unesco as their technical adviser or operational
agency, with the result that Unesco's influence permeates to a considerable degree the educational sectors of their programs. Since
the UNDP and Unicef are both directly part of the UN system, their
cooperation is standard practice, but in the case of the World Bank
Group, it is based on a special interagency agreement under which
the World Bank contributes to staffing and backstopping operations
in Unesco to support bank lending programs.

The UNDP policy for educational assistance had its origin in
its task of assisting urgent priority projects of economic development. Accordingly, the criteria for aid resulted in the early 1960s
largely in the setting up of technological institutions, technical training, and university and second-level fields of study closely related
to economic growth.

Later, as a wider conception of the role of education in development gained ground, these criteria were extended and embraced
general secondary education, teacher training for the primary level,
and a major experimental program in work-oriented literacy. The
point was reached where teacher training (predominantly for the
second level) took up nearly half the total allotment. The UNDP has
been greatly concerned over the recent period in revising its own
procedures and in the introduction of country programing. The latter represents its largest single contribution to the improvement of
educational aid, since it provides machinery for coordination at the
formal level that supplements the less formal arrangements mentioned earlier.

The share of UNDP funds for execution through Unesco has
varied between 15 to 16 percent and 12 to 13 percent of the total over
the last five or six years, the trend being a slight diminution of the
share. The order of magnitude is around $25 million annually for
projects resulting from country programing and another $11 million
for large-scale projects approved directly by the UNDP administrator. These amounts cover educational and training programs, institution building, science, and technology, as well as education in the
more general sense, the latter coming to more than half the total.
Just over half the new projects in the latter field adopted in 1973
were in the area of planning and research and in basic education,
indicating a response to these new priorities.

The evolution of the UNDP program over the years and the difficulties it is still encountering are a microcosm of aid problems and
of the workings of the United Nations and its specialized agencies for
educational aid.

In the second part of the 1960s there was considerable criticism of the working of the United Nations system as a whole, and a commission was appointed under Sir Robert Jackson to study the capacity of the United Nations machinery as an instrument of development aid. As a result of the Jackson Report and the study of it made by the United Nations, a number of new procedures were introduced that now govern the main lines of the program and are therefore worth citing.

The basis of the changes introduced in 1972 and now governing the system are as follows:

1. The adoption of the concept of a United Nations Development Cycle. The cycle consists of programing at the country level; project formulation, appraisal, and approval; and implementation, evaluation, follow-up, and periodic reviews. It also means forward programing to fit as far as possible the life span of countries' five-year development plan.

2. Country programing, that is, the assessment of needs in the different sectors in an integrated manner having regard to the capacity of the sectors to provide mutual support to each other and the establishment of indicative planning figures for aid for each country. The program is formulated by the recipient government in cooperation, at an appropriate stage with representatives of the UN system, the latter under the leadership of the resident representative of the program. Needs are identified within the country's objectives and internal resources for inputs from the UN system, and a preliminary list of projects is established. It is for the government to take into account other external inputs, multilateral and bilateral. The Resident Representative submits each country program to the Administrator, who in turn submits it to the Governing Council for approval with his recommendations.

3. Special consideration is given to least developed and newly independent countries where lack of administrative structure has previously hampered their formulation of needs.

4. In addition to the country programing, a proportion of total resources is allocated directly by the Administrator to certain large-scale or regional projects involving several countries.

5. The new system of assessing local costs permits more flexibility, providing for full or partial waiver where necessary.

6. Advice is furnished on follow-up investment possibilities from bilateral and multilateral sources of finance arising from UNDP aid.

7. The Resident UNDP Director has greater delegated powers.

A number of important difficulties in implementing UNDP projects, even though by 1974 the country program is in the third year of

its activities, are felt by Unesco to be still present. The first relates to the system of country programing under which each of the
agencies of the United Nations concerned with specific sectors has
to provide position papers on the countries' development situation in
their sector and their needs for aid. The time required for the
preparation of the papers has not been adequate, and the position
papers have not been discussed sufficiently with the governments.

Reporting on this matter to the 94th session of the Unesco Executive Board held in June 1974, Mr. Maheu, the then Director General, stated, "As a general remark it can be said that governments
are not always aware of agencies' briefs." He added, "it is not that
governments are not interested in observation and advice, it is
rather than such 'input' must be 'timely' and readily usable by the
officials concerned."

The second difficulty is what the Director General called "the
rigidity and seemingly excessive detail required by the present project documents, which it is felt could be simplified without impinging
on the UNDP's monitoring responsibility." The UNDP has been
greatly concerned with the management aspects of its work and has
introduced a "management plan," which is a timetable for all concerned for the preparation of new projects and the review of ongoing
projects. This is combined with the delegation of authority to the
UNDP Resident Representatives to submit proposals for approval "in
principle" without prior submission of a full project document and to
authorize the start of preparatory assistance. This represents a
considerable effort on the part of the UNDP to streamline its management.

There were, however, difficulties of implementation, which
still trouble Unesco. The Director General, in the statement already
cited, said, "Project implementation continues to encounter the more
traditional difficulties: recruitment of specialists, delays in the
nomination of candidates for fellowships and in the delivery of equipment. These difficulties arise from factors vesting both with the
Secretariat and the Governments."

In the Introduction to his Report on the Activities of the Organization in 1973, Mr. Maheu had stated:

> So far as the execution of projects financed by
> the United Nations Development Programme
> (UNDP) is concerned, two points to which I
> drew attention in my introduction to the Report
> on the Activities of the Organisation in 1972
> may perhaps be remembered. I mentioned
> first of all the complexity and unwieldiness of
> the procedures followed. Although during the

past year those responsible have become more
clearly aware of the disadvantages of these procedures, it is still necessary to improve cooperation between the Secretariats in order to
achieve more flexible project implementation
and more imaginative programming, particularly with respect to the launching of innovatory projects.

I further noted that in 1971-1972 the total
funds for projects financed by UNDP had shown
an increase of 13 percent over the estimated
amounts. Encouraged by this expansion, the
Secretariat had made provision in the 1973-1974
Programme and Budget for an even greater advance with respect to projects entrusted by
UNDP to Unesco. It must be admitted, however, that the total amount actually obligated
for carrying out UNDP projects during the first
year of the biennium has not justified this optimism.

(A table was introduced here showing that only 38.3 percent of the
expenditure provided for the biennium 1973-74 had been actually expended in 1973.)

The main reasons why the activities financed by UNDP fall short of the target shown
in document 17 C/5 are, in my opinion, the
following:
(a) on UNDP's side:
the funds allocated by UNDP for projects entrusted to Unesco for execution did
not reach the expected level;
authorisation to undertake certain projects was limited to approval for "preparatory assistance" instead of full approval;
there has therefore been relatively little
work on these projects;
country programming procedures entail
abnormally long delays: the final versions
of project documents, for example, can
still be drawn up only after patient and complex negotiations, particularly when UNDP
Headquarters is involved;

(b) on Unesco's side:

the Secretariat has encountered serious
difficulties in drawing up the lists of equipment to be ordered, placing the orders, and
obtaining delivery within the time-limits
laid down by the plans of operation;

where experts are concerned, the preparation of post descriptions, the search for competent candidates able to accept appointment
and the obtaining of governmental approval,
far from being expedited, are all taking
more and more time, owing inter alia, to
the increasing diversity of developing countries' needs and the dearth of good candidates in certain fields;

the selection of candidates for fellowships is often considerably delayed in the
various countries because of poor syn-
chronisation with the work of the experts.

The Governing Council of the UNDP agreed at its session in
November 1973 on the following three points:

(a) Continuous and systematic consultations between UNDP and the agencies should take
place at both the field and Headquarters level,
and a more active representation by both parties
in meetings of the respective governing bodies
was needed. In this connexion, agencies were
urged to participate fully in the Council's proceedings;

(b) There should be greater utilisation of
the agencies as sources of technical expertise
at all phases of the development cycle;

(c) Requirements for sectoral support to
Resident Representatives should be examined
in terms of the particular needs of each country at each phase of the development cycle; in
this connexion it was stressed that a flexible
approach might be more productive than a
uniform pattern of arrangements.

Nevertheless, it is to be noted that Maheu remarked (94 EX
SR 9, p. 9):

It is strange that an education project worked
out over a long period with the competent
Minister of the interested country can be
judged as a bad one by the UNDP. In this
respect I draw attention to the possible unfortunate implications of the notion of ac-
countability which the UNDP has recently
adopted and which imposes on the directorate
the need to take account of the execution of
projects. The UNDP has thus been led to set
up dispositions to commit itself to verify the
work of the executing agents. There thus exist two systems of control which causes duplication and adds to the general expense.

Other criticisms expressed by the Director General were that
the governments of many countries found it difficult to find counterpart personnel for launching and continuing projects, and some did
not seem to understand that this was an essential aspect of the
UNDP's international aid. They seemed to think that international
experts were considered simply as specialists or as trainers of
local people. In his view, unless counterparts were well chosen and
played a full role, the very idea of the aid operation, which was that
they should take over from the outside experts, was defeated.

He also criticized the delays in appointing fellows, who sometimes lost a whole year when an attempt was made to marry the op-
timal time period for the fellowships in relation to the project and
the calendar of the institutions abroad that trained them. He was of
the opinion that it was possible to work out a variety of methods,
some of which would be cheaper and more efficient, which would re-
inforce the creation of national institutions and development in the
countries themselves, rather than adhere fixedly to the notion of the
transfer of knowledge and technology that had governed aid principles
over the last 20 years.

The second largest source of funds for educational assistance
in the United Nations system is Unicef, which for 1973 amounted to
$15.6 million and for 1974 to $22 million. Originally conceived as a
welfare and relief agency, it became in the late 1950s and 1960s progressively interested in child development as part of the overall development problem. Early in the 1960s education figured prominent-
ly, along with health and nutrition, as a substantial part of the Unicef
program.

The program was carried out with the cooperation of Unesco,
and on the educational side it took on many of the characteristics of

Unesco's own educational assistance work during the 1960s. Unesco
was concerned with the second as well as the primary and preprimary
levels of education and with educational planning. The Unicef contribution was distributed among these components, and by the end of the
decade about 40 percent of the funds were going to second-level education.

At the same time, Unicef was continuing to maintain its overall view of the child, thereby taking a wider than purely educational
view, even in its educational aid, and placing special emphasis upon
such items as the reduction of wastage through poor home conditions
and health and nutrition education. At the end of the 1960s a review
was made of progress, and a number of recommendations were
jointly agreed on by the Unicef and Unesco Executive Boards to improve the efficiency of the joint educational program. However, the
main lines of the previous criteria were not disturbed, and it was
not until 1972 that, as a result of a further review, a fundamental
change was made in the scope of the program. It was decided to
phase out the aid given to second-level education and to concentrate
as much as possible upon bringing as many children as possible above
the educational poverty line. Thus, there was a special interest in
the first part of the primary cycle, often called elementary education, and in the situation of children in the underdeveloped rural
areas and in depressed conditions in shanty towns.

A revised joint program was thus born, aiming at helping primary education and educationally deprived children. Preprimary
education and the plight of the handicapped were recognized as important fields of action, but it was felt, since governments gave
priority to the education of normal children of school age who were
not being educated and since preprimary education was largely en-
joyed by the more, rather than the less, privileged children, that
these two deserving causes should be left to other programs rather
than figure in any substantial way in joint Unicef-Unesco effort.

The joint revised program became incorporated into guidelines
and was approved by both Executive Boards. An extract follows:

> Modifications are proposed in the policy for
> Unicef-Unesco cooperation in educational as-
> sistance in order to respond more effectively
> to the changing needs of developing nations,
> and to render it more consistent with Unicef's
> general assistance policy. The latter is focused
> upon collaboration with developing countries in
> their efforts to plan and implement effectively
> national welfare and development programmes
> for children and adolescents. Within this

context, the resources of Unicef are being
directed increasingly to assist countries to improve the situation of children deprived of a
basic practicable level of services and opportunity, particularly those in rural areas, urban
slums and shanty towns, and in the least developed countries.

This focus is to be applied progressively to
Unicef's aid for education. In this connection,
other external aid agencies such as UNDP and
the International Bank for Reconstruction and
Development (IBRD) are devoting increasing resources to the educational systems of developing countries. However, these efforts tend to
concentrate largely on programmes most likely
to have rapid impact upon national socioeconomic development. Thus, Unicef's orientation to the deprived child and its overall view of
children's development complement the assistance provided by other external agencies. In
this regard, the education of girls and women
is of particular importance, partly because help
to mothers is one of the best ways to help young
children, and partly because more equal educational opportunities for girls and women will
facilitate their increasing occupational role in
national development.

Governments and external aid agencies,
such as Unesco, are emphasizing increasingly
the need to evaluate existing structures of education and to consider alternative organisations,
since the traditional formal systems tend to be
too expensive and relatively inefficient to be gen-
eralised rapidly in developing countries. In the
majority of these countries, over 50 percent of
the population are under 20 years of age. Given
this fact and the limited reach of the existing
systems, new approaches are essential to provide the mass of educationally deprived children and youth with basic and continuing educational opportunities. Unicef, in collaboration
with Unesco, should place a priority on this
field, which includes out-of-school education
and the use of new media.

Unicef's operational role in this endeavour
should be oriented primarily to the target population through experiments at the field level,
and to the diffusion of successful pilot projects.
Unicef, in collaboration with Unesco, should
support also studies and specialist training
oriented to the finding of innovative solutions
to the problems of the target population.

The foregoing implies a progressive shift
of emphasis from secondary to primary and
out-of-school education, as other resources
are found to carry on existing viable projects
(notably in the field of secondary-level science
education), or as they can be phased out con-
veniently. In this regard, Unicef will support
efforts to develop a more integrated primary
school programme, such as the relating of
science courses to such fields as nutrition,
health and practical subjects. Further, Unicef
endorses and supports Unesco's initiative to
promote international understanding through
education.

Thus, the reform of primary education
constitutes a major concern of Unicef-Unesco
cooperation. Encouragement should be provided
to curriculum development activities that will
improve the child's performance in his present
and possible future environment, rather than to
those which place a more exclusive emphasis on
academic achievement as a step in preparation
for further formal education. In this regard, it
must be emphasised that only a small minority
of primary students continue to secondary education, particularly in the least developed countries. This is likely to be true for the next
decades in rural areas where the majority of
children live. While certain common standards
must be maintained throughout a country, rural
education should contain a special practical
component to prepare the child to develop the
rural environment rather than to swell the numbers of the unemployed in the towns.

Further, endeavors to reduce the high wastage rate in terms of drop-outs and excessive
repetition should be assisted at the primary

> level. This includes the identification of the
> pedagogical and non-pedagogical causes for
> this widespread phenomenon, and the develop-
> ment and application of appropriate remedial
> actions.

This revised Unicef/Unesco program is now in operation in its second year and is already having a considerable impact. Table 6.1 in Chapter 6 on basic education shows the impact. An important feature of the program is its large delegation of authority to field staff in the regions and its greater flexibility of operation than the UNDP program. Other references to educational projects under the Unicef/Unesco program are contained in Chapter 6.

A new line in Unesco technical assistance to governments began in 1972 following the wishes of the General Conference of that year, under which, in addition to giving advice on specific subjects, Unesco was called upon to advise over the whole range of the formulation and implementation of educational policy. To a certain extent this had already been done previously, since in order to ascertain particular priorities for assistance it was necessary to undertake overall studies of countries' priorities. The new factor was the specific recognition of Unesco undertaking a policy role instead of its technical assistance being based on the assumption that the government policy was fixed and that the assistance was purely technical.

Writing on progress in this new line of assistance, the Director General in the Draft Programme and Budget for 1975-76 (18 C/5) stated,

> As regards methods, I would draw attention to
> the growing importance of the advisory services
> made available to Member States on request by
> their governments. Two features distinguish
> such services from the classic type of technical
> assistance. Firstly, whereas the main purpose
> of technical assistance is to further the estab-
> lishment and operation of basic institutions by
> training the necessary national personnel, these
> advisory services are specifically intended to
> help national authorities, by means of a critical
> dialogue in which the international contribution
> consists in the comparison with relevant ex-
> periments in other countries, to formulate,
> evaluate or think out afresh their educational
> policies and strategies after reflection on the
> basic issues involved. Their place is therefore

at the highest levels of decision-making and
they cover the widest possible field, whereas
the classic type of technical assistance is
geared to operational action which, however
important the area with which it is concerned,
is by definition applied at fairly narrowly cir-
cumscribed points.

Secondly, technical assistance usually consists in supplying Member States with the services of experts recruited abroad, who stay in
the country for periods of varying length, depending on what is required for training counterpart staff and running the institution or pilot
project to which they are assigned; on the other
hand, in accordance with the wishes expressed
by governments themselves, advisory services
are more likely to be provided by specially experienced Secretariat officials, assisted in case
of need by high-level outside consultants. The
time required for such services is variable:
generally missions are of short duration, though
they are prepared well in advance by thorough
documentation and information-gathering work,
but sometimes, as in the case of senior advisers,
a mission may last several years.

The World Bank Group has also, since the early 1960s, taken
an active role in assisting the formulation and carrying out of educational aid policy. Its criteria at first, like those of the UNDP, were
what would be considered today of an overly narrow economic orientation. This was largely because it was entering a field relatively
unknown to it, but as the program developed, wider conceptions of
education were introduced step by step. Today the President of the
World Bank Group, Robert McNamara, has been a leading advocate
of resources for reforming education with the help of international
assistance in the direction of maximizing its social and egalitarian
as well as its economic role, and for the regeneration of entire educational systems.

In 1971 the World Bank published a Sector Working Paper that
stated,

A deeper and more continuous dialogue between
the Bank and the borrower is necessary if we
are to encourage in the borrower a greater willingness to reform and innovate and if we want to

succeed with the projected financing of education as indicated in this paper. On the Bank side, more intensive sector analysis, particularly with a longer time perspective, can improve the Bank's understanding of the sector and the credibility of its advice. On the borrower's side, improvement in management and planning practices should lead to a better appreciation of priorities and readier availability of soundly conceived projects. Unesco's present effort to strengthen its planning services for member countries should contribute to this end as well as financial assistance for planning and management analysis for which the Bank has begun to provide financing in selected cases. In all these activities the prime objective is to develop local capability and self reliance.

From this combination of factors, we hope to develop a better basic strategy agreed between the Bank and the borrower within which we can identify a phased sequence of projects covering a period of up to ten years. In this phased sequence we would expect to find capital and technical assistance financing interspersed so as to constitute a rational and orderly application of resources for development of the sector.

Although we anticipate that the volume of Bank lending will continue to increase rapidly as it has done since 1968, it is a major point of this paper that the success of the Bank's efforts in the education field is not to be measured primarily by the amount of money we lend but rather by the effectiveness with which Bank and country resources are deployed to meet crucial needs. We expect the Bank to become the largest financer of educational assistance and to continue in most cases to finance projects of such size that a qualitative and quantitative impact is secured. However, since all external assistance to education will probably continue to be less than 10% of total expenditure by developing countries, the motivating and multiplying effects of external assistance will be the principal test of success.

The Bank's position was usefully summed up in its <u>Annual Report</u> for 1973.

> Over the years, as the Bank gained more experience, it diversified its activities. A few years ago, it decided that it should broaden its approach further by determining priorities and selecting projects on the basis of a thorough examination of the education system as a whole. In particular, apart from projects which produce trained manpower directly, it should consider other types of projects which could have important long term significance for economic development. Such projects would be "designed to encourage changes which improve the relevance, efficiency and economy of education systems."
>
> In the earlier years, the overwhelming proportion of the assistance was for educational "hardware"--for the construction and equipment of school buildings. But, more recently greater attention has been given to the "software"--to such aspects as improving the curriculum, producing better teaching materials, and planning systematically the education that is offered.
>
> The greater emphasis on objectives of social equity is reflected in several of the education projects which have been financed during the last five years. It is reflected also in the studies and research which are being done. Both actual operations and studies reflect a new strategy, with greater stress on people in the traditional-transitional sectors of the economy which have hitherto been left outside education systems. The aim is to find appropriate ways to enable education systems to promote both economic growth and social justice. This has required a comprehensive approach at all levels and areas of both formal and non-formal education and training.

During the fiscal year ending June 1973, countries received loans or long-term credits for education totaling $293.5 million. Between fiscal years 1963 and 1973, 89 educational projects were approved costing $1,652 million--of which $906 million came from

the World Bank Group ($502 million in the form of loans and $404
million in 50-year credits free of interest).

In 1972 the department of the World Bank dealing with education was reorganized into regional project divisions. The Director
General of Unesco refers to this in his Report on the Activities of
the Organization in 1973 as follows:

> While the general policy regarding the coopera-
> tive programme as a partnership has remained
> unaltered, the practical effect of the new struc-
> ture has been to accentuate the problems of co-
> ordinating and scheduling missions and to in-
> crease the demand for experienced Unesco staff
> to participate in missions organised by the Bank.
> Greater emphasis is also being given to basic
> education sector studies.

A further development has been some telescoping of the procedures for feasibility study, project preparation and appraisal, and
programing of implementation, which had in the past been the subject of separate missions.

The World Bank program for 1974-78 is for an allocation of
$1,075 million in constant prices for the Bank/IDA lending to the
education sector, as compared with actual lending between 1969-73
of $947 million, namely an increase of about 14 percent. In addition,
nearly $350 million for education training is expected to be included
in lending for other sectors. The 1974-78 program is expected to
permit "tooling up" for a substantial expansion beginning about 1978.

A major feature of the program is a substantial increase to
about 27 percent of the total in lending for primary and basic education with a proportional decrease for intermediate and higher. Support for technical education and teacher training is expected to remain at the same levels while lending for general education will decline. Large increases for education for rural populations are expected, and technical assistance is expected to rise from 7 to 9 percent of the total.

The Bank hopes to ensure as far as possible an equitable distribution of lending by income levels both between and within countries, but differences in absorptive capacity, educational technology,
and the greater availability of funds for Bank loans rather than for
IDA credits are limiting factors.

The World Food Program (WFP) aids education mostly through
supplying food to children and students at the different educational
levels, thereby improving learning capacity, reducing dropout, and
increasing the school attendance of a number of children who have

long daily journeys to school and could not otherwise enroll. In addition, certain funds released from national budgets for the governments' school food budget are used in cooperation with Unesco as
well as the recipient country in promoting specific educational programs and projects.

According to the publication by the Food and Agriculture Organization (FAO) titled Ten Years of World Food Programme Development Aid 1963-72,[1] 21 percent of WFP assistance "is earmarked
to support projects largely or exclusively designed to develop and
expand the educational sector." Through all WFP-supported projects, assistance reaches some 3.7 million primary-school children,
285,000 second-level school pupils, 384,000 students in higher education, and 123,000 participants in adult education and literacy
courses. In financial terms the amounts were $172 million for pri-
mary, $38.3 million for secondary, $31.5 million for higher, and
$2 million for adult education.

WFP resources, however, have been affected by adverse
changes in the surplus food situation and in commodity prices. Assistance for education, therefore, will be concentrated on the least
developed countries and children in primary schools.

Within the United Nations system, both the ILO and the FAO
have programs of assistance that, though based primarily on their
own fields of competence, interlock with the educational work of
Unesco, as have also to a lesser extent the World Health Organization (WHO), ICAO, and WMO. Cooperation and coordination between
the agencies is ensured not only by day-to-day contacts, but also
through the Education and Training Subcommittee of the UN Secretary
General's Administration Coordination Committee.

Of particular interest on the ILO side has been its preemployment and its vocational training programs and projects as well as
the Employment Program, which has made a number of original employment studies in developing countries in which important educational analysis and recommendations have been made in cooperation
with Unesco. On the FAO side, rural development activities have
called for an interlocking interest with Unesco in agricultural and
rural education at all levels.

Although the progress that can be made in eliminating the unemployment of school-leavers depends heavily on the actual employment situation (the outlook for which is unfortunately poor), much
can be done with assistance to fill the existing gaps in the skills and
types of education that continue to be in high demand and scarce supply. This refers particularly to the supply of technologists, businessmen, and scientists, as well as social service and civil servant
personnel of the requisite quality for modernization of society. The
challenge of the New Economic Order, if it is to be brought into being,

will involve the creation of the necessary manpower and human resource skills backed by research, which a closer integration between
the developing and the developed countries requires.

The other multilateral agencies that have had or maintain considerable activity in educational aid are the European Development
Fund of the European Economic Community (EEC), the Inter-
American Development Bank (IDB), and the Inter-American Council
for Education, Science and Culture of the Organization of American
States. The Colombo Plan has also been instrumental in securing
cooperation among the main suppliers of aid to Asia, but it is extremely loosely knit and does not have policy initiatives and funds,
other than those of its individual members. A similar type of organization is the Commonwealth Fund for Technical Cooperation.

The main focus of the educational aid of the Commission of
European Communities (CEC) has been on capital aid, mainly to the
associated African and Malagasy states.* Since its inception, around
$200 million has been allocated to education for capital equipment.
In addition, 14,000 grants have been awarded in the field of education
since 1958. The policy trend is to move from capital aid toward
scholarship and training grants and to reduce the numbers being
trained in European countries and increase the numbers trained locally or in third countries.

The IDB began operating in the early 1960s in the educational
field, utilizing funds provided under the Social Progress Trust Fund
from the United States. Up to 1965, the IDB's loans were limited to
university-level education, despite the word "social" in the title of
the Trust Fund. Its policy was then changed to include technical and
vocational training, teacher training, and the support of administrative services of universities.

The IDB is considering how it could extend or revise its field of
activity to include assistance in areas of wider social impact, in the
sense of covering larger numbers of the population (for example, by
assisting primary education), and some projects are under consideration. The IDB, by the end of fiscal year 1973, had allotted $91 million
for education, representing 10.3 percent of its total operation.

The Inter-American Council for Education, Science, and Culture has been concerned mostly with science and technology (including
research in educational areas such as audiovisual aid and research

----

*The 18 associated states are Burundi, the Federal Republic of
Cameroun, the Central African Republic, the People's Republic of the
Congo, the Ivory Coast, Dahomes, the Republic of Gabon, Upper Volta,
the Republic of Madagascar, Mali, the Islamic Republic of Mauritania,
Niger, Rwanda, Senegal, Somalia, Chad, and Togo. Agreements also
have been concluded with Uganda, Kenya, and Tanzania.

and experimentation), though it also has put considerable effort into vocational and technical education. The amount for the year 1972-73 was about $2.7 million.

The Southeast Asia Ministers of Education Organization (SEAMEO)* has operated mostly through six regional centers, of which three are specifically in the educational field, namely the Regional Center for Educational Innovation and Technology (INNOTECH), the Regional Center for Education in Science and Mathematics (RECSAM), and the Regional English Language Center (RELC).

The regional centers are financed primarily by the countries in which they are located--INNOTECH in Vietnam, RECSAM in Malaysia, and RELC in Singapore, with the United States paying half during the first five years of operation. There is, in addition, a SEAMEO Educational Development Fund, which is based largely on a bond issue (SEAMEO Educational Development Bonds) to which friendly governments, organizations, and individuals can subscribe. More than 5,000 professionals benefited in one way or another up to 1972 by participating in seminars or training courses.

The Colombo Plan, which groups together loosely with a minimal secretariat the main traditional bilateral suppliers of aid to Southern Asia, covers fellowships and other educational activities. A special interest has been taken in third-country training and the supply of middle-level technicians. The assistance given is shown in the aid statistics and reports of the various bilateral donors. A similar type of organization is the Commonwealth Fund for Technical Cooperation recently launched with an initial budget of £300,000--the United Kingdom and Canada being the largest contributors, but with 17 countries taking part in all. Some portion of the funds will be devoted to education.

Other Commonwealth activities provide technical assistance under various regional funds, for example, the Special Commonwealth African Assistance Plan (SCAAP), the plan for Technical Assistance to Non-Commonwealth Countries in Africa (TANCA), and the Commonwealth Scholarship and Bursary Scheme.

It will have been seen that the different sources of funds for educational aid at the multilateral level have a varying degree of involvement in the question of educational reform and regeneration. The tendency of any funding agency would normally be somewhat inclined to support the status quo, especially if the agency were moving in an area in which it did not have previous technical experience.

---

*Its members, as of 1974, were Indonesia, the Khmer Republic, Laos, Malaysia, Philippines, Singapore, Thailand, and Vietnam. Associate members were Australia, France, and New Zealand.

Thus, the extent to which new policies and changes of criteria have been adopted has depended on technical advisers, in most cases from Unesco, but also on the general climate of opinion in the educational profession. Unesco, as has been seen, has had a major impact on the UNDP, the World Bank, and Unicef, with which it has cooperation agreements for advice on and execution of educational projects, but less on the regional organizations such as the EEC, the European Development Fund, the IDB, and the OAS. A cooperation agreement with the IDB is under consideration.

A form of assistance that falls under both multilateral and bilateral headings is the system of Funds-in-Trust, which began in 1963. Under this arrangement Unesco serves as the executing agency for funds provided by individual donor governments, nongovernmental organizations, or private firms.

The Secretariat of Unesco, through its field staff, discusses possible projects with governments of developing countries and explores their financing with potential donors. It also maintains an inventory of unmet needs. At the end of 1973, there were 157 project requests for assistance under study for aid under the Funds-in-Trust procedures, and 13 projects had been agreed on during the year, totaling about $2.5 million. This form of assistance, sometimes known as "multi-bi" aid, combines a number of advantages of both multilateral and bilateral aid and has, it would seem, an important future.

Summarizing, it may be said that at the multilateral level, Unesco, Unicef, and the World Bank are showing considerable initiative, but nevertheless the demand for more radical change is mounting.

The Director General of Unesco summed up the situation as follows in the Introduction (page xxix) to his Report on the Activities of the Organization in 1973:

> My discussions with the governments of developing countries in the course of my official journeys and visits to projects being carried out in the Field, and the general supervision of planning and management at Headquarters, convince me more and more each day of the need to carry out a thorough review of the aid provided to the countries in question through the United Nations system--particularly UNDP assistance--as regards alike the aims pursued, the methods followed and the machinery employed.
>
> Not that such aid does not have beneficial effects at the points where it is applied. On the

contrary, there is no doubt that in many instances the results secured by this means are
very good. And there is no doubt either that,
taken overall, such aid deserves something
much better than the ignorance, indifference
and even disparagement which it too often en-
counters in the so-called donor countries.
Moreover, if it were not so, how could we account for the high opinion held of such aid by
the recipient countries, which see at first hand
the efforts made and are best placed to judge of
their results? Their high opinion is sincere,
and all the more valuable because, in many
cases, it is combined with lively criticism, evi-
dencing a clear-sighted approach. But when
this is recognised--which is not, I repeat, always so to the extent deserved--I still think--
to judge from Unesco's experience at least--
that the general conception of international aid
needs to be reconsidered, as regards both
principles and practice.

We revert to these matters in Chapter 5, which discusses
criticisms and evaluations of educational cooperation. In Chapters
9 and 13 there are discussed a number of suggestions as to how the
methods, organization, and techniques of educational cooperation
might be further improved, and how various built-in delays to change
might be reduced.

NOTE

1. Rome: FAO, 1973.

4

By the mid-1960s, considerable experience had been acquired by donor governments in working within the parallel frameworks of bilateral cooperation with the newly independent countries and participation in the multilateral agencies. Educational assistance, because of its rapid rate of expansion, began increasingly to attract evaluation--not only in individual donor countries but also in the forum of the Development Assistance Committee, which initiated in 1966 some preliminary studies and exchanges of view among its mem bers as to the efficiency of the educational aid process and possible improvements.

Considerable changes were taking place in the distribution by source of educational aid. In 1963 about 96 percent of the total bilateral technical assistance of the DAC Member Countries (of which just over a half was for education) was supplied by four countries: France, the United Kingdom, the United States, and Belgium. More than half the bilateral educational assistance was supplied by France alone, and the 13 other OECD Member States together provided only a little more than Belgium. By 1969, however, while France, the United Kingdom, and the United States still provided together the bulk of educational aid, the German Federal Republic was spending half as much as France; Canada had almost reached a par with Belgium and Italy; and Sweden, the Netherlands, Australia, and Japan also had developed substantial programs.

Belgium, France, and the United Kingdom continued to concentrate on the countries with which they have historical links, mainly in Africa. Those countries absorbed 77 percent of the educational personnel and 56 percent of the experts and advisers out of the total of DAC members' aid. Some 20 African countries were still dependent to a considerable degree for their second and higher levels of education on teachers supplied under French and British schemes.

As of 1973, the amount of official bilateral educational aid supplied by the countries represented on the DAC was $1,142 million, as shown in Table 4.1. Table 4.2 shows the percentage of total aid devoted to education for the same countries. The number of publicly financed students and trainees within the sums is given in Table 4.3. Table 4.4 shows the number of educational experts (teachers, administrators, and advisers) in the totals shown in Table 4.1.

The French Government, the largest supplier of educational aid, was among the first to face problems of policy changes and redeployment, as it had large-scale programs of direct teacher supply that were called in question under the criticism that aid should not consist of mere substitution of resources. French educational aid came under criticism for the presence of too many French teachers utilizing curricula more suited to France itself than to African countries, a tendency often encouraged by the francophone elite of the ex-colonies.* Nevertheless, experiments, some not wholly successful, were initiated in a number of countries with French cooperation and assistance, to introduce new types of rural education to suit local conditions, following recommendations made in 1964 and 1966 at Conferences of Ministers of Education of the African francophone countries; and innovatory projects involving the use of television were set up in Niger and the Ivory Coast.

M. Laurent of the Ministry of Foreign Affairs summed up the situation in an OECD report.

> The road that leads to human and cultural adulthood is that of training. But we cannot ourselves directly provide this training, and we should not do so lest in effect we hold back the advancement of those countries we have undertaken to assist. Cooperation through substitution is neither very effective nor durable.
>
> In those countries where substitution is still somewhat too prominent a feature of our programmes--as in the North African States for obvious historical reasons--it is our duty to reshape our aims and our means of action by directing our major efforts towards the training of teachers and senior management. The time has

---

*A report of a committee of the National Assembly of Madagascar on the 1972 budget for cooperation with France stated, "The younger generation of Malagasy students strongly oppose older African leaders who, because of nostalgia for the education they received, would like universities which are identical to pre-World War II French universities."

TABLE 4.1

Official Bilateral Educational Commitments
(millions of dollars)

Australia	Austria	Belgium	Canada	Denmark	France	Germany	Japan
35.7	1.3	2.2	66.2	3.7	592.2	149.7	18.2

Netherlands	New Zealand	Norway	Sweden	Switzerland	U.K.	U.S.	Total*
38.5	4.0	19.1	21.9	3.1	88.3	95.0	1,142.1

*Of which total, technical cooperation was 926.13, the rest being capital aid.

Source: Development Cooperation (Paris: OECD, 1974), p. 250.

TABLE 4.2

Percentage Allocated to Education in Total Official Bilateral Aid

Australia	Austria	Belgium	Canada	Denmark	France	Germany	Japan
10.8	9.4	1.2	9.6	5.1	37.1	12.3	1.7

Netherlands	New Zealand	Norway	Sweden	Switzerland	U.K.	U.S.	Total
15.3	14.4	28.3	8.8	7.0	14.0	3.1	11.7*

*Of which total, technical cooperation was 36.5 percent, the rest being capital aid.

Source: Development Cooperation (Paris: OECD, 1974), p. 252.

come to give practical effect to a policy line
that has often been proclaimed but too seldom
followed in reality, to put an end to the dispersal of resources and concentrate them on
getting countries to train their own management personnel and their own educators.[1]

TABLE 4.3

Students and Trainees: Publicly Financed Fellowships
by Individual Donors, 1973

Country	Number of Persons Financed
Australia	4,433
Austria	564
Belgium	7,585
Canada	2,245
Denmark	321
France	14,559
Germany	24,242
Italy	1,694
Japan	5,743
Netherlands	3,123
New Zealand	1,133
Norway	424
Sweden	1,527
Switzerland	800
United Kingdom	15,002
United States	14,628
Total	98,023

Source: Development Cooperation (Paris: OECD, 1974).

TABLE 4.4

Donor Programs, 1972: Bilateral Technical Cooperation
Contributions to Developing Countries

	Teachers	Administrators	Advisers	Total Educational Experts
Australia	44	--	7	51
Austria	65	--	2	67
Belgium	1,445	41	41	1,527
Canada	1,036	73	46	1,155
Denmark	173	3	8	184
France	22,367	736	--	23,103
Germany	2,388	457	259	3,104
Italy	784	--	1	785
Japan	54	--	--	54
Netherlands	170	7	12	189
New Zealand	21	--	14	35
Norway	201	3	1	205
Sweden	70	3	3	76
Switzerland	25	--	--	25
United Kingdom	5,528	495	186	6,209
United States	283	2	669	954

Source: Development Cooperation (Paris: OECD, 1974).

Later, an interdepartmental committee was established under
M. Gorse to review, at the commencement of the United Nations
Second Development Decade, French aid to developing countries.
This document had not been published at the writing of this book, but
it is reported that recommendations were that French aid should
promote educational reform, the better relation of educational aid
to local development needs, and new methods of rapid teacher training to permit a faster takeover by Africans. This should be accompanied by a change in the nature of aid to higher education so as to
transfer responsibility directly to the countries themselves. Emphasis should be placed on education for rural development as first
priority, to be followed by industrial training as industry grew, on
adult literacy, research and development in education, and on technical and scientific education.

Although the Gorse report has not been adopted officially, it
has undoubtedly had an important effect on policy. The tendency of
the African nations to seek a fuller national consciousness both individually and as part of the African continent is leading to France
taking a wider continental view than that related earlier to its ex-
colonies. This, as shall be seen, is also a characteristic of change
in British aid. Further efforts are being made to reduce substitution and to aid experimentation in rural education more linked to development needs. But major overall policy changes remain to be
announced.

French cooperation consists heavily in the supply of teachers
at the second and third levels, the cooperation given at the technical
and professional level being of particular importance for the development of the recipient countries. This assistance is given within
the formal educational systems of the recipient countries, but a
major effort, perhaps the largest of any such efforts by donor agencies, has been made to stimulate educational reforms using nonformal or restructured forms of education. A panorama of these experiences going back over a number of years is set out in Economie
et Education en Milieu Rural by Andre Cruiziat. [2]

The Federal Republic of Germany, which has been increasing
its aid for education since 1965, is now the largest educational donor
after France, coming before the United States and the United Kingdom. West Germany was one of the countries that took very seriously the United Nations proposals for the Second Development Decade,
and in 1971 the Cabinet adopted a set of principle objectives and activities for the Decade. [3] The policy statement indicates,

In keeping with the recommendations and programmes of the multilateral organisations, the
Federal Government will take into account in

the Second Development Decade the importance
of education and science for all sectors of development through greater qualitative and
quantitative efforts. Promotional measures
should aim at a flexible adjustment of education syllabuses and methods to the changing
demands of the labour market and the social
environment. Effective measures towards
structural changes in the educational system
and the development of new teaching and
learning methods have priority over contributions effecting merely the quantitative expansion of existing educational systems.

Educational and scientific aid will enjoy
an increasing proportion of the growth of technical assistance. In suitable cases, capital
aid should also be allocated for investment in
this sector.

Increased support should be given to the
following fields in educational and scientific
aid: education administration, educational
planning and research, educational measures
outside the traditional school system including the use of mass media, flexible vocational
education systems, material infrastructure in
the educational system, and application-
oriented research.

As regards methods of operation the policy declaration states,

Educational and scientific aid will utilize all
the possibilities of cooperation in the spirit of
partnership between institutions in the developing countries and in the Federal Republic of
Germany. In this cooperation, priority is to
be given to the requirements of the developing
countries. In particular, in the provision of
educational aid, the indiscriminate transfer of
German educational models is to be avoided.

A more detailed policy statement on educational assistance
was contained in The Educational and Scientific Aid Programme of
the Federal Republic of Germany, adopted by the Federal Government in December 1971.[4]

This policy statement includes the following points:

Taking into account international thinking on
priorities and the experience gained to date,
educational aid during the Second Development
Decade will be concentrated on functional basic
education, initial and further occupational
training, educational planning and services in
support of education. These areas of concentration have been selected in order to establish closer links between the various fields of
school and out-of-school youth and adult education which hitherto have been to a larger extent unrelated. . . .

The German Federal Government will give
preferential support to measures carried out
by institutions and groups outside the formal
school system and aimed at providing a large
number of people with practical and environ-
ment-related basic knowledge. . . .

As part of its effort to widen the scope of
functional basic education, the Federal Government will intensify its aid for the reform
of primary education proceeding from the approaches found feasible so far. For this purpose it will send out teams of advisers and will
help to establish educational centres at national or regional level. . . .

Measures for the promotion of occupational
education should generally be implemented in
the developing countries. . . . The criteria
will be: the demand for skilled labour oriented
to employment, growth and social policy objectives, the prospects for their integration into the
economic and social life of the country, as well
as structural requirements within the education
system. . . .

Services for education--such as the building of educational establishments, the provision
of teaching and learning aids--are the prerequi-
site to qualitative and quantitative improvements and for ensuring the dependence and
autonomous character of the educational system in developing countries. Assistance in
this field will be intensified. . . .

> The Federal Government intends to step
> up its assistance for the application of mass
> media in education, especially for courses
> of training outside the traditional school sys-
> tem. [5]

The policy statement also makes it clear that the Federal Republic will cooperate in projects supported by a number of multilateral or bilateral agencies and will provide special grants for
projects carried out by other organizations on a transfer basis.

Among the areas to which particular attention has been given
are higher-level education and middle-level vocational training.
Study grants have also been a favored method, and large numbers of
students from the developing countries come to Germany at the
middle, higher, and postgraduate level to continue their education in
special fields, both academic and industrial.

Over the more recent years, a deepening interest has been
taken in education in the developing countries as a whole, with emphasis on projects that involve curriculum restructuring and redevel-
opment; there has also developed an interest in aid for the reform of
primary education.

In addition to official aid, there is a large amount of educational aid given from German voluntary sources, notably church organizations. Trade unions also have cooperated in projects for vocational training. There is a substantial volunteer program consisting mainly of middle-level personnel with vocational training background.

It would seem that the German aid program has had a valuable
influence on developing educational institutions such as universities,
colleges, and research institutes and in the modernization of teaching methods and teacher training. At the middle level the experience
has been more patchy. The policy was originally to use aid to set up
model vocational education centers, which it was thought would later
be taken over by the national authorities. In fact, this was found difficult to achieve since governments were not necessarily very active
in taking over the pilot institutions. Also, a satisfactory number of
the students did not go into the fields in which they had been trained.
The tendency now, therefore, is to modernize existing institutions
rather than to try to create new pilot models.

An interesting feature of the German administration of aid is
the existence of evaluation teams at headquarters, which are able to
go on short notice to study the progress of projects and to make
recommendations for changes while the operations are still in an
early stage. This procedure is discussed in later chapters of this
book and recommended for use by other agencies, since serious

difficulties often result from projects being evaluated so late that changes cannot be introduced in time to correct operations.

During the same period, U.S. aid was also changing its focus. The trend toward social objectives and reform in education in the thinking of the U.S. aid authorities was illustrated by a statement by John Hannah, the then Administrator of the United States Agency for International Development (USAID), quoted in a background paper provided by the USAID to a meeting on Educational Innovation of the Development Assistance Committee of the OECD. He stated,

> General social progress cannot be achieved by a small elite commanding a huge constituency of illiterate and disoriented people. Success in development requires that at least the majority of people be supplied with the knowledge and opportunity to participate to some reasonable degree in economic, social, and political activity.

The background paper goes on to say:

> Our perception of the current state of education, in terms of reaching this broad human development objective, is that traditional educational systems in most of the developing nations are reaching too few people with the wrong kind of education, at prohibitive cost. In recognition of this discrepancy between current systems and current needs, AID has started an organized search for alternatives.

The USAID adopted at the beginning of the decade[6] an increased interest in the sectoral, as distinct from the project by project, approach, for the purpose of "Attacking comprehensively the interrelated policy, financial and physical restraints on change." The USAID states, "While difficult to plan and execute, such integrated and comprehensive sectoral programs promise to yield far more significant results than efforts aimed at only segments of the education system." The general policy toward aid was altered, the main reforms being to "distinguish clearly between our security, development and humanitarian assistance programs and create separate organizational structures for each." An increasing share of aid was to be channeled through multilateral institutions and to be operated through the policy framework they establish. The initiatives of the developing countries themselves would be more heavily relied on, and aid implementation through the private sector would be encouraged. Aid would be concentrated in countries of special interest to the United States and in areas of special U.S. competence.

The innovative focus is being directed to three key areas: educational technology and communications, nonformal education, and educational finance and the reduction of unit costs. It is set out as follows:

> Problem Area One: To explore the potential of education technology, as broadly defined, to achieve major gains or breakthroughs in quantity, quality and cost factors in LDC [least developed countries] education and human resource development.
>
> Problem Area Two: To evaluate the experience of the LDCs (and the U.S.) with nonformal educational programs and to foster experimentation and transfer of knowledge of successful experiences between the LDCs.
>
> Problem Area Three: To foster evaluation, research, and experimentation with various modes of educational finance, and to increase the usefulness and use of economic measurements tools in educational planning, decision-making and management.
>
> All these problem areas are of concern to many other official and private assistance agencies. Every effort will be made to concert and coordinate our efforts with them in order to achieve maximum impact of research, experimentation and implementation. Similarly, it is recognized that any successful attack on these problems must be made as a joint enterprise between the TA/EHR, Regional Bureaus, Missions, governments and private institutions in the LDCs. Particular attention will be given to fostering such partnerships.

Since the adoption of the new approach reflected in the 1972 background paper, a number of sound projects have been developed in these three areas, but the amount of official U.S. educational aid has shown a decline. In 1973, it was only half ($93 million) of what it was in 1966 ($182 million). There has also been a reduction in the size of the Peace Corps, as discussed in Chapter 5.

For the years 1974 and 1975 the appropriation was $90 million a year under Section 105 of the Foreign Assistance Act of 1973. This Act states:

> Sec. 2 (2) Future United States bilateral sup-
> port for development should focus on critical
> problems in those functional sectors which
> affect the lives of the majority of the people
> in the developing countries: food production;
> rural development and nutrition; population
> planning and health; and education, public ad-
> ministration, and human resource development.
>   (5) United States bilateral development as-
> sistance should give the highest priority to
> undertakings submitted by host governments
> which directly improve the lives of the poorest
> of their people and their capacity to participate
> in the development of their countries.
>   Sec. 105. Education and Human Resources
> Development.--In order to reduce illiteracy,
> to extend basic education and to increase man-
> power training in skills related to development,
> the President is authorized to furnish assis-
> tance on such terms and conditions as he may
> determine, for education, public administra-
> tion, and human resource development.

John Hilliard, who was director of the Office of Education and Human Resources, USAID, from 1969 to 1973, gave in the summer of 1974 an illuminating account of the strategy and efforts of U.S. educational cooperation for development in an article in Prospects. [7] The criteria for overall guidance he sets out as needing careful consideration beyond the individual country approach required for sector analysis are as follows:

> Does the project, or cluster of projects, ap-
> pear to have a significant potential for:
>   Providing more useful (relevant) education/
> learning on an expanding scale. (Subject matter,
> quality methodology, delivery systems.)
>   Providing useful education to a significantly
> larger clientele at acceptable unit and total
> costs. (Relevant materials, mass media.)
>   Reaching populations which are disadvan-
> taged educationally. (Rural, urban poor,
> women, families.)

Improving "holding power" of schools to reduce dropouts and repeaters. (Making learning more real, more interesting, more participatory.)

Improving articulation of components of the education system. (Between levels of formal system and between formal and non-formal.)

Improving the content, methodology and technology of school systems or out-of-school education. (Educational system reform.)

Introducing innovations for the foregoing purposes in delivery of knowledge, skills and attitudes in respect to critical development sectors. (Effective components of education in other sector projects--health, population, nutrition, agriculture.)

Providing more effective approaches to financing, cost reduction and efficiency of school systems. (New resources, more effective allocation and utilization, greater equity in educational costs.)

Encouraging and assisting institutions in evolving and playing a more effective role in education for development. (Universities, industries, labor unions, co-operatives.)

Advancing the "state of the art" in any of the above, with particular reference to communications technology for development, out-of-school education/learning, and educational finance, costs and efficiency.

He goes on to say, "Obviously, no project or group of related projects is likely to meet more than a few of such criteria. But every project should clearly meet at least some of them, and in so doing include a generative or multiplier effect which will continue with or without further AID funding."

As regards its overall method, the USAID approaches development problems through sector analysis, that is, planning its cooperation in terms of the framework of the whole educational system concerned and the possibilities of its support or renovation.

The policy of the United Kingdom also underwent revision, and in 1971 a White Paper for Parliament on "Education in Developing Countries" was issued, based on a far-reaching review made in 1970. The main points in the White Paper were as follows:[8]

Teacher supply was to continue for Africa "in order both to sustain the expansion of their secondary school systems and to help them create or consolidate institutions of higher learning." In Asia the emphasis was on "special subjects, such as English language teaching and technical education, with some help in staff and equipment in subjects relevant to development."

New factors emphasized were that education must turn more to the agricultural sector, since jobs in the wage earning economy remain in short supply; education must be more systematically planned in relation to the needs of the economy; this must be done in closer cooperation with other aid suppliers; and "our knowledge and experience need to be adapted to changing situations--in which we may nevertheless be expected (as an ex-colonial power) to provide kinds of help which are ceasing to be appropriate."

On the question of the nature of future cooperation and the procedures to be used, the White Paper states, "There should be no question of meeting requests uncritically," and a frank dialogue is involved. Areas of development in which U.K. aid would be most helpful had to be analyzed, and the geographical distribution might come in question, since there are programs that would not continue at these present levels.

The problem of rural development had to be tackled by curriculum reform in the schools and a broad program of adult education, in which aid could supply training programs, expertise, and educational media. In both rural and urban areas, "we should be ready to help in experimental projects which may point the way to far-reaching developments."

In rural areas, aid might be offered "to one or more projects for adult education (including literacy). This might be done in association with an appropriate international agency. Furthermore, such a policy might attract private funds from within Britain." In towns and cities "there are immense problems on the outer periphery of the formal education system." The possibility of "community schools serving the needs of children, adolescents and adults should be experimented with and aid given."

As regards the supply of teachers, "there are increasing indications that we could, with advantage, put a larger part of the aid which goes to teacher supply to more selected arrangements than the present supplementation schemes." This would involve reducing the supply of contract teachers at the second level and increasing the supply going to supervision, teacher training, technical and vocational education, science and mathematics teaching, and in general help for the modernization of education. Primary teacher training also has to be increased by aid to institutes of education and training colleges.

As regards universities, their needs should be studied individually. "We shall need to consolidate our programme for the development of local staff while continuing to provide academic staff for shorter or longer periods as well as external examiners and consultants in the light of advice on the Inter-University Council and the British Council." University-to-university aid should be increased.

Aid for vocational and technical training should be given a higher priority and improved as the degree of success in the past has been varied. A Technical Education Resource Group had been set up to improve technical teacher training effort. The U.K. aid expenditure in this field was at present not large, and should be expanded, especially as it is now tending to move toward non-Commonwealth areas as well.

Currently a number of changes in policy and method are under way in the British educational cooperation program. Priority attention is to be given to the poorest countries and the poorest people in those countries and hence to the development and improvement of living conditions in rural areas. Assistance in other areas will be continued, but it would not normally be increased. Greater collaboration with voluntary agencies is being encouraged.

From outward appearances British bilateral aid is organized in a very complicated way. The main provider of funds is the Ministry of Overseas Development, but a large proportion of them are spent through the British Council, which not only is an education aid agency but also is undertaking, outside the aid program proper, on its own responsibility though in consultation with the other British governmental agencies concerned, paid educational services for certain developing countries (such as Iran, Saudi Arabia, and Venezuela).

Various forms of cooperation are looked after by specialized bodies, for example, the British Volunteer Programme (BVP), the Inter-University Council for Higher Education (IUC), and the Organisation for Technical Education and Training in Overseas Countries (TETOC). It is clearly of major concern that these agencies, which enjoy a considerable measure of autonomy, should be in a position to advise on policy, and to work in an integrated and coordinated way within the general lines of governmental policy; formal and informal steps are currently being taken accordingly.

As regards the regeneration and modernization of education, the White Paper stated,

> In most poor countries there is a wide gap between the education arrangements and their present and future needs. Addiction to obsolete and inappropriate metropolitan models

and to rote learning, undue emphasis on overseas examinations, chronic shortages of
trained staff, buildings and equipment, and
grave administrative weakness all ensure that
the gap will not be an easy one to close. The
position is often made worse by voracious public demand for more of the educational mixture
as before.

Efforts in promoting new educational techniques had been
sporadic and not well coordinated," and a new organization for this
purpose had been set up.

In the next ten years the impact of new ideas
about learning, new teaching methods, new
equipment and the pervasive influence of the
mass media might offer the possibility of radical change, though it is a matter of judgement
how far they should be allowed to alter the existing methods. The organisational strains on
overseas Ministries of Education and on the
other departments of government concerned
with education and training will be immense.
So will the opportunities for wasting money and
dissipating resources in ill-planned and uncoordinated activities, undertaken not only by
local governments but by a great variety of
donors. On the other hand, the positive possibilities for change will obviously also be of
tremendous significance. We have made arrangements to help in this context by setting
up a new organisation, the Centre for Educational
Development Overseas, which will deal not only
with curricula but with educational technology
and with the organisational implications of change.
We are ensuring that the new body is properly related to our own aid efforts and to that of other
donors and operators in adjacent fields.

An annual expenditure of around £1.2 million was a rough forecast
of the center's initial resources. U.K. aid in one sector or another
had, by 1971, extended into 100 developing countries. The same
trend of moving into a wider group of countries than those in which
they were traditionally interested is true also of the French and Belgian programs, which also cover a great variety of countries.

Belgian aid has been concentrated in the 1960s on its ex-colonies: Zaire, Rwanda, and Burundi. Later it was extended to other francophone African countries and also into Latin America and Asia. It has mostly been vocational and technical, and as compared with the aid of the other ex-colonial powers, less directed to secondary and higher education and more toward vocational and technical education, though Belgian teachers work also in the second and higher educational levels.

An interesting feature of the approach Belgium has taken to education is that--unlike the other powers, which tended to support types of education that supplied the administrative cadres and the national elite--it has acted to favor universal primary education. The enrollment ratios at the primary level are much higher in Zaire and Rwanda than in other African countries at a similar level of economic development. This has been due to national efforts, but these undoubtedly have been influenced by Belgian policy when it was the colonial power, as well as by the work of Belgian missionaries who took a very effective practical view of educational needs at the village level, onto which the national governments have grafted new initiatives and resources.

Belgium has also undertaken a number of joint projects, for example, with Germany and the United Kingdom on educational radio and with the Netherlands on technical education. A considerable number of trainees and students are also received in Belgium and given study grants. In this connection there has been a move toward group courses as opposed to grants to individuals, which is also one of the recommendations made later in the chapter on study abroad.

Educational aid from Canada, given through the Canadian International Development Agency (CIDA), has grown rapidly in volume in recent years, making it the next largest donor after the previous countries listed. The relative newness of the Canadian effort has permitted it to move into new areas of assistance, both in geographical terms and in the types and methods of aid, and to show considerable innovatory spirit.

Canada has, in particular, redeployed its previous effort of direct provision of teachers to fill gaps in the second level in developing countries. Help is still given in this respect, including the francophone and some of the anglophone countries of Africa, but the movement now is toward expert help in curriculum development and assistance to educational reform and to the spread of basic education.

Teacher training, however, continues to be an important item, and emphasis is being placed on assistance to technical and vocational training and on basic education and nonformal education. The main geographical concentration is on Africa south of the Sahara, but educational aid is also given to South Asian countries.

Canadian aid has been particularly active in promoting third-country training of students. Although receiving considerable numbers of students from developing countries, by her "third-country" method, Canada enables students from one developing country to study in another, so as to reduce "brain drain" and to encourage types of instruction particularly related to the problems of the developing countries. Canada has joined in an important scheme, supported predominantly by the United States and the United Kingdom, for third-country training in Africa, conducted under the auspices of the Association of African Universities.

The trend in Canadian technical assistance, the heading under which educational assistance falls, is described in Canada and the Developing World, the annual review of CIDA for 1970-71. It is an interesting summary of the change in demand, which is general and applies to other aid agencies also.

> During the years under review, there has been an encouraging growth of the capability of many developing countries to provide their own senior and middle-level manpower, and to take over positions previously filled by foreign personnel. In education, for example, there was a substantial lessening of the demand for Canadian primary and secondary school teachers, and even for university professors. On the other hand, there was an increased demand for teacher-trainers and various types of education specialists and planners. As the developing countries began to plan increased facilities for the training of craftsmen and technicians, a very strong demand arose for qualified Canadian instructors in technical and vocational subjects: the demand became so great that some requests had to be declined because no suitable candidates could be found.
>
> In other sectors the scope for generalists seems to be rapidly diminishing. The need now is for senior experts with advanced professional training who have had several years relevant experience in positions of responsibility. There is a general trend away from operational personnel toward individuals who can serve as advisers to government departments and public corporations.

Australian aid for education (other than for Papua and New Guinea) consists mostly of receiving students from Asian universities into Australian institutions, though it is now starting to move toward a strategy of aiding the growth of institutions in the countries from which the students come and toward third-country training. Difficulties have arisen about the choices of the students to study in Australia, and as regards their return to development work in the countries from which they come, which have led to some revision of selection policy. Educational experts are also abroad from Australia in limited numbers, and heavy support is given, both financial and in terms of expertise, to Papua and New Guinea.

Swedish aid to education has played a particularly important role owing to the clarity of its objectives and priorities and the high level of its operational performance, although it is less in quantity than that of the major powers. It doubled in amount between 1968-69 and 1972-73 and has also gone up rapidly since 1972-73.

The objectives of Swedish aid have been described by the Swedish International Development Authority (SIDA) in Aid and Education-- Policy and Programme, 1972 as follows:

> Among the goals of the educational system, SIDA places especial importance on the following: to provide vocational knowledge; to provide the foundations for communication and cooperation; to contribute to the achievement of equality; and to permit social changes. . . . In the present situation priority should be given to the following subsectors: non-formal education, elementary education, vocational training and supplementary vocational training, including agricultural training and training of teachers and administrators within these fields. The second priority will then be secondary education, especially in science, technology and agriculture, training of secondary school teachers and administrators. The third priority will be tertiary education.

Swedish aid has concentrated on a selection of countries, notably Botswana, Cuba, Ethiopia, India, Kenya, Pakistan, Tanzania, Tunisia, Zambia, Afghanistan, Lesotho, Liberia, Sri Lanka, and Swaziland. Swedish resources are offered in the form of material resources (teaching aids, equipment, buildings) accompanied often by technical assistance, field personnel (expert advisers or teachers and teacher training staff), and courses and seminars. The granting of scholarships for study in Sweden, a method in use

earlier, has been largely discontinued in favor of grants for study
in the developing countries themselves.

The concept of close integration of educational aid with the
country's own educational system, the employment situation, and
social objectives is leading to an increased interest in basic education. Emphasis in the past on direct aid to technical and vocational
schools also has been reduced in favor of teacher training. Sweden
has shown a special interest in the education of women and girls.

Sweden has made more use than the other bilateral agencies of
the Funds-in-Trust system, under which the agencies provide funds
for jointly selected projects administered through Unesco.

The Netherlands are also a substantial provider of assistance
under educational cooperation programs with an influence greater
than that indicated by its volume, owing to its quality. In addition
to financing considerable numbers of students and trainees in countries of origin and in third countries as well as in the Netherlands,
a substantial number of teachers and educational advisers are at
work in a considerable range of countries.

Norway, Denmark, Austria, New Zealand, and Switzerland
mostly divide their effort between scholarships and experts, with a
preponderance to the former.

The efforts of the smaller aid-suppliers have often had a usefulness well out of proportion to their volume. Some of them have
specialized in particularly important fields of study where they have
special facilities to offer; others have undertaken novel and experimental projects. In general, they have supported increased use of
multilateral aid, and they value and use Unesco's Funds-in-Trust
system, as it relieves them of the burden of setting up local missions to identify and carry out projects.

Other countries giving educational aid, apart from the socialist
countries of Eastern Europe, which are dealt with in a separate section, are notably Spain, India, the United Arab Republic, and Israel.
There are also arrangements in the developing regions by which different countries assist each other by exchange of students and pool-
ing of training facilities, but these are relatively small. Spain has
been concerned mainly with technical and vocational training in Latin
America, the UAR has aided universities and secondary schools in
the Arab states, and Kuwait and other Arab states also have contributed financial aid to education in the Arab world. India and
Israel have assisted African countries south of the Sahara with
training and study grants.

Additions to the ranks of the bilateral donor countries will be
likely to emerge during the next decade particularly from those that
are at present increasing both their income and their educational development at a fast rate. This should assist the process of educational

cooperation between countries of the same region with similar cultures and educational problems.

Italian aid to education is largely in the form of the maintenance of public Italian schools and subsidies to private ones in countries in which it has had historical connections (Libya, Ethiopia,
Somalia, UAR, and certain Latin American countries). Originally
intended to meet the needs of expatriate Italians, those schools are
now used mainly by the nationals of the countries concerned. There
is also a considerable program of scholarships and training grants
and officially organized courses for students from the developing
countries.

The assistance given by Japan consists mostly of grants for
individual training in Japan, though there are also some training
centers set up in Asian countries. There is, however, a program
for aid to secondary education, in the form of experts and equipment,
for science teaching in second-level education and some supply of
teachers at the university level. An important contribution to educational research is made by the Japanese National Institute of Educational Research (NIER), which works in close cooperation with
Unesco and 18 Asian countries to meet research needs in the Asian
region.

EDUCATIONAL AID FROM THE SOCIALIST
COUNTRIES OF EASTERN EUROPE

Educational aid from the socialist countries of Eastern Europe
was small between 1955 and 1960, consisting of financing the education in the USSR of a small number of students from the developing
countries. In 1960 there was a radical change of policy, and since
then most Soviet agreements have included provision for education
and training, educational aid being integrated with overall aid projects. After 1960 the other socialist countries of Eastern Europe
also started programs, which together represent about half the total
socialist educational aid effort. Educational aid from this source
became concentrated on technological institutions and technical
schools mainly in Africa and Asia and study in the donor country for
students from those regions.

A study by the Institute of Economics of the World Socialist
System (Moscow), prepared for UNCTAD[9] in 1970, deals with "innovations in the practice of trade and economic cooperation between
the socialist countries of Eastern Europe and the developing countries." It points out that the "Number of intergovernmental trade
agreements and agreements on economic, scientific, and technical
cooperation increased many times over during the last ten to fifteen

years. "[10] At the same time, it states that the level "does not as
yet fully reflect either the place held by the socialist countries of
Eastern Europe in the world economy or the potentialities of the
Third World." While each country organizes its own external relations independently, cooperation is provided for by CMEA (Council
for Mutual Economic Assistance). [11]

The basic principle guiding the cooperation is mutual benefit,
and is expressed as follows by the Moscow Institute: "mutual benefit, assistance in bridging the economic abyss between highly developed and less advanced countries, equality of both parties, the transfer of scientific, technical, and production 'know-how' by the more
developed to the less developed countries, prevention of unjustified
one-sided concentration of the benefits of cooperation." While, as
stated by the Moscow Institute, "this cooperation is concentrated
above all in the sphere of material production," the socialist countries of Eastern Europe "train personnel for the developing countries at all levels, both in their own educational establishments and
within the developing countries themselves. They are building higher
and secondary educational establishments and vocational training
centres, and also send their teachers and instructors to other countries. "[12]

Assistance is mainly rendered on the basis of intergovernmental agreements and also under scientific and cultural cooperation
plans between the interested countries. In part it is also effected
through the United Nations and its specialized agencies and by under-
standings between public organizations of a socialist and developing
country. Some countries accept students as a result of individual
applications and also students who pay for their own tuition. The
diverse cooperation channels ensure flexibility of operation and the
possibility of adjustment to the specific conditions of the various
countries. Personnel is trained in those specialties that suffer from
the greatest shortages in a particular developing country; a mutually
complementary system of training personnel in different skills is
applied in a developing and a socialist country.

More than 20 higher-education establishments are being set up
in developing countries with the help of the socialist countries of
Eastern Europe. They will have an overall student body of more
than 155,000 (in Burma, India, Ethiopia, Cambodia, Guinea, Indonesia, Mali, Tunisia, Algeria, Kenya, and other developing countries). Some 30 establishments of secondary technical education
are also being created. Middle-grade personnel and skilled workers
are being trained in over 100 special vocational training centers.
These centers are usually set up on the construction sites, and a
socialist country assumes full responsibility for designing and building such centers and providing them with instructional equipment

and study aids. But wherever possible local specialists are drawn
into this work.

As regards study abroad, in 1967, there were 19,400 citizens
of developing countries studying in higher and secondary educational
establishments of the socialist countries of Eastern Europe; of these,
8,400 (44.4 percent) were from Asian countries, 9,000 (46 percent)
were from African countries, and 2,000 (about 10 percent) were
from Latin America. As compared with 1963, the number of these
students had almost doubled (10,900 and 19,400, respectively).[13]
Most of the students, postgraduates, and those undergoing practical
training become specialists in industry, agriculture, and education.
Large groups of skilled workers and specialists of average and high
qualification also undergo practical training directly at factories,
in designing and research institutes, state farms, governmental offices, and vocational training establishments of the socialist countries of Eastern Europe. In the USSR, for example, about 23,000
people had received such training by 1965;[14] in Czechoslovakia more
than 2,500 specialists from developing countries were trained from
1959-64 (at present about 1,000 people receive training annually).[15]
Training is done either in connection with deliveries of complete
plants or independently in a broader specialty.

Special higher-education establishments for training highly
competent personnel from among citizens of Asian, African, and
Latin American countries have been set up in the Soviet Union and
Czechoslovakia and are functioning successfully. The Patrice
Lumumba Friendship University was founded in the USSR in 1960
and has large material and technical facilities. It is now attended
by more than 3,600 students and over 120 postgraduates from 83
countries. * Czechoslovakia and the German Democratic Republic
also train large numbers of students.

Other new forms of training personnel from developing countries have been introduced recently in the socialist countries of
Eastern Europe. Among them are the advanced training of planning
experts and specialists in the location of the productive forces in

―――――――――――――

*The Patrice Lumumba Friendship University has six main
departments. The engineering department prepares specialists in
power machinery, engineering, construction, geology, and mineral
prospecting. The agricultural department trains a broad range of
agronomists. The department of physical, mathematical, and
natural sciences prepares physicists, mathematicians, and chem-
ists. Historians, specialists in Russian language and literature,
and journalists are trained in the historical-philological department.
There are also departments of medicine, economics, and law.

newly independent countries, together with specialists in town development and local planning and economic planning courses, organized
along the lines laid down by the United Nations (for example, at the
Higher School of Planning and Statistics in Warsaw, where 150 people
from 30 newly independent countries have already graduated).

The trend in numbers and geographical distribution over recent
years as regards students and trainees from the developing countries
in the USSR and the other socialist countries of Eastern Europe can
be seen from Table 4.5. If the socialist developing countries are
included, the total reaches 19,400 in 1967.

The distribution by subjects of the students as at 1967 is shown
in Table 4.6.

The rate of expansion of education and training programs of the
Eastern European socialist countries can be seen from the fact that
they have multiplied 12 times since 1958 and nearly twice since 1963.
The number of teachers involved is 10,000, with a yearly input of
about 2,000. Aid for education and training is regarded as a priority area for the future as well as at present. The proportion of educational aid given by the USSR and the other socialist countries of
Eastern Europe has changed owing to the increased activities of the
latter, from 65 percent earlier in the decade to 55 percent.

In the matter of training, the most favored method in use is
that of mass training of national personnel directly on the construction site of the enterprises and other projects built with the help of
the aid-supplying countries. As of 1968, more than 200,000 skilled
workers, technicians, and other specialists in many developing countries had been trained on the job individually and in groups, as well
as in training centers of the enterprises, including 150,000 with the
help of Soviet specialists. This method accounted for more than
four-fifths of the total national personnel trained with the help of the
socialist countries of Eastern Europe.

The amounts of educational assistance for development for this
group of countries are not published in that form and have to be estimated from the overall assistance figures. Overall assistance
from the USSR amounted in 1970 to around 25 percent of its GNP, of
which about $850 million went to communist developing countries and
$300 million to others. A change of trend took place in 1971, and
the amount going to noncommunist countries (for example, Egypt,
Algeria, Iraq, and Pakistan) increased nearly threefold. Most USSR
assistance consists of loans at rates of interest of 2.5 to 3 percent
to be repaid in 8 to 12 years and of commercial credits at 3 to 3.5
percent. Educational cooperation usually forms part of such development or trade assistance.

TABLE 4.5

Students and Trainees from Nonsocialist Developing Countries
in the USSR and Eastern European Socialist Countries

	Africa	Asia and Middle East	Latin America	Total
		Students		
1965				
USSR	5,065	4,435	935	10,435
Other socialist countries of				
Eastern Europe	2,800	1,920	305	5,025
Total	7,865	6,355	1,240	15,460
1966				
USSR	6,305	3,795	1,115	11,215
Eastern Europe	2,920	1,805	355	5,080
Total	9,225	5,600	1,470	16,395
1967				
USSR	5,750	3,425	1,100	10,275
Eastern Europe	2,250	1,600	300	4,150
Total	8,000	5,025	1,400	14,425
1968				
USSR	6,080	4,200	1,500	11,780
Eastern Europe	1,840	1,650	480	3,970
Total	7,920	5,850	1,980	15,750
		Trainees		
1965				
USSR	330	1,030	--	1,360
Eastern Europe	440	345	--	785
Total	770	1,375	--	2,145
1966				
USSR	180	1,335	5	1,520
Eastern Europe	365	555	15	935
Total	545	1,890	20	2,455
1967				
USSR	375	600	10	985
Eastern Europe	375	700	15	1,090
Total	750	1,300	25	2,075
1968				
USSR	220	735	--	955
Eastern Europe	220	480	--	700
Total	440	1,220	--	1,655

Source: United Nations (E/7011/D6), 1970.

TABLE 4.6

Student Distribution by Subject

Subject	Number	Percentage
Industry	5,800	35.9
Health services	3,800	23.9
Education arts	3,700	23.1
Economics, science, and law	1,400	8.8
Agriculture	1,300	8.3

Note: The figures exclude students attending preparatory courses not yet classified by specialties.

Source: United Nations (E/7011/D6), 1970.

China in 1971 is reported to have supplied $400 million to developing countries (communist and noncommunist), but the educational component has been only a small fraction of the total. Of the total, by far the greater part consists of grants; the rest (perhaps 15 percent) consists of interest-free loans repayable over 10 to 15 years after a period of grace of about 10 years. Some 26 noncommunist countries (among them, Ethiopia and the Sudan) took part in cooperation agreements with China.

The countries of Eastern Europe are also active in both overall cooperation and in education especially in the form of study and training in their countries of students and fellows from developing countries. The estimate for 1971 was at just under $300 million of overall aid from these countries. These countries in general operate, as does the USSR, through loan agreements, but usually on more rigorous interest and repayment terms.

PRIVATE BUSINESS AND EDUCATION AND TRAINING

No figures are available showing the contribution to education and training in the developing countries resulting from the activities of foreign private business. Considerable effort, however, is expended on the training of staff in local enterprises and by bringing them to headquarters. There are also schemes for sending personnel to universities in their own countries, in third countries, or in the headquarters country. A few foreign businesses also contribute actual schools for the children of their employees.

In any final assessment of benefit, the profits by the foreign business have to be taken into account if the matter is viewed from the financial angle. From a resource angle, the operative question is whether the education and training would in fact have been carried out without the foreign contribution and whether more substitution of expatriates by local staff is possible. Educationally, the presence of such companies usually has both direct and indirect favorable influences in stimulating educational development. These could be exploited more appropriately if foreign firms were willing to combine to make a special direct contribution to training or to public educational systems in areas where they were drawing heavily on the output of the educational system. In a number of developing countries in Latin America local employers have themselves set up such schemes, for example, SENAI in Brazil, SENA in Colombia, SENATI in Peru, and INCI in Venezuela. Such systems could be usefully extended with the participation of foreign enterprises.

A pilot survey of technical assistance expended by private enterprise was undertaken by the OECD in 1967. It suggests that the number of people from developing countries trained in member countries by private enterprise at its own expense probably exceeds substantially the number of officially financed trainees in industry and trade, and that the number of persons trained by foreign private enterprise in developing countries is probably considerably superior to the number trained in the OECD Development Assistance Committee's member countries. It showed, too, that a number of foreign firms extend--especially in Africa--fellowship grants for studies at local universities.

The role of multinational business corporations has become a matter of increasing international concern. The largest of them have revenues exceeding the GNP of quite a large number of the developing countries taken individually. Their profits are far in excess of the regular budgets and voluntary contributions of the entire UN family. If these corporations were able, in addition to their present educational and training contribution, to offer even a small percentage of their profits for use as educational aid under a Funds-in-Trust system of Unesco, a very substantial sum could be made available for education in the developing countries, while at the same time only making an extremely small difference to their profits.

NOTES

1. Aid to Education in Less Developed Countries (Paris: Organisation for Economic Cooperation and Development, 1971), p. 97.
2. Andre Cruiziat, Economie et Education en Milieu Rural, vol. 1, Panorama des experiences non conventionnelles de formation

pour 14 Etats africains et malgache (Paris: Secretariat d'Etat aux Affaires Etrangeres, Direction de l'Aide au Developpement).

3. These are set out in full in Development Policy Concept of the Federal Republic of Germany for the Second Development Decade (Bonn: Federal Ministry of Economic Cooperation and Press and Information Office of the Federal Government, 1971), in English.

4. (Bonn: German Foundation for Developing Countries, 1972), DOK 640 a/72.

5. Ibid.

6. See U.S. Agency for International Development, "United States Foreign Aid and the Alliance for Progress: Proposed Fiscal Year 1970 Program."

7. John Hilliard, "Towards an AID Strategy in Education," Prospects 4, no. 2 (Summer 1974).

8. United Kingdom, Ministry of Overseas Development, Education in Developing Countries: A Review of Current Problems and of British Aid (London: Her Majesty's Stationery Office, 1970).

9. United Nations (E/7011/D6), 1970.

10. See also UNCTAD, Review of Trade Relations Among Countries Having Different Economic and Social Systems, para. 62 in Proceedings of the United Nations Conference on Trade and Development, Second Session, Vol. 5, Special Problems in World Trade and Development (E/68/IID18), and Hungarian Institute for Economic and Market Research, The Use of Long-Term Agreements as an Instrument for Promoting Trade Between Socialist and Developing Countries (TD/18/Supp. 2), p. 18.

11. As regards the membership, the UNCTAD paper, op. cit., states, "At present Bulgaria, Czechoslovakia, German Democratic Republic, Hungary, Mongolia, Poland, Romania, and the Soviet Union are taking part in the work of CMEA. In conformity with an agreement between CMEA and Yugoslavia, the latter cooperates in CMEA on questions of mutual interest. Other socialist countries also participate in the work of CMEA agencies as observers."

12. UN (E/7011/D6), op. cit.

13. See Diplomatiia i kadry (Moscow, 1968), p. 86.

14. See Vneshniaia torgovlia, no. 3 (Moscow, 1966): 10.

15. See Mezinarodni Vztahy, no. 1 (Prague, 1966): 33.

5

NONGOVERNMENTAL
COOPERATION

Governments contribute obligatorily to the international organizations of which they are members with amounts fixed according to
the size of their national income. But they also make general moral
commitments as in the case of the expressed intention, approved in
the UN Strategy for the First Development Decade, to raise their
annual official development assistance to 1 percent of their gross
national product, including voluntary contributions to multilateral
agencies and bilateral aid.

The International Development Association, the part of the
World Bank that gives soft credits on easy terms, and the UNDP are
financed entirely from voluntary contributions by governments.
Unicef receives its resources both from voluntary allocations by
governments and from fund-raising from private sources. Moreover, bilateral aid is voluntary in the sense that no country is under
an obligation to conclude a cooperation agreement with another.

Governments also give support to individual volunteers who
wish to serve in the developing countries, either entirely voluntary
or as an alternative to national military service. This movement
has been considerable in the past but has been found to be expensive,
since the moment governments intervene, questions arise of adjusting the conditions of volunteers to national and international standards.
For this reason, as well as because of uncertainties over recruitment, this form of cooperation has not developed internationally on
a large scale. Important efforts have been made by the U.S. Peace
Corps and volunteers from other countries such as the United Kingdom, where there are strong traditions of voluntary contributions to
public efforts. Nevertheless the cost has been high[1]--the average
expenditure for a Peace Corps volunteer (including administrative
costs) in 1967 was set at around $7,600 a year to the United States.

The figures for Swedish volunteers was around $5,000 a year (ex-
cluding administrative costs).

Volunteers going from one developing country to another cost
between $2,400 and $3,000 (excluding travel and administrative cost),
while a domestic volunteer working in his own country costs much
less. In 1968-69, the average minimum cost of an Ethiopian university service man was around $900, whereas in 1967-68 each volun-
teer of the Company of Young Canadians required an outlay of $10,500.

The initiative started by the United Nations for an International
Volunteer Service has been disappointing, and the general outlook is
poor except for schemes, as in Iran, where it is an alternative to
military service.

The UN study already cited states,

> Some observers of the situation with regard to
> youth suggested the possibility of achieving "a
> civilization of service," in which, in contrast
> to the basically self-centered consumer society,
> citizens, with their material needs easily satis-
> fied thanks to technological advances, would de-
> vote a significant proportion of their lives to
> serving their fellow men. Other commentators
> were not convinced that service was more than a
> passing fad, whose very modishness among the
> younger generation jeopardised its survival as a
> major youth activity. They pointed to a succes-
> sion of organizational crisis in a number of
> schemes, to the reduction in financial appropria-
> tions accorded by Governments to certain pro-
> grammes, to recruitment figures that were
> levelling off or falling off, to the shift of youth-
> ful interest from social to political action or in-
> action (in the case of the "hippies"), even to the
> disappearance of a number of schemes that only
> a few months earlier seemed to promise great
> expansion. The 1950s had been the decade of
> service to youth, they pointed out, when the num-
> ber of Governments making administrative and
> financial provision for aid to out-of-school youth
> activities had grown nearly tenfold. Then came
> the 1960s, the decade of service by youth, when
> Governments began assisting youth to volunteer.
> What reason was there to suppose the evolution
> should stop?

The study concludes, "The 1970s may be either a decade of increased participation by youth in society through development-oriented voluntary service, or of rejection of that society by youth. It remains to be seen whether the world is moving towards a civilization of service."

Proposals have been made at various times for a Voluntary Fund to dispense educational aid; the 15th Unesco General Conference called for a Secretariat study; and a feasibility study was made in 1969. The conclusions of the study were that there appeared little chance of obtaining additional funds for education by setting up a new international fund, owing to lack of support and the proposal has not been raised again in Unesco since then. Apart from doubt as to achieving the required measure of additional funds to justify the project, there was opposition to the multiplication of voluntary funds.

It was, however, found that there was some support for the idea of establishing with voluntary contributions an international center for research and innovation in education, which might finance research and experimentation in pilot projects set up in different parts of the world. The result might be expected to add to the efficiency and relevance of education and thereby make an impact going well beyond the normal application of relatively small amounts of money. In addition, the feasibility study drew attention to the possibilities of mobilizing additional resources from countries, voluntary organizations, and multinational businesses by a greater use of Unesco's Funds-in-Trust system. The Executive Board approved the general tenor of the feasibility study but took no specific action, except to ask for other reports in due course on how further progress could be made on the positive elements in the feasibility study.

In his Report of the activities of the organization of 1970, the Director General comments as follows in respect of the resources voluntarily provided by individual governments and by Unesco under its Funds-in-Trust scheme:

> . . . the expansion of the Funds-in-Trust de-
> serves special mention, in spite of the relative-
> ly small amount involved, for I am convinced
> that this formula, which combines the best
> features of bilateral and of international cooper-
> ation, has a great future before it. I am en-
> deavouring to take full advantage of all the pos-
> sibilities offered in this respect, and I would
> take this opportunity of appealing again to the
> developed countries to make more use of the
> Organisation's services in this way for the
> benefit of the developing countries.

The Funds-in-Trust system is a way of overcoming the obstacles created, particularly for smaller aid-givers, by the cost and difficulty of maintaining a staff for project identification and preparation purposes. The expansion of this system would be likely to reflect a genuine addition to aid funds and not a substitution, because the facilities offered ease the task of aid-giving for the governments. Moreover, this system can, it may be hoped, tap new sources of funds, such as from multinational industry.

The largest of such businesses have a turnover greater than the budgets of many countries and than the GNP of the smallest countries. Even if only a very small percentage of their revenue were to be devoted annually to educational aid undertaken through Unesco, the total amount would be very large. Certain of such businesses traditionally have interested themselves in education, and at least one concern is at present studying the question of giving a percentage of its revenue for educational aid. Since multinational businesses are, as a whole, under considerable criticism for overall economic and political reasons, a disinterested contribution to education to be administered by Unesco would be a happy step for them to take.

A field in which there has been considerable and growing success is in the work of the nonprofit sector (voluntary agencies, foundations, and such) in educational cooperation.

The main contributors under this heading are the churches and foundations and nongovernmental organizations,[2] many of whom have expertise based on a long history of providing assistance. The OECD has estimated that for the year 1970 net private foreign aid for all purposes amounted to $858 million, rising to $1,362 million in 1973. If government subventions to voluntary agencies are added, the total is increased to $1,676 million, of which 67 percent come from the United States, followed in size of contribution by the Federal Republic of Germany, Canada, and the United Kingdom. There are no statistics collected of the amount of voluntary agency assistance to education, but informed opinion believes it is about half of total regular voluntary agency activities abroad, though a deduction has to be made for special contributions, for example the large remittances to Israel from the United States. Somewhat under half is allotted to education. Having in mind that the subventions from public funds are in some cases counted in official aid, it would seem that between $300 and $350 million a year was in 1973 being added to education from this source.

The merit of private aid of this kind is that it is generally a net addition to the educational flow, as it is not competing with official bilateral or multilateral aid. Further, it tends to be operated with close regard to the technical and educational factors involved and adjusts to local circumstances with considerable skill. On the other hand, there is the danger of lack of integration with overall national

planning and with the contributions from other agencies due to the
aid being unofficial. Sometimes, too, there is the disadvantage of
"pet" projects being adopted or of particular sections of the community, in the case of aid by religious organizations, being favored
over others. Many of these possible disadvantages can be overcome,
and the experience of this type of aid drawn upon, if the regular
practice could be adopted of closer consultation with such agencies
by governments, while respecting their independence. Action might
include inviting the larger sources of private aid to take part in consortia and consultative groups dealing with program planning and
educational aid.

A valuable recommendation in this sense was made at the conference on Christian Education in Africa in 1963.[3]

> We recommend that in every country the Churches
> examine the possibility of establishing an asso-
> ciation for their cooperation in educational plan-
> ning, and service it with an adequate secretariat
> to enable effective consultation with their govern-
> ments and liaison with Churches in other parts of
> Africa and in countries overseas.

No information is immediately available as to how far their recommendations have been carried out, but it would obviously have value
in connection with country programing procedures.

Certain aid-supplying governments (for example, the United
States) widely use private nonprofit organizations for the carrying
out of projects and make considerable use of contracts with universities in the donor country to deal directly with their counterparts in
developing countries.

The voluntary agencies in the United States and the Federal Republic of Germany are the largest contributors. The World Council
of Churches has its own budget of educational assistance, which is
relatively small scale, but its constituent organizations have large
educational assistance programs. The U.S. Government supports
the voluntary agencies with funds for specific purposes, including
education, and the German Federal Government acts similarly.
There is no direct control in either case, though the USAID encourages them to form consortia for improving program planning, management, and evaluation.

There was a decline in the trend of the flow from voluntary organizations and foundations from the United States during the late
1960s, and a rise in Europe. The Advisory Committee of the USAID
on Voluntary Foreign Aid reported that the dollar remittances of the
registered U.S. voluntary agencies active in international development

was just over $557 million in 1970 but that this represented a reduction of 17 percent from 1968. By 1973 it had more than recovered this reduction and in 1974 totaled $949 million.

Little material exists, and few studies have been made, showing the volume, distribution, and trend of educational assistance to the developing countries from voluntary organizations. A case study by John D. Lange Jr., issued by the U.S. Foreign Service Institute,[4] contains the following tables showing assistance for all purposes, in which education takes a large share, from private nonprofit organizations, and indicating the use of such organizations as channels of government funds. (See Tables 5.1 and 5.2.)

The international programs of U.S. foundations also vary in volume according to economic fluctuations.

The Ford and Rockefeller Foundations are important examples of the role of foundations in educational cooperation. Between 1950 and the end of 1972, the Ford Foundation made commitments totaling $4.2 billion. The volume of its specifically educational assistance going to the developing countries was $14.8 million in 1973. The Foundation's brochure "International Programs of the Ford Foundation" points out, however, that "Support of education is common to all divisions and offices of the Foundation. All in all, some two thirds of the funds granted annually by the Foundation support activities that could be described as 'educational'." This brings the total to about 30 million for 1973. The Foundation is now making a cutback, owing to a reduction of the income of the Foundation due to economic conditions.

The method employed by the Ford Foundation has been to use the advantages it has as regards flexibility and objectivity, and ability to draw on high-level skills to assist in the building up of the capacities of individual countries to meet their educational needs. It maintains a network of highly qualified field offices to assess opportunities to respond to requests for support. Over recent years, the effort has been increasingly directed to helping the development of capacities for educational planning and research, particularly with reference to improving the educational opportunities of the less privileged and the poor and improving the overall quality and relevance of education. Examples of Ford Foundation cooperation projects are the support given to a national assessment of education in Indonesia; the research on the distribution and performance of elementary education in Thailand; the study of dropouts in Malaysia; assistance to planning and research centers in six Latin American countries designed to strengthen their analytical capacity and to enlarge their communication with each other on common problems; support to the Center for Educational Research and Development and the Science and Mathematics Education Center in Lebanon, advanced

TABLE 5.1

Worldwide Private Foreign Aid (Net)[a]

(remittances in millions of dollars to LDCs)

	1970	1971	1972	1973
Worldwide	858.3	912.8	1,035.9	1,362.2
As a percent of official aid	12%	12%	12%	15%
United States	651.0	621.7	697.2	905.3[b]
As a percent of official aid	21%	19%	21%	30%
Germany	77.8	108.3	123.6	157.2
As a percent of official aid	13%	14%	15%	14%
Canada	51.6	49.0	54.0	78.4
As a percent of official aid	15%	12%	11%	15%
United Kingdom	33.6	46.2	50.0	53.9
As a percent of official aid	7%	8%	8%	9%
Sweden	25.2	23.6	27.2	29.9
As a percent of official aid	22%	15%	13%	11%
France	6.3	7.2	7.9	10.0
As a percent of official aid	1%	1%	1%	1%
Others	12.8	56.8	76.0	127.5
As a percent of official aid	1%	3%	4%	5%

[a]Net of any government contributions.

[b]About half of this sum consists of assistance to Israel.

Source: OECD.

social science training of educational researchers in Brazil; and, starting in 1975, a long-term effort to enlarge West African capabilities in educational research.

TABLE 5.2

Total Aid through Private Agencies to LDCs
(remittances in millions of U.S. dollars)

| | Amount | | | Percent Change | | |
	1971	1972	1973	1971	1972	1973
Worldwide	1,199	1,338	1,676	8%	12%	25%
Private	913	1,036	1,362			
Government	286	302	314			
United States	841	927	1,122	--	10%	21%
Private	622	697	905			
Government	219	230	217			
Germany	129	150	192	38%	16%	28%
Private	108	124	157			
Government	21	26	35			
Canada	60	61	91	2%	2%	49%
Private	49	54	78			
Government	11	7	13			
United Kingdom	48	51	55	41%	6%	8%
Private	46	50	54			
Government	2	1	1			
Sweden	32	34	40	-6%	6%	18%
Private	24	27	30			
Government	8	7	10			
France	7	8	10	17%	14%	25%
Private	7	8	10			
Government	--	--	--			
Others	82	107	166	156%	30%	55%
Private	57	76	128			
Government*	25	31	38			

*Rough estimates.

Source: OECD with some data adjusted by country authorities.

A still more recent trend, which may continue to take a larger proportion of the Ford Foundation's effort, is the support given to the study of problems at the international level. An example of this is its collaboration with the Rockefeller Foundation in the Bellagio conferences, which have brought together the major cooperating agencies and representatives of the developing countries to study and take joint action on problems of world educational development, some of the results of which are described below.

In supporting projects in individual countries, the Foundation has particularly in mind the interest of those projects for countries that may be similarly placed. Thus, the reduction in volume of their support to individual countries may be counterbalanced to some extent by the wider international impact of a more concentrated program.

The Rockefeller Foundation has a longer history but has been engaged in forms of support that have ranged less widely over the total educational system but have rather concentrated on human resource development and institution-building in higher education, science, technology, and medicine. In 1973 the Rockefeller Foundation alloted $13.3 million to education ($8.8 million of this was in education, and $4.5 million in other subject areas. It has undertaken wide-ranging support at the higher level through its major University Development Program, the basic premise of which is that universities can be instruments for economic and social improvements.

In "The Course Ahead: The Rockefeller Foundation in the Next Five Years," issued in 1974, it is stated:

> The Foundation therefore will continue to emphasize the strengthening of selected institutions that show a capacity to be national and regional models. The objective will be to help the institutions to reach a level of excellence that can be maintained without further assistance from abroad. This point is being reached at several of the universities supported over the past decade. As Foundation assistance is phased out, work is beginning with other universities with similar promise. The Foundation will seek to effect improvements in the quality of education and research within these universities and, more importantly, to assist them to break out of their walls and extend their activities into the communities, confronting the real problems facing a nation in the throes of development. . . . Particular

attention will continue to be placed on departments of agriculture, public health, medicine,
and social sciences. Assistance will generally
entail the provision of especially needed faculty
competence and an extensive fellowship program
for the training of present or projected staff. . . .
        This approach may be extended to depart-
ments of education. The problems of primary
and secondary education in the less-developed
countries become progressively more serious,
limiting the number of candidates for higher education and thus for national leadership. Research
involving the education departments of universities,
together with model programs which can be tested,
may demonstrate how to strengthen lower school
systems. . . . Universities will also be encouraged to develop, on an experimental and demonstration basis, applied programs and extension
activities adapted to the needs of their countries
or regions. Such programs should provide a
more rapid transmission of the knowledge and
skills which apply to the real needs of the people.

The Rockefeller Foundation has made great use in its educational cooperation programs of the method of granting fellowships
and scholarships as part of its policy of placing emphasis on the
human factor in development. Over 10,000 awards were made between 1917 and 1970, many of which went to developing countries.
The other main method, associated with its policy of concentrating
on institution-building, has been staff training of higher-level specialists, especially in agriculture and medicine, but it also has been
concerned with the reshaping of universities for development, and it
has provided both expert help and equipment to universities for this
purpose in each of the main developing regions. The different phases
of its work are described in more detail in Chapter 7.
        The Carnegie Corporation assists universities in the developing
countries of the Commonwealth in their role of providing leadership
and direction for educational change. Examples of projects are the
designing of new teaching methods to make social studies more relevant to the young citizens of African countries, and aid for a satellite
communication system among the different islands participating in
the University of the South Pacific.
        The Commonwealth program has also been active in bringing
together members of teachers colleges from many African countries
through the Association for Teacher Education in Africa (ATEA) to

discuss curriculum reform and the teacher's role in fostering economic and social development. An African Social Studies Program in which the Ford Foundation also participates encourages and assists national efforts to improve social studies curricula for primary and secondary schools for the purposes of development and nation building. Assistance has also been given to the publication of educational reviews in Africa.

There are numerous other foundations which have a concern with educational cooperation in addition to the big three (the Ford, Rockefeller, and Carnegie Foundations). Among these are the Asia Foundation and the Near East Foundation.

In addition to the voluntary agencies and foundations there are a number of independent nonprofit international organizations concerned with the development of education that either directly or through contracts with aid agencies provide educational analysis and advice to the developing countries. An example is the International Council for Educational Development (ICED). This organization, which has an international Board of Trustees, was founded in 1970 and has already produced major studies on both higher education and nonformal education.

The Bellagio conferences, held as a result of a Ford/Rockefeller-Foundation initiative to reassess the impact of education on development and the needs for cooperation, have attracted heads of educational cooperation agencies and experts in discussion of some fundamental issues and resulted in four projects. An International Educational Reporting Service has been set up to provide an exchange of information among countries on innovating projects under the direction of the International Bureau of Education. A total funding for the first three years of just over $1.25 million was arranged from the following sources: Unicef, CIDA, Canadian International Development Research Centre (IDRC), ODM (U.K.), SIDA, and USAID. A major study costing nearly half a million dollars was initiated on University Roles in Developing Countries, contributed to by the Rockefeller and Ford Foundations, USAID, UNDP, Unicef, IBRD, CIDA, IDRC, and IBD. Support for research on education and development in Latin America undertaken through ECIEL has been granted in studies in education and income distribution amounting to $3 million; possible funders for that project include the Rockefeller Foundation, the International Development Research Centre, USAID, the IDB, the World Bank, and the Inter-American Foundation with ECIEL. Task forces also have been set up to study problems of basic education.

NOTES

1. See United Nations, New Trends in Service by Youth
(E/71/IV/1), 1971, p. 24.

2. See OECD/ICVA, Development Aid of Non-Governmental,
Non-Profit Organisations (1967). U.S. organizations are listed in
the Directory of U.S. Non-Profit Organizations Participating in
Technical Assistance Abroad (New York: American Council of Vol-
untary Agencies for Foreign Services, 1971). See also "Private
Foreign Aid from Europe and North America" by John Lange, U.S.
Department of State (Senior Seminar in Foreign Policy, 17th Session
1974/5).

3. Christian Education in Africa (London: Oxford University
Press, 1964).

4. Lange, op. cit.

6

The appeal and importance of cooperation for basic education is a strong one in connection with the conception of cooperation to establish at least minimum standards of education and living levels on a world scale, since basic education is a human right. This field of activity presents a special challenge to international cooperation.[1] Illiteracy and excessive fertility are linked, and a continuance of the present high and yearly increasing illiteracy rates in the developing countries can touch off another population explosion. Assistance to basic education also differs from aid to the other levels in the sense that the demand for higher and second-level education is practically unlimited, whereas universal basic education on a world scale is a limited and feasible objective. It is, in any case, the only educational level that the mass of the population are likely to attain.

There are two meanings of basic education. The one is the amount and type of education, varying from country to country, provided at the first level in the primary cycle, or in the case of adults, the provision of simple forms of training for employment. This meaning relates to the amount of education, formal or nonformal, required before second-level education or the skilled trades can be acquired.

The other meaning relates to the elementary educational minimum, usually represented by the first part of the primary cycle and consisting of about four years of education in school. It is also represented by nonformal education, which aims to bring youth and adults who have missed school up to a standard of functional literacy and numeracy and is really preemployment education rather than training for actual employment.

Cooperation for the first type of basic education was at one time considerable, in the form of the provision of primary-school teachers, especially by France. This provision has now almost entirely ceased, apart from some volunteer and nongovernmental groups and the work of missionaries. Official cooperation, whether multilateral or bilateral, now inclines to teacher training for primary education, expertise in curriculum development, material supplies, and the provision in the case of the least developed countries of administrative and supervisory staff.

Since most of the resources for primary education, apart from textbooks and certain materials, can usually be produced locally, aid agencies did not in the 1960s feel the need for special attention to this level of education. They did, however, tend to become involved either where the language of an ex-colonial power was that used in schools as the language of instruction (for historical reasons or because of the multiplicity of local languages) or where governments were giving particular attention to first level education. There was some substantial involvement under the UNDP/Unesco Program in teacher training. A substantial number of teacher training projects were carried out, even though the priority was toward secondary, technical, vocational, and higher-level education, and Unesco operated for a number of years a Major Project for Primary Education in Latin America, mostly from its regular budget. Unicef devoted some 60 percent of its funds allocated to education to projects at the first level, the rest going to secondary education. But broadly, as recommended by the Unesco Regional Conference of Ministers of Education and Those Responsible for Overall Planning, the second level was given priority in national plans and in cooperation programs.

The extension of primary education, moreover, was seen to involve decisions of a political or social nature, which most countries felt they could handle without advice. Aid agencies, therefore, started to interest themselves mostly in the promotion of nonformal educational projects, which provided a seemingly promising ground for experimentation, and they assumed a certain technical leadership in this difficult and not always successful field of educational development.

The major agencies, multilateral and bilateral, also began in the late 1960s to take a new interest in the use of the new media as a means of raising educational productivity. The Ivory Coast Project for televised teaching throughout the whole of the educational system of the country attracted a wide range of donor support and was aided by bilateral as well as multilateral donors.* The French Government, which gave considerable assistance, also developed projects for the

---

*A fuller description and critique of this project is contained in Chapter 12.

use of the mass media in some other African countries, and the U.S. aid administration was active in El Salvador and Western Samoa in the same field.

During the same period the USAID cooperated with the Guatemalan Government in a program of modernizing primary education and utilizing modern teaching methods, though this project still was based on a longer primary cycle than the country would appear to be able to bear if education were to be extended to the present sections of the population, mostly Indian, who are deprived of it.

Thus a number of experiments took place in which the more classical forms of aid to primary education were being replaced by attempts to solve problems of quantity and quality by the use of the new communication technologies. It is too early to evaluate this effort fully, and a certain amount of controversy still exists as to the value on a cost-benefit basis of large-scale efforts of this kind. [2]

An important project, however, illustrative of the more classical approach, was being carried out in Colombia by the Federal Republic of Germany, [3] which can usefully be described in some detail.

German advisers worked with the Colombian Government in such measures to increase enrollment as shift working, coeducation, and cutting down the unusually long numbers of instruction hours in the lower grades of primary schools (for example, in the first grade from 33 to 22 hours a week). This number was found more economical in the sense that it set free teachers and classroom hours to enroll additional pupils, and, at the same time, pedagogically it was found to improve the rate of learning.

The project also included measures to reduce repetition by new classes designed to compensate pupils who had fallen behind, and an additional program of classroom instruction was planned by the government for the purpose.

The project undertook an appraisal of the existing primary education system relating to the extent to which the primary school prepared the student for adult life, and to what extent for further education; the teaching methods used and causes of pupils' successes and failures; teacher training; the structure of the curriculum and the learning process; and the effect of social and climatic differences on school performance.

A Colombian team together with German experts worked jointly for a year on this fact-finding review, and changes in the teaching program were introduced for each grade following three stages: planning; trial and modifications; actual introduction of changes. Training manuals for teachers and teaching materials were produced in large numbers on the basis of financial contributions from Germany as well as the Colombian Government. Standard sets of teaching aids were produced, the experimental sets being financed from German project funds, based on the national production possibility, and avoiding dependence on imports. Textbooks also were prepared jointly by German and Colombian specialists accompanied by teacher guidance sheets.

The German aid, in addition to financing experimental materials, was mostly in the form of help to organize the survey of the country's schools, to provide training for Colombian personnel to work on the project, and collaboration in preparation of the modified curricula and work instructions for teachers. Seminars were conducted for the training of experts, and the German advisers were coauthors of the model textbooks. Scholarships were provided for specialized studies in Germany for the Colombian school supervisors.

This project, which has not yet been fully evaluated, is understood to have had an important impact on improving the methods of survey and the development of curricula and teacher training in the Colombian educational services. What is less clear is whether the project may not have been "overeffective" in the sense that the teaching material is not as wholly Colombian and related to local needs and possibilities as would have been the case if the assistance had been more indirect. This might have meant spreading the project over a longer period of years to develop the Colombian expertise and resources more, making reliance on the foreign advisers less necessary.

The project has involved the expenditure of some $3 million of German aid. One of the comments that might be made is that it is a pity that a full evaluation has not been made; nor was there built into the project a regular evaluation system by which the use of the aid resources were tested regularly against the development of comparable Colombian resources to replace the work of the advisers.

A number of joint efforts were made during this period, largely at the initiative of external sources of assistance, to ruralize primary education. These usually were rejected by the local population, for whom education was a means of escape from rural tasks into clerical employment, and who regarded a rural practical bent in the curriculum as resulting in "second-best" education.

A number of French-aided programs of this kind in Africa met with this difficulty (as in Upper Volta and Madagascar). Experimentation is still continuing, with special efforts, as in the Mandoul Valley project, to secure local participation in the design and carrying out of the new forms of rural education.

Multilateral agencies, such as Unesco, the ILO, and the FAO, as well as bilateral ones, also experimented with assistance to pilot projects. Difficulties frequently arose, however, from the fact that, even when the pilot project itself was a success, it was difficult to duplicate elsewhere the conditions of its success, which were frequently due to individual local circumstances and leadership.

Many hopes had been placed by international agencies at one time in the possibilities of using ambitious programs of primary education with six- or seven-year cycles and comprehensive forms of adult education as part of community development, as instruments to spark rural progress. Too often, however, it became clear that education itself could not contribute its catalytic influence unless the other requirements for development--capital, credit, communication, and agricultural markets--were also present, in substantial quantities, and these were usually in short supply.

Thus, some rethinking took place, and a concern developed with the more realistic approach of promoting basic education in the second of the meanings we indicated at the outset of this chapter; namely, how to meet at least minimum learning needs for all, geared to the necessities of different environments.

As the 1970s advanced, this problem attracted special interest, and the question of the shortening and restructuring of the primary cycle, in order to speed up the universal attainment of at least a minimum basic education, came into prominence, together with that of an enlarged use of nonformal education to fill the educational gap, which was reducing productivity and adding to the number of illiterates. The motivation was partly because a minimum of basic education was seen as a human right of all and a means of increasing and spreading as wide as possible the economic and social benefits of development, and partly because overproduction in relation to employment opportunities was appearing at the other levels.

We have mentioned in Chapters 2, 3, and 4 the initiatives by the UNDP/Unesco Experimental Literacy Program, started in the 1960s, and the redeployment toward basic education by the Unicef/Unesco and World Bank/Unesco cooperative programs, which have taken place in the mid-1970s.

The decision of the Unicef/Unesco program in 1972 to shift its effort toward the elementary part of the first-level cycle, and to phase out its aid to secondary education except in respect to nutrition and health, was the first of its kind. The elementary education to be assisted was seen as being literacy, numeracy, and some measures for understanding the economic and social environment and health and nutrition, rather than the more academic studies needed for progression to secondary education.

Unicef also sponsored in 1973 a study of the possibilities of using nonformal education as an instrument of accelerating the extension of basic education for children and adolescents who had missed schooling, and a number of projects in this area are being identified and supported.

The results of these policy shifts are shown in the General Progress Report of the Executive Director,[4] which states that

"Unicef has practically terminated its assistance to education at the secondary level." This is illustrated by Table 6.1.

TABLE 6.1

Number of National Personnel Who Received Training
with Unicef Stipends

Formal Education	1973	1974 (estimated)	1975 (planned)
Primary education teachers	60,200	85,700	77,300
Secondary education teachers	2,900	1,500	700
Teacher training instructors	6,100	6,300	6,000
Other educational personnel	3,400	2,500	1,900
Total formal education	72,600	96,000	85,900

Note: Figures are rounded to nearest hundred; zero is less than 50.

Source: Unicef, General Progress Report of the Executive Director, Part 2 (E/ICEF/637), April 19, 1975.

As regards nonformal education, the comparable numbers for women's education and training rise from 8,100 in 1973 to 12,600 in 1975, for local, village, youth leaders, and such from 6,200 in 1973 to 15,300 in 1975, and in vocational preparation from 600 in 1973 to 1,700 in 1974.

The Unicef-sponsored study prepared by the International Council for Educational Development (ICED) and issued under the title New Paths to Learning reviewed documentation on 145 nonformal educational projects. It states,

> There are numerous ways in which countries
> can help one another--both directly and through
> international organizations--to mount new and
> more effective efforts on the frontiers of

nonformal education. The few suggested below
for immediate attention aim primarily at reducing two universal obstacles to such efforts,
affecting developing countries and international
agencies alike: the acute shortage of broad-
gauged analysts and planners in this field, and
a corresponding shortage of pertinent knowledge
needed to advance these frontiers. . . .

Before presenting these suggestions, a
word of caution is in order. The current rapid
growth of interest in nonformal education is encouraging, but it also carries certain dangers.
The greatest dangers we see are: (1) that nonformal education may be regarded by many as
a panacea, which it surely is not; (2) that it will
become another worldwide fashion resulting, as
fads so often do, in superficiality and eventual
disillusionment; and (3) that countries and international agencies may try to do too much too fast--
before having developed the necessary human
talents and knowledge--with resulting waste and
disappointment. . . .

The best preventative, we suggest, is for
countries and international agencies, even those
besieged with requests, to be highly selective
in what and how much they attempt in the next
few years. . . . The plain truth is--and we say
this with no hint of criticism--that no international agency or individual country is equipped
at the moment to render or to use such help effectively on the massive scale required. Thus
their first priority should be to get equipped as
quickly as possible, by working together to develop the necessary personnel, methods and new
knowledge required to move ahead rapidly in
this field. . . .

The study concludes:

Finally, we suggest that the time is ripe for a
massive new infusion of international assistance from all quarters to give rural children,
especially in the poorer developing nations, a
decent opportunity in life. . . .

> The richer nations in years past have con-
> tributed much to the building up of secondary
> and higher educational institutions, mainly in
> urban centres. But they have done compara-
> tively little to broaden and strengthen the criti-
> cal foundations of education at the bottom of the
> pyramid, especially in the rural areas where
> the bulk of people live. A shift of priorities is
> now in order that would put much more help
> where it is most needed--into the education of
> rural children and youth. . . .
> We venture to suggest that a change is also
> needed in the priorities of the richer nations
> themselves. To take the clearest example,
> even a small marginal shift of funds from mili-
> tary uses into positive international assistance
> could not only make a massive difference in the
> life prospects of millions of disenfranchised
> rural children but at the same time help build
> firmer foundations for enduring peace through-
> out the world.[5]

The types of nonformal basic education that have received foreign aid are adult education and preemployment training. These may
take the form of functional literacy programs or less closely organized activities, such as agricultural clubs, youth groups, extension
work, or community schools. The problem in this area of activity
is that most of the projects, other than those specifically dealing
with literacy and usually for adults, presuppose a substantial measure of literacy and basic education of a minimum kind. The gap is
in respect of projects that aid adolescents and adults who missed
minimum basic education when they were younger.

Almost simultaneously with the ICED study for Unicef, the
World Bank also sponsored through the ICED a study of nonformal
education dealing with adults, rather than children and youth, and
concerned with programs of employment and productivity. Under the
title Attacking Rural Poverty: How Nonformal Education Can Help,
the study examines a great many cases and problems in rural areas.
Its main approach is what countries can do themselves, but the theme
of external assistance is developed. The conclusions, in brief, are
that nonformal education is an indispensable and potent instrument of
rural development; that, given a favorable political climate, even the
poorest of countries should be able to mobilize the resources for a
considerable expansion of nonformal education in rural areas; that
critical types of help from the outside are needed to hasten the process,

but assistance agencies will be required to alter considerably their past policies, doctrines, and modes of operation.

The emphasis is placed on self-instruction and the production of well-programed print materials, radio broadcasts, and simple learning devices, which people can operate on their own or inside some organized education program. Emphasis is also placed, as in New Paths to Learning, on planning and the training of "broad-gauged national and international personnel" and on the need to revise existing project preparation and procedures to cover broader perspectives. In addition, short-term professional assistance is recommended for diagnosing situations and formulating fresh approaches.

Some criticisms are reported of existing assistance. It, for instance, states:

> In the course of our field work we heard many complaints from external agencies that developing countries often failed to assign their ablest people as counterparts to take over assisted projects as soon as possible from foreign experts. We heard at least as many (diplomatically expressed) complaints from developing country officials about foreign experts: too many were being sent; they stayed too long or did not stay long enough, and absorbed too much of the budget; their high salaries and life-styles were a troublesome contrast to those of their local counterparts.

Nevertheless the view is taken that

> the various multilateral, bilateral and private organizations clearly have a great fund of experience and expertise which can be of invaluable assistance to developing countries in broadening and strengthening rural nonformal education. Moreover, they are in a unique position to undertake useful activities on a transnational basis, which individual countries cannot do alone, such as comparative research, collection and dissemination of pertinent information from different countries, certain types of advanced training that individual countries cannot afford, and the bringing together of people from different countries with common problems to learn from one another's experiences in workshops and seminars. . . .

But there are also serious practical con-
straints--far more than with formal education--
on what outsiders can do to assist in nonformal
education. [6]

As a result of the studies made by the ICED, it became clear
that, while nonformal education was a potent and largely unused instrument for basic education, caution was indicated as to the possibilities of its rapid extension in the immediate future. Unlike in-
school education at the primary level, nonformal education is not
backed by a single Ministry and a large state-organized system with
schools and teachers throughout the country. For large-scale, immediate progress to prevent educational poverty at the source, a
renovated or transformed primary school system was required.

The World Bank had already given assistance in 1973 to Lebanon
and Indonesia for the development of primary education in the form of,
respectively, a loan of $6.6 million and a credit of $12 million. In
the proposed allocations for 1974-78, basic education, as shown in
Chapter 3, is due to be increased by 27 percent at the expense of the
second and higher levels. But when drawing up its program for
1974-78, the World Bank decided to move into the assistance of basic
education with much larger resources. It hoped to provide around
$350 million for the purpose over the four years, mostly for school
education, but assisting nonformal education also, especially programs for young adults who missed schooling. This was to represent a 27 percent increase in assistance to basic education with a
proportionate reduction of that to other levels. The World Bank's
Sector Paper also rendered a valuable service by showing that, while
each country had its own unique problem, a broad solution to universal basic education on a world scale over the next decade or two was
not unfeasible financially.

On this issue, the Sector Working Paper (December 1974) of
the World Bank estimates additional costs, including the necessary
teachers and teacher training as follows:

Approximately 140 million new student places
would be required by 1985 in primary education
in the Group I and II [that is, those with under
$250 per capita income containing about 70 per-
cent of the population of the developing coun-
tries] countries to take care of the out-of-school
group if the existing primary education systems
of the world (averaging about six years for the
cycle) were expanded without change. If we assume a four-year cycle of primary education,

it might be possible to achieve the same aim by
adding approximately 60 million new student
places. An expansion of the primary education
system without a structural change might require an average annual capital spending equal
to about 18 percent of the total public expenditures in 1974 on education in the Group I and
II countries. A restructured, four-year system
might require capital expenditure equaling 8
percent of the same total. The annual recurrent increases in cost caused by the expansion
would also be lower in a restructured primary
system, and possibly average 2 percent, as
against 5 percent in the traditional system.

The number of illiterates in the age group
15-44 increased during the last decade and will
continue to increase. Unless existing adult
education programs serving this age group and
enrolling about 5 million students are expanded,
the number of illiterates in Group I and II countries will continue to increase during the next
decade from a current 355 million to 405 million.

Adult education is in its very early stages
in most Group I and II countries. It is estimated, however, that all illiterates in the 15-
44 age group could have an opportunity to participate in functional literacy or other basic
education and training programs by the end of
this century if programs for 12 million or 13
million adults per year were organised in addition to those already in existence. The programs would require capital expenditures of
only about 1 percent of the total public education expenditures of Group I and II countries
in 1974. The annual recurrent costs might be
about 6 percent of their total public education
expenditures. [7]

One of the most important features of basic education is its relation to population growth. This takes three forms. First, the influence of basic education on fertility. Since there is a good deal of
evidence that as the education of individuals increases, they tend to
have fewer children and space their births better, a major extension
of basic education to people at present deprived of it could have a

significant effect on excessive population growth. Assistance for
basic education has not to date figured largely in educational cooperative programs, but the new initiatives, especially of the World Bank
and Unicef, are a significant change of trend that is likely to make
its contribution to better population balance in the years to come.

The second impact of basic education is at the level of direct
use and instruction regarding the use of family-planning techniques.
Clinics find it much easier to conduct family-planning programs when
the population is literate and has some elementary education of a
civic nature.

The third impact is education about population problems in
schools, both at the basic and second level in nonformal education
and at the higher level and in universities. This type of impact cannot be expected to be as important as that of the other two, which are
direct influences on behavior, but it is also valuable. The United
Nations Population Fund has provided finance for Unesco to assist developing countries to incorporate population education into the curricula
of both school and out-of-school education at the different levels, as
well as in the universities. As of 1973, there were 12 such projects in
operation.

Another important need is for more basic education for women
and girls, not only for population purposes but also as a contribution
to the productivity of the labor force and to the raising of living levels.
The contribution to productivity is both direct, since women work a
great deal in agriculture, and indirect, through their impact on the
other members of the household. Some agencies--notably Unesco,
Unicef, and SIDA--have valuable cooperation programs in this field,
which could well be initiated in other cooperation programs.

Thus, this chapter may be summarized by noting that basic education has a particular appeal for outside assistance, since it is a limited objective, both social and economic, linked to the idea of creating
minimum standards of welfare throughout the world. On the other
hand, it does not make the demand on assistance for large capital investment as in the case of universities and technological institutions.
The assistance required is largely organizational and for the promotion of research experimentation and the development of new teaching
and learning patterns, both formal and nonformal especially in rural
areas. This type of expertise is in short supply both in developed and
developing countries, and internationally financed training courses
and career services could help to relieve this bottleneck. There is
considerable experience of pilot projects in bilateral, multilateral,
and nongovernmental organizations, but miscalculations and mal-
assessments of the feasibility of success are still common. One of
the requirements is a form of manual or set of challenging operational guidelines and checklists, which would help administrators and

local personnel working within this field. At present this experience
is scattered among and within the donor agencies, and there is need
for it to be brought together and evaluated to help future operations.

An increase is taking place in resources available for educational cooperation for basic education. In addition to the decision of
the World Bank Group already mentioned, this field of education is
given special mention in Section 5 of the U.S. Foreign Assistance
Act. Further, the cooperation policies of the United Kingdom and of
other bilateral agencies, as well as strategies suggested by the
United Nations and the ILO, are also being turned toward the solution of problems of poverty, especially in rural areas.

It remains to be seen how far the additional emphasis on the
aid-supply side designed to educate the poorer sections of the population in developing countries receives a commensurate response in
terms of cooperation requests from the developing countries themselves.

NOTES

1. See H. M. Phillips, Basic Education: A World Challenge
(London: John Wiley and Sons, 1975).

2. See the articles in Prospects 3, no. 3 (1973).

3. See Aid to Education in Less Developed Countries (Paris:
OECD, 1971), p. 239.

4. Unicef, General Progress Report of the Executive Director,
Part 2 (E/ICEF/637), April 9, 1975.

5. Philip H. Coombs, with Roy C. Prosser and Manzoor
Ahmed, New Paths to Learning (New York: International Council
for Educational Development, 1973), pp. 102-3.

6. Philip H. Coombs with Manzoor Ahmed, Attacking Rural
Poverty: How Nonformal Education Can Help (Baltimore: Johns
Hopkins Press, 1974), pp. 218-19.

7. World Bank, Sector Working Paper, December 1974, pp.
32-33.

There were five main influences affecting educational expansion in the 1960s. Each of these influences had a different impact depending on the particular time at which the individual emergent countries concerned achieved independence, and on their degree of development, and thereby on their needs for educational assistance.

The first main influence was the need to create, or increase the number of members of a high-grade national elite that would guarantee in diplomatic, administrative, and managerial circles the immediate future of the newly independent nation. The supply position as regards clerical and, to some extent, middle-grade personnel was easier initially since the colonial powers had trained many people in these grades. There was a need, however, to replace higher middle-level foreign personnel who directed administration and frequently commerce, as well as the public utilities.

The second main influence derived from the manpower factor in economic growth. The growth targets set for greater economic development and self-sufficiency implied increases and the development of high- and middle-level cadres of qualified and technical personnel and workers in the skilled trades in agriculture, industry, and commerce. Industry and agriculture did not have the organization and background capacity to provide the necessary manpower itself, and this pointed to a greater proportion of public technical education than took place in the developed countries.

The third influence was social and political, namely, the requirements of building integrated and viable nations. Nation-building meant the growth of a substantial section of the population having more than primary education and of a middle and lower middle class that would influence social integration and political stability.

The fourth influence was the one that, in many cases, became dominant. This was the automatic pressure of parents of pupils who attained primary education that their children should be able to continue into the second level. Since education was seen as providing an escape route from hard conditions into clerical and white-collar work and was also the road to the "glittering prizes" of new jobs, prestige, and wealth (which independence was expected to bring), inevitably this pressure was great. The effect of this influence was that carefully laid educational and manpower plans became distorted as a result of politically uncontrollable forces exercised by the most influential sections of the population.

The fifth influence was educational aid itself. Teachers, curricula, textbooks, examinations, and the structure of the education system could not be changed overnight. What was previously a colonial education system became an assisted independent system. But the system and its teachers continued largely as before, if for no other reason than that there was nothing else to replace them.

The first four influences dominated the supply of external assistance, though the fourth was accepted with reluctance since cooperating agencies often felt some uneasiness, and still do, about the development nature of needs emanating from this influence, even though they also felt unable to refuse to meet them. Cooperating agencies also had to face the difficult problem of how to gear a system of educational assistance, with the necessary technical backstopping, to a set of countries moving at a different pace of development and starting from different bases.

Thus, some countries already had an educated elite, frequently educated abroad, that demanded the same standards as abroad in the new universities to be created at home, while other countries, which had been left much on their own, did not have the resources, human and material, to feed such universities and needed different educational development models. The nature of the challenge produced by over 70 different countries becoming independent over a small span of years was a prodigious one and obviously placed a great strain on donor agencies, and it was not surprising that failures and setbacks, as well as successes, resulted.

In the early 1960s, Unesco initiated a set of regional conferences of Ministers of Education and Those Responsible for Overall Planning. Models and objectives for balanced educational growth were adopted by them, region by region, and economists and manpower specialists entered the educational field in force. Priority was accorded to secondary and technical education, and this not only influenced national plans and programs but also had a more than proportionate influence on foreign aid, since most of the economists and manpower advisers were from the developed countries and were frequently associated with aid programs.

Thus the UNDP started its assistance to education by restricting it to projects that could be judged to have an urgent effect on economic development, such as the filling of gaps in skilled manpower and qualified personnel and technological training. Emphasis was placed on the spread of science and technology and on the creation of the necessary institutions and qualified personnel at the recipient end to utilize it according to national needs. Similarly when the World Bank entered the field of educational aid in the early 1960s, assistance was restricted to technical education and other types of training to respond to the demands of industry.

Soon, however, both the UNDP and the World Bank Group moved into general secondary education, since it was seen to be the indispensable basis for technological and higher education and the manpower component of development. At first the UNDP applied ratios between second level and primary as a criterion for assistance, under the influence of the concept of an educational pyramid geared to development needs. As the 1960s developed, both the UNDP and the World Bank Group, followed by others, took on a wider view of the whole educational process and broadened their criteria to cover assistance to achieving educational balance as well as action to aid economic productivity. To a considerable extent this was a change due to expressed national needs at the recipient end, but it was also due to changes at the world level and in the donor agencies (especially the multilateral organizations) in attitudes to development and to the evolution of an understanding of the social factors in development.

Thus the developing countries, although asserting themselves in their own particular requests and in a growing way in the meetings they held under UNCTAD auspices about development in general, remained considerably influenced by the developed countries and by the multilateral agencies, where the developed countries carried considerable weight. Many experts from developed countries wanted the recipient countries to apply educational planning techniques and decision-making, which their own countries did not feel they were ready to adopt.

A similar situation arose at the end of the 1960s and beginning of the 1970s in respect to educational reform. Developing countries were expected to make hard decisions of a political as well as an educational nature, decisions that most of the developed countries had avoided. However, the greater degree of sophistication and administrative capacity that emerged (partly as a result of external assistance) in the developing countries enabled them to take a stronger and more independent position than previously. They were not, however, yet fully equipped, research-wise, to work out and apply new models--

though there were some striking reforms introduced in some countries such as Tanzania and Peru. Generally, the amount of actual
fundamental change that was taking place at the recipient end was
small and not enough to change the broad direction and disposition
of education cooperation.

Nevertheless changes are proposed, such as the decision of
the World Bank and other agencies to slow down on assistance to general second-level education and comprehensive schools. The experience of educational assistance of almost all the agencies at the
general secondary level has reflected an inevitable tendency when
educators meet to work out proposals which are to be financed from
abroad. This is that the projects often become too refined and too
expensive in relation to possibilities of their upkeep and further
spread on a nationwide level. The experience of the Canadian loan
for comprehensive schools in Thailand is discussed in some detail
in Chapter 10.

The World Bank had been making substantial loans and long-
term credits for secondary-school buildings. The standards applied
were high, as required by good architects, but it was sometimes
anomalous to go into poor towns to see that the only good buildings
were schools put up with Bank money. The premises and equipment
were not always well kept up and used. Further, in many aid projects at the second level, it was not uncommon to find that science
equipment and books provided by donor agencies were kept locked up
by the teachers, who did not want to risk their loss or destruction
and, therefore, did not use them.

Thus there emerged out of this experience one of the factors
we discuss in the concluding chapters, namely the need to avoid what
may be called the "Midas" touch. The emphasis today is on relating
projects more closely to what the local conditions can bear and to
recognize that an even more indispensable condition that money is
the creation of a local spirit of self-dependence, with which many
obstacles, it has been shown, can be overcome.

How foreign aid can help to create such local attitudes is easier
to express negatively, in the form of what it should not do, rather
than in program terms. Nevertheless, new approaches are being
tried out under which the participants in all the aspects of education--
teachers, parents, and the community--are being regarded as a fundamental aspect of project preparation. There is, however, still a
long way to go in this direction, and there is a lack of experience and
techniques of surveying local conditions and attitudes affecting those
most concerned, which is a gap needing to be filled. As will be seen
in Chapter 10 on Peru, a major experiment in this regard is being
undertaken in that country. In addition there are a number of other
efforts to develop tools to relate education more closely to local felt

and real needs, such as the studies being undertaken by SEAMEO through its center INNOTECH.

Perhaps the greatest single difficulty with aid projects at the level of technical schools and training centers for skilled trades is the tendency of the students to use them as stepping stones to other types of education than those for which they are intended. Thus, if a good technical school is set up to help to meet the general shortage of middle-level technicians, it will frequently be regarded by parents and students, and even by the teachers themselves, as a lower form of higher education rather than a terminal form of middle education. This leads to its output being overacademic and not related to actual work needs.

Much disappointment has been caused by this factor, particularly among the smaller bilateral donors, to whom model centers of technical training have seemed a clear way of aiding educational development with limited resources. In some cases whole educational assistance programs of this kind, sometimes supported by trade union groups as well as donor governments, have been abandoned because of the difficulties of being able to ensure that the students actually enter the jobs for which they are trained or are suitably trained for the jobs available.

The author once inspected a second-level technical school for the training of maritime personnel set up with external assistance. The need was clear, since the country was greatly expanding its number of fishing trawlers, as well as its commercial fleet. The school was well equipped and managed, and the instruction was good. However, when the question was posed as to the actual jobs the school-leavers took up, it turned out that only a tiny percentage went into seafaring. The rest used the school as a form of general second-level education in order to acquire clerical jobs on shore in commerce and industry.

The reasons for this lie deep in the socioeconomic conditions of the developing countries. There are also some simpler factors: donor-sponsored middle-level schools and centers are often superior in equipment and organization to their national counterparts, and aspirations for higher diplomas are generated in the student (even though they are not obtainable and, alas, are usually not likely to be obtained).

Further, the more the training center or school becomes academic, the less the output fits the employers' needs at the middle level. In the field of technical training this points to a greater use of the facilities of industry, agriculture, and commerce for technical training rather than regarding technical education as a part of the formal system. The difficulty, however, is that not many developing countries have the volume of industry or the organizations of employers to create such projects, though there are notable exceptions in

Latin America such as Servicio Nacional de Aprendizage (SENA) in
Colombia, which combine private and state resources to educate
people and to acquire types of technical capacity more related to employers' actual needs than is often the case with public technical
schools.

Aid to higher education would at first sight also appear to be
one of the most successful forms of cooperation, since there are
many universities and higher-learning and technical institutions that
owe their existence, and often the initiatives that set them up, to external sources of aid and encouragement. Moreover an impressive
number of able graduates from those institutions are also clearly
visible.

Yet the universities as a whole in the developing countries are,
according to most analysts, in bad shape. In "Education for National
Development: The University,"[1] Michael Todaro and his colleagues
of the Rockefeller Foundation write,

> Yet universities in the developing countries have
> been found by practically all informed observers
> to be as dysfunctional and disoriented as educa-
> tional institutions in lower levels. Many of the
> problems basic to primary and secondary educa-
> tion recur in more or less aggravated form in
> universities: annual increases in the order of
> 10 percent in student enrollment, rising costs,
> declining pupil-teacher ratios, deficient facili-
> ties, inappropriate curricula, administrative
> inertia, and ever more serious problems of
> unemployment or malemployment for university
> graduates.

Malcolm Adiseshiah, in 1970 when still Deputy Director General of Unesco, described the situation as follows:[2]

> . . . the current university situation in the un-
> derdeveloped world can only be described as
> bleak. The prevailing syndrome of wastage,
> drop-outs, inefficiencies, repetitions, unin-
> spired teaching, prescription of pre-digested
> and erroneous "bazaar notes" as texts, over-
> crowded class-rooms, lack of time for reflec-
> tion and research, examination systems--all
> these inhibit thought and act as superficial
> classification machines. . . . Add to this the
> lack of relation between employment opportunities

and development demands for skills on the one
hand, and the streams and specialisation offered in the colleges and universities on the
other. Crown it with the moral confusion and
material corruption creeping into university
administrations and staff life, the atmosphere
of terrible boredom and shiftless unreality,
and one then sees the whole sad picture.

It would appear, therefore, that either the assistance given
over the last 30 years was insufficient to influence the overall situation, or that its effect did not take root because it was not continued
long enough, or that it was wrongly conceived and operated as far as
its general impact was concerned, as distinct from specific particular successes.

One answer is perhaps that the volume of aid and its impact
and duration was in fact insufficient to influence higher educational
systems as a whole, and in most countries it fell short of the critical mass and duration. Another is that a higher university system
cannot move much in advance of national general economic and social
conditions, whatever the outside stimulus. Yet another answer is
that, while on the whole the assistance was well conceived and operated, having regard to the difficulties at the time, there were choices
made and actions taken initially, which on hindsight would better
have been different.

In the early period of educational assistance higher education
was the main priority area of bilateral aid, not only because of the
national needs but also because this was the form of educational assistance the developed countries favored and found most easy to give,
there having been little official experience of assistance at the other
levels. This resulted in the setting up of a number of "quality" universities with the aim that they should have first-class standards,
be multifaculty, be centers of research, and usually be fully residen-
tial. Examples were the University College of the Gold Coast; the
University College of Khartoum; University College, Ibadan; Makerere
University College; and the University College of the West Indies.
This aim was broadly achieved, and the "quality"-oriented universities played their part in producing the first ranks of the leaders and
qualified personnel that independence demanded. But this was at a high
unit cost in relation to local resources, and the pattern of studies they
utilized was not well related to the particular needs of economic and
social development of the new countries. Rather, it relied too much
on imitation of the older institutions of the educationally advanced
countries, especially those of the then colonial powers.

As development needs became better understood, this pattern came under criticism, and there was a switch to assistance in creating the development-oriented type of institution of higher education with a greater utilitarian concern and emphasis on producing qualified professional personnel, such as engineers and agronomists, and on technological training and research. This new type of demand took root, assisted by the arrival on the scene in considerable force of educational aid from the United States and the multilateral agencies. The latter, being international, were able to offer a wider range of institutional examples to the emergent countries, though at the time they suffered too from the fallacy of overimitation of existing models. The Anglo-American-Nigerian Commission's Report Investment in Education (1960) had, for instance, an important impact, as had the work of Unesco. Also in the home countries of the colonial powers themselves during the 1950s, different university patterns were emerging. The new provincial universities were taking shape in the United Kingdom, colleges of advanced technology were attaining university status, and new perspectives for university organization were opening.

At the outset, the reproduction of the European type of university required the new universities to work for the degrees of universities of the metropolitan power. These seemingly antiquated and "colonialistic" measures were in fact based on pragmatic rather than political considerations, since, on the one hand, there was little alternative basis on which to build, and, on the other, they reflected the desire of public opinion in the colonies. Both in the British and the French colonies there was a fear of being provided with "second-best" education.

As the first universities took root and experience of development grew, a second phase of aid activities emerged aimed at measures for the modernization of the original universities and the creation of new and more utilitarian patterns of higher education with an orientation to manpower and practical research needs. Examples of universities founded with external assistance in this phase were the Ahmadu Bello University in Northern Nigeria, which contained both academic and practical faculties. Another was the University of Malawi, covering all post-second-level education with many more students working for diplomas than for degrees, in order to conform with the country's employment possibilities.

In a number of countries, such as Botswana, Lesotho, Swaziland, Guyana, and the Pacific islands, the emphasis in aid to the new institutions was on the science of public administration, the faculties of education, and community services; subdegree courses at the post-secondary level were covered, as well as the normal higher-level studies designed to have an intellectual impact on national affairs.

The United States moved vigorously into the educational aid field following the Truman Point Four program and opened up important programs at the university level. From 1960 on, about half the U.S. official development aid funds obligated were for higher education. In addition there was important assistance at this level from other public and private sources including the foundations.

The further phase that developed was one of continuing to help in specialized fields, especially science and technology, but of moving away from institution-building. This was partly because the original basic institutional gap had largely been filled but also because an excess of supply of higher-educated graduates over the demand, except in some of the fields of the natural sciences and advanced technology, was beginning to emerge.

Institution-building is still favored in respect to "centers of excellence," national or regional, to cover a number of countries that lack the necessary resources for their universities to embrace all modern, scientific, and technological fields important for development. Regional institutions such as the Asian Institute of Technology in Bangkok and the SEAMEO Centers in Southeast Asia allow countries to economize in extending their educational services, as do also well-conceived study abroad programs in the more developed countries.

There has been a good deal of reliance upon university-to-university cooperation, sometimes officially sponsored, sometimes part of the general mutual exchange of knowledge and personnel instituted directly by the universities themselves. Not all the latter type of cooperation has been development oriented, and, even with the officially sponsored cooperation that takes place under contract, there has been often a tendency for the two universities to work in partnership on the more academic rather than the more utilitarian aspects of study and research. Nevertheless, there are also successful examples of such cooperation for development purposes.

A number of attempts were made to promote regional universities or to federate the universities of small neighboring countries to enable them to pool their resources, but without success. The most ambitious effort resulted in the setting up of the federated University of East Africa. This attracted almost all the major bilateral, multilateral, and foundation donors into offers of assistance. After some progress the university federation was dissolved and replaced by the establishment of various functional ties and a common Inter-University Committee. However, universities that served a number of neighboring countries de facto rather than de jure, as in the case of the University of Dakar, have made a valuable contribution to solving the problems of new states with small resources.

The phases of bilateral aid correspond to a considerable extent to those of the great foundations that have played an important part in university aid, such as the Rockefeller, Ford, and Carnegie Foundations. Kenneth Thompson and his colleagues of the Rockefeller Foundation have traced[3] four phases in the Rockefeller Foundation's assistance to university development. The first was helping the transition from colonial to national universities, by providing assistance in the form of visiting professors, deans, and heads of departments or research institutes, skilled in institution-building from universities in the developed countries.

The second phase was assistance to developing universities after they had assumed their own leadership. This took the form of advisory services. The third phase was one of consolidation: the planning of graduate courses and research to establish the universities' role in national life and its contribution to the solution of the country's problems. The fourth phase was university-to-university help within developing countries or, as described by Thompson, a process of "first generation university development centres helping second generation centres."

Examples of the four phases quoted by Thompson are, as regards the first, the establishment, in which the Foundation was "virtually a coequal partner," of the Universidad del Valle at Cali in Colombia, which differed from the usual Latin American university pattern in that the fundamental approach was service to the community rather than the pursuit of knowledge for its own sake. An example of the second phase is the Foundation's help first to the University of East Africa and then to the three national universities it had covered. The third phase is illustrated by the assistance the Foundation gave to the University of the Philippines, and the fourth by the cooperation that took place between the East African University and that of Zaire, between the University del Valle Colombia and that of Bahia, Brazil, and between Thai, Indonesian, and Philippine universities.

A further difficulty that has arisen is that institutions have in the past sometimes been sponsored by bilateral agencies in competition with each other, and without too close a regard to whether employment would be available for the trained manpower produced in the form of highly qualified engineers and technologists. This created in a number of countries an excess supply of qualified persons in those fields.

The types of aid given to higher education under cooperation programs have included capital assistance for buildings and equipment; the provision of fellowships; help in university administration and providing academic and technical advice for the setting up of new faculties with adequate standards of attainment and examination systems; and assistance in devising or reforming the organization,

structure, and content of study and research to bring them more into
line with development needs. In addition there have been the more
intangible forms of cooperation: in the form of exchange of knowledge and personal contacts among the world community of scholars
and help in curricula and modernizing teaching and research methods. The comparability of degrees between countries has also been
a subject of assistance by Unesco.

Most donor agencies are now conscious of the need to shift resources somewhat away from higher education to the other levels.
The reasons are usefully summarized in guidelines produced by the
United Kingdom Inter-University Council for Higher Education Overseas, entitled IUC and Related Services:

> (1) the growing maturity of the older univer-
> sities--Ibadan, Ghana, UWI--with others on the
> same road. The priority need in the field of
> staff recruitment is increasingly for higher-level
> posts, short-term secondments and visits and
> for help in new developments;
> (2) For the first time, graduate production in
> certain fields is getting near the limits of man-
> power requirements.
> (3) In some countries there are dangers of
> overproliferation of universities and duplication
> of facilities and of demands for staff;
> (4) The provision of IUC services involves an
> increasing element of financial support which
> must be considered in relation to the total aid
> programme;
> (5) Because almost all the countries con-
> cerned are now independent, and because capital
> and recurrent funds for universities are increas-
> ingly determined by the national development
> plans, it is necessary to take more fully into
> account relations between universities and their
> Governments;
> (6) Because many universities, especially
> those most recently established, are accepting
> responsibilities for teacher-training, technical
> education and professional education at diploma
> as well as degree level, increasing coordination
> is needed with other bodies, notably TETOC,
> CEDO [Center for Educational Development
> Overseas], and the British Council, and with
> potential donors in other advanced countries.[4]

The shift in emphasis required and the redeployment of resources away from the expansive trend of the 1960s does not mean
that higher education should not be an important target of aid. The
needs on development grounds are in many countries now for a slack-
ening of the increase of student enrollment and increased initiatives
to put their qualified manpower in the position to participate in the
streams of technical progress and the transfer or adaptation of the
technologies suited to their economic and resource conjuncture and
social needs. The need also remains for the application of improved
methods of planning and administration.

Other items are the development of self-instructional techniques and of open universities; the provision of audiovisual material
for science and language laboratories; the financing of scholarships
both within the countries themselves and abroad to encourage merit,
opportunity, and international understanding; the establishment of
more linkages among universities in the developing countries themselves; the devotion of university research and teaching resources to
problems in the educational field at the other levels and to research
and experimentation and the pursuit of innovation in education; the
democratization of education in the sense of greater responsible participation of the students in curriculum design and university administration; and the adoption of counseling and guidance services to
prevent student frustration and graduate unemployment.

An important long-term program for the study of experiments
made with alternative university structures has been launched by
Unesco, and case studies have already been initiated in Canada, the
United Kingdom, the United States, and the Soviet Union.

The other most significant recent multilateral contribution to
higher education has been the establishment of the United Nations
University, which came into being in 1974. A University Council
has been appointed to set up the university, with a contribution of
$100 million from Japan, payable over five years, together with the
capital costs for its establishment. Japan has also offered to be one
of the host countries of a research and training unit of the university
outside of Tokyo, and to contribute to the capital costs for similar
units in the developing countries. A private individual in Japan has
offered the facilities of a ship for possible use by the university.

By the end of 1973, 21 countries had offered contributions for
certain facilities, and suggestions for affiliation or association have
been received from a number of universities and research institutions.
The building and running of the university is to be financed from voluntary contributions, by governments directly, or through the UN or
nongovernmental organizations. The Rector may also accept assistance for projects, for example, for fellowships financed by intergovernmental organizations, whether or not they belong to the UN system.

As at the beginning of 1975 there was, however, a situation that the Director General of Unesco, Mr. M'Bow, described as a vicious circle. The university was waiting to receive the promised aid in order to commence its work, and the contributors were waiting to see what were the concrete programs they should support.

This project is a culminating point of an idea raised as long ago as 1921 by the Commission for Intellectual Cooperation and the League of Nations and on which preparatory studies and consultations have been proceeding actively since 1971, when Unesco carried out a favorable feasibility study.

The principal features of the university's charter are as follows:

The United Nations University shall be an international community of scholars, engaged in research, post-graduate training and dissemination of knowledge in furtherance of the purposes and principles of the Charter of the United Nations. In achieving its stated objectives, it shall function under the joint sponsorship of the United Nations and the United Nations Education, Scientific and Cultural Organisation (hereinafter referred to as "Unesco"), through a central programming and coordinating body and a network of research and post-graduate training centres and programmes located in the developed and developing countries.

The University shall devote its work to research into the pressing global problems of human survival, development and welfare, that are the concern of the United Nations and its agencies, with due attention to the social sciences and the humanities as well as natural sciences, pure and applied.

The research programmes of the institutions of the University shall include, among other subjects, coexistence between peoples having different cultures, languages and social systems; peaceful relations between States and the maintenance of peace and security; human rights; economic and social change and development; the environment and the proper use of resources; basic scientific research and the application of the results of science and technology in the interests of development; universal human values related to the improvement of the quality of life. [5]

Although the university is to serve all members of the United
Nations, it will be particularly concerned with the developing countries. The Charter states, "It shall endeavour to alleviate the intellectual isolation of persons in such communities in the developing
countries which might otherwise become a reason for their moving
to developed countries." The university is granted autonomy within
the framework of the United Nations and both academic and financial
freedom in the allocation of its resources.

Assistance problems at the higher level of education have
tended to have a character and momentum of their own, distinct from
the other levels. As regards methods of carrying out operation programs in higher education, aid agencies have utilized the scholarly
traditions of cooperation among universities, and a number have
adopted the practice of giving aid through contracts with their own
universities to work with those in the developing countries.

The advantages of this system are those that flow from the use
of existing resources and machinery, which do not have to be duplicated bureaucratically in the aid agencies. In addition, a great deal
of natural academic support is mobilized among scholars, which goes
beyond the terms of contract or particular aid projects.

However, there are also certain disadvantages. Universities
themselves are usually powerful entities and have their own ideas
about the type of aid required, which may not necessarily be those of
the aid agency or even as closely linked as is desirable to development objectives. The search for knowledge for its own sake is deeply rooted in the university pattern, and the fellowship of scholars in
both recipient and donor countries sometimes develops into help
among colleagues, which necessarily does not maximize the national
good. There is always the danger that when contracts are made with
large organizations, the organizations further their own plans and
projects rather than making the positive redeployments required to
further long-term projects in terms of staff time and the assignment
of high-level personnel. One of the problems in this connection is
that academics live in a fairly rigorous career and promotion system,
and detachment for types of work that do not have a career future is
not always welcomed, or, alternatively, the work is taken and treated
more from a scholastic than a development angle.

These problems have been encountered by aid agencies in a
number of countries. They are not sufficient to undermine the desirability of university-to-university aid but call rather for greater care
in the selection and supervision of the administration of such projects.
Contracts should have built into them procedures for ex-ante as well
as post-facto evaluation in which wider interests than that of any individual university are represented.

The United Kingdom Inter-University Council for Higher Education Overseas has filled this role to a large extent. In its guidelines, IUC and Related Services, it states, "The provision of IUC services involves an increasing element of financial support which must be considered in relation to the total aid programme."[6] But, as suggested elsewhere, there is room in the United Kingdom and other donor countries for an overall intermediate body to deal with educational cooperation, which links--from the standpoint of information rather than actual control--more closely the government and the private-sector policies in respect of educational aid, regardless of the source of funds. At the international level, some similar action is required.

One of the anomalies of assistance in higher education is the donor's attempt to prescribe criteria for the planning and development of universities, which they do not themselves adopt or which many of the academic profession reject. Most universities of high standing in the developed countries pay heavy regard to the pursuit of knowledge and scholarship for its own sake, but advisers from these universities frequently have to urge that the developing countries adopt approaches that are more vocational and related to economic and social needs.

While bilateral and foundation aid was at first devoted to institution-building in the sense of covering the whole range of higher education and has moved now to that of specialized development activities, the multilateral agencies, coming later as they did upon the aid scene, began with the more specialized approach (other than the general help given by Unesco from its regular program). The United Nations Expanded Technical Assistance Program and the Special Fund (now combined in the UNDP) were mandated to relate their aid to economic development and to the creation of institutional infrastructures to meet urgent manpower and research needs. This tendency still continues with UNDP and also with the World Bank Group, the emphasis being on science, engineering, and agricultural facilities.

The current trend is a reduction of the volume of educational assistance cooperation going to the higher and university level, but with a strong effort being maintained on the qualitative side. The future perspective for cooperation at this level as well as for secondary and technical education depends in most developing countries on the rate of economic progress and employment creation, since the supply of school-leavers and graduates at these levels is exceeding demand in many countries, though shortages remain in specialized categories and for middle-level technicians. This shortage is partly due to socioeconomic factors such as levels of pay, the prestige in which different occupations are held, and other noneducational factors.

It is to a lesser extent due to failure of educational systems to change their structures and curricula.

Since cooperation from abroad is usually sought for fields in which there are gaps, cooperation agencies sometimes are faced with the task of helping to fill educational gaps by the educational means they are able to provide, whereas in reality solutions lie with the country itself, since it alone can deal with its socioeconomic problems of occupational structure, remuneration, and prestige. A good many cooperation projects have encountered difficulty and failure on this account, particularly in the area of technical training.

What often happens is that the externally supported institution has both facilities and educational quality somewhat higher than the similar nonaided institution. The effect of this is frequently to make the students feel their training is already part of higher education and to induce them to go up the educational pyramid rather than fill needed posts at the middle level.

The perspectives for cooperation in higher education, which depend on the rate of economic growth, are for this reason related to the question of the New Economic Order, proposed by the United Nations. If there were substantial economic changes in the sense of the New Economic Order, then education at all levels would be affected. The need would be twofold. First that the education system should be able to produce the necessary increase of human resource potential required. This requires forward planning at the level of educational infrastructure, since educational output takes longer to create than physical capital. Secondly, as particular economic proposals were adopted they would have to be interpreted into educational needs and cooperation possibilities.

The prospects of substantial progress toward the New Economic Order are at present poor, though sooner or later further efforts may have better results. It is, therefore, difficult for developing countries, particularly in the difficult economic circumstances of the mid-1970s, to undertake switches of their educational resources or greatly expand certain types of education to meet hypothetical situations. On the other hand, it is possible to look at the education infrastructure and to see whether there are serious weaknesses that would damage development opportunities as they opened up.

The concern with infrastructure is basically a problem of quality, organization, and innovation, and of relating the existing system closer to development possibilities, rather than one of quantitative increase. The developing countries are in fact expanding their higher levels extremely fast, as can be seen from Table 7.1 showing the increases by level of education between 1970 and 1971 (the latest figures available) for the developing countries.

TABLE 7.1

Annual Percentage Increase in Enrollments by Level, 1970-71

	First	Second	Third
Africa (excluding Arab states)	1.6	3.4	19.8
Asia (excluding Arab states)	1.6	4.6	17.7
Latin America	4.7	7.6	17.3
Arab states	8.9	7.2	17.5
Developing countries	2.8	7.1	19.5

Source: Unesco Statistical Yearbook 1973.

Since higher and university education by definition produces persons with higher-level qualifications, this should be an area where it is possible for external cooperation assistance to decline as natural capabilities grow. Such a situation would be near at hand but for the fact that the problem of the planning of universities for change is a complex one troubling universities all over the world, in the developed as well as the developing countries. This, therefore, is likely to be an area where much cooperation is required. In the next chapter an example is mentioned in the case of Peru. The International Institute for Educational Planning (IIEP) has made an important study (Planning Universities for Change), which deals mostly with the developed countries but from which important indications for developing countries and cooperation programs emerge.

NOTES

1. F. Champion Ward, ed., Education and Development Reconsidered: The Bellagio Conference Papers (New York: Praeger Publishers, 1974), p. 205.
2. Let My Country Awake (New York: Unesco, 1970), p. 251.
3. Ward, op. cit., pp. 195, 204.
4. IUC and Related Services: A Guide, a manual issued by the IUC, p. 32.
5. See UN General Assembly Resolution 3081 (XXVII) of 6 December, 1973.
6. IUC and Related Services, op. cit.

8

ASSISTANCE TO STUDENTS
AND TRAINEES: FELLOWSHIPS
AND MATERIAL SUPPLIES

Travel has long been an important force in the spread of knowledge, inspired by religion, commerce, and sheer inquiry, as in the appeal of the Kublai Khan for knowledge of Christian doctrine and for the sending of Dominican friars overland to China. As well, the Prophet Muhammad had already said in the seventh century, "Acquire knowledge even if you have to travel to China."

Study and training abroad in modern dimensions was already in operation in the first decade of our century. In 1911 the proportion of foreign students in German universities was higher than it was in the late 1960s, despite the considerable use today by the German Federal Republic of this type of educational assistance. The situation is similar for the United Kingdom and France, the decline in the proportion of foreign students at the same time as there was an increase in their number being due to the great increase over the period of the enrollment of university students who are nationals of the recipient countries.

Study and training abroad has remained one of the main tools of educational cooperation, but with two differences. First the need has in one sense become greater owing to the rapidity with which new types of knowledge and technologies have proliferated; and the pressure of rapid educational expansion at the first and second educational levels has meant that it is often cheaper to send students abroad than to set up institutes or particular branches of training when specialization is intense and equipment costly. The second difference is in the contrary sense. The enormous increase in communication facilities of all kinds has meant that much knowledge can be transmitted by other means, and the countries that once sent students are now equipped with their own universities and training institutions to a much larger degree. The position of study abroad and its growth over the last decade on the basis of the latest published statistics can be seen from Table 8.1.

TABLE 8.1

Estimated Foreign Student Enrollment
at Third Level of Education

	1960	1971
World total*	238,671	528,774
Africa	18,238	27,999
America	72,892	200,153
Asia	22,294	73,565
Europe	105,742	199,591
Oceania	5,505	10,066
USSR	14,000	17,400
Developed countries	190,748	412,443
Developing countries	47,923	116,331
Africa (excluding Arab states)	3,032	9,466
Northern America	60,358	171,084
Latin America	12,534	29,069
Asia (excluding Arab states)	16,290	39,857
Arab states	21,210	52,241

*Except the following, for which data are unavailable: South Africa, Southern Rhodesia, Peru, Venezuela, China, Democratic People's Republic of Korea, Mongolia, Democratic Republic of Vietnam, and Fiji Islands.

Source: Unesco Statistical Yearbook, 1973.

It will be noticed that the movement of students and fellows for training purposes from one developing country to another is increasing (for example, from Malaysia to India and from Iran and Afghanistan to other Asian countries). Another trend among the developing countries is the establishment of regional or national centers serving several countries for training purposes. Examples are the Asian Institute of Technology in Bangkok, the centers established in different Southeast Asian countries by SEAMEO, and the Associated National Centers affiliated with the Asian Program of Educational Innovation for Development sponsored by Unesco.

Of the world total of just over half a million people studying in other countries than their own, about one in five was financed by official educational assistance from the OECD member countries and the centrally planned economies of Eastern Europe. The number of foreign students aided by the OECD member countries can be seen from Table 8.2.

For many years little attention was paid to the planning and evaluation of study and training abroad programs, which was regarded as a natural process rather than a conscious instrument of educational policy. But in the 1960s, with the spread of educational planning, three major criticisms emerged.

The first was the negative effects of the brain drain. The second was the insufficiency of the effort to integrate study abroad programs with national development objectives and needs. Training and study abroad need to be part of both each country's educational plan and its overall development plan. The third area of criticism was that the management of such programs was often poor, leading to weak or nepotic selection of candidates and to lack of arrangements to ensure that the studies were afterwards put to good use in the profession for which they had been given.

The criticisms still apply in varying degrees to the different categories of study abroad, which are (1) study to provide individuals with qualifications in a particular field or profession, (2) study that trains an individual for a specific task on a specific project, and (3) study by those already qualified to bring their knowledge up to date or solve a special problem.

The first category is less easy to adapt to development purposes than the others. Nevertheless, the application of manpower and employment criteria can make this kind of study abroad a means of supplementing the output in educational systems of qualified personnel in short supply. The second category is, by definition, linked to a selected objective and, therefore, controllable. The third category may or may not be easy to keep in development channels according to the degree of latitude allowed the individual. The problem of ensuring the incorporation of the individual in the development process on his return is also easier in the second category, but often more elusive in the first and third. A number of countries, therefore, have incorporated guarantees of employment on return after study and penalties for nonreturn.

A further difficulty is that often the individual fails to acculturate himself to his new surroundings, especially when the language is different from his own. This factor, together with problems of adjustment to different environmental and cultural conditions, can easily reduce a student's performance. Data exist on this problem, and one of the most interesting examples is the inquiry made in 1967

TABLE 8.2

Students and Trainees Assisted by DAC Countries

Number and Place of Study	Assisting Country or Agency									
	Australia	Austria	Belgium	Canada	Denmark	France	Germany	Italy	Japan	Netherlands
Total number of students and trainees	3,194	265	4,036	2,468	432	13,792	14,419	1,666	4,611	2,578
Students	1,906	204	2,271	1,619	68	8,888	5,391	1,246	674	2,147
in the donor country	1,867	204	2,268	1,348	(68)	6,734	4,909	(1,246)	674	1,562
in the country of origin	6	--	3	--	--	2,154	437	--	--	222
in third countries	33	--	--	271	--	--	45	--	--	363
Trainees	1,288	61	1,765	849	364	4,904	9,028	420	3,937	431
in the donor country	1,277	61	871	849	(364)	4,904	7,674	(420)	3,937	421
in the country of origin	--	--	894	--	--	--	--	--	--	10
in third countries	11	--	--	--	--	--	1,354	--	--	--

Number and Place of Study	Assisting Country or Agency								
	New Zealand	Norway	Portugal	Sweden	Switzerland	United Kingdom	United States	Total DAC Countries	EEC
Total number of students and trainees	1,247	382	--	1,593	873	13,800	16,269	81,625	2,322
Students	904	292	--	43	279	9,210	9,933	45,075	1,420
in the donor country	846	232	--	28	238	9,210	8,444	39,878	912
in the country of origin	12	43	--	3	28	--	124	3,032	508
in third countries	46	17	--	12	13	--	1,365	2,165	--
Trainees	343	90	--	1,550	594	4,590	4,590	36,550	902
in the donor country	341	79	--	470	208	4,590	4,454	30,920	163
in the country of origin	--	3	--	609	199	--	--	1,715	689
in third countries	2	8	--	471	187	--	1,882	3,915	50

Source: "Development Cooperation," 1974 Review, OECD, p. 291.

in the German Federal Republic.[1] These figures demonstrate serious losses on the operation. Out of each 100 new foreign students enrolled in 1957-58, the result after eight years of study was that the number who passed their final examinations successfully were medicine 40 percent, science 32.7 percent, engineering 31 percent, economics and the social sciences 20.7 percent, and agriculture 57.4 percent.

A later study made in 1974 gave improved results, as can be seen from Table 8.3.

A measure that has been found useful is to use group fellowships so that there is a process of mutual reinforcement among the students and a constant exchange of ideas about the applicability of what they learn to conditions in their own countries. The advantages are that the trainees have greater confidence in a group and are able to exchange ideas and experiences with each other so as to facilitate learning; further, a group is easier to handle at the reciprocal institution and can have a more thorough program prepared for it than is the case with isolated individuals. Disadvantages are that presence in a group may make acculturation more difficult. French experience, described in detail in a recent report[2] prepared by the French National Commission for Unesco, favors a system of alternation between group and individual training. This is on the condition that the stay is of at least the length of an academic year and that after training the trainees are likely to take part in team activities when they return home.

In general group fellowships have been found to reduce brain drain and to aid the impact of study abroad on development by avoiding the fragmentation and compartmentalization that is often rife in the administration of study abroad programs. In 1971, Unesco convened an International Committee of Experts on Training Abroad policies, which recommended[3] that study-abroad programs should be administered as part of the total training effort. It pointed out that such an integrated approach required a major effort of cooperation between the various national and external agencies concerned. The UNDP suggested to the committee a framework for training-abroad policy including recognition of the need for centralization of training in development programs; improvement of methods to determine needs and priorities and to coordinate planning and administration both of training programs in general and of specific projects; and increasing the "trainer" role of outside experts, and improving the training of local counterparts on projects. In 1973 the IIEP (Unesco) issued a monograph[4] that set out these and other measures to make programs more effective.

A number of developing countries have established national organizations to deal with programs of study and training abroad. In

TABLE 8.3

Rates of Success and Failure of Scholarship Students of the
German Academic Exchange Service, 1956–70

	Total Number of Scholarships Terminated	No Finishing Intended	Exam Passed	Studies Interrupted	Withdrawn	Unclear
Ethiopia	44	--	26	10	8	--
Ghana	74	14	44	9	7	--
Guinea	6	--	2	1	3	--
Cameroon	19	--	14	1	4	--
Kenya	7	--	7	--	--	--
Congo	9	5	1	--	3	--
Liberia	37	3	13	4	17	--
Madagascar	15	10	5	--	--	--
Nigeria	99	7	78	7	7	--
Sierra Leone	11	--	8	1	2	--
Somalia	15	1	5	4	5	--
Sudan	65	4	32	7	17	5
Togo	20	1	14	1	4	--
Uganda	8	--	5	--	3	--
Zaire	3	1	2	--	--	--
Total	432	46	256	45	80	5
Percent	99.9	10.8	59.6	10.6	18.8	0.1

Source: Peter Kasprzyk, Die Forderung afrikanischer Studenten durch den DAAD, DAAD-FORUM Studien, Berichte, Materialien Deutscher Akademischer Austauschdienst (Bonn-Bad Godesberg, 1974), p. 32.

Venezuela, for instance, an office in the Ministry of Planning has been set up to coordinate national and international training. Colombia has an Institute of Educational Credit and Technical Training Abroad, linked to the Ministry of Labor and the Department of Planning, which is responsible for all loans to students in Colombia and abroad, administers funds contributed by different institutions for the training and retraining of their staff, and distributes information to students about training possibilities. Other Latin American countries have similar semiautonomous organizations.

In Asian countries the program is usually handled by the Technical Cooperation authorities, but the departments of external relations, of education, and of economic affairs are also involved in varying degrees in most countries. The extent of the administration problem can be seen from the example of India, which reports[5] it receives some 500 offers of fellowships each year from 38 countries and organizations. In addition the Government of India itself has a scheme for national scholarships for study abroad under which 50 selected Indians are sent to other countries for higher studies and training. In some North African countries a fellowship office distributes all awards for study abroad and at home. A number of organizations concerned in the countries of origin offer language training facilities and cooperate with donors for the selection, guidance, and supervision of students going abroad or already there.

Donor agencies have also taken action to improve the management of study abroad. Unesco recently established an Interdepartmental Committee on International Training, so that all units get together on problems and policies. The Division of Study and Training Abroad acts as the secretariat of this Committee and serves as a link between planning elements and training administration. It has also made arrangements for specialists to come from Member States to observe its training administration in action and has sent out advisory missions. The FAO also has a Division of Study and Training Abroad, which is responsible for all group training for all departments and for the orientation of experts. The World Bank has a special unit to ensure that account is taken of training abroad in all projects.

No country has made a full cost-benefit study of the advantages and disadvantages of the movement of its students abroad, whether on their own or sponsored from national or foreign sources, which takes into account the alternative possible uses of the funds for developing local resources. Such a study would be complex but feasible. There has, however, been a good deal of evaluation of individual fellowship programs and also analysis in connection with the problem of brain drain. One such study,[6] made on the donor-country side in respect to the movement to the United States, estimated that over the first part of the 1960s,

the net cost to the United States of foreign students . . . was $45 million annually; that when
the value of the education absorbed by U.S.
students abroad was added the balance was reduced to $18 million; and that when the non-
returning foreign students were taken into account there was a benefit to the United States
of $16 million. Many of the students had of
course been studying privately and not as a
result of aid programs.

What can be said about the future of study and training abroad?
Its value in broadening people's understanding of each other across
frontiers will give it a potential long life as a cultural and educational instrument varying only with the state of the world economy
and the degree of harmony in international relations. As a traditional instrument of educational aid for development from the advanced to the less advanced countries, however, its future is likely
to be a more restricted one, and it would seem this should be so.
There should be, as the developing countries acquire their own educational resources, a redeployment of aid away from training abroad
toward training in the recipient countries themselves, since this type
of aid amounts only at present to around one-tenth of aid funds devoted to training and study abroad.

The experience of the German Federal Republic, which we referred to illustratively on other aspects of the problems of study
abroad, gives a good demonstration of this trend in operation. Tables
8.4 and 8.5, for Nigerian and Ethiopian students, respectively, show
the division between grants for studies to be pursued in the Federal
Republic and those in the country of the students' origin.

There will of course always be a need in fields of heavy specialization for study in other countries. Further, the value of study
abroad as a general educative influence and means of promoting international understanding will remain and no doubt will continue to
produce an important flow of students and fellows between countries,
both privately and as a result of cooperation programs.

MATERIAL SUPPLIES

The material needs of educational programs are for capital investment and maintenance and the annual flow of educational materials
and equipment. Capital expenditure represents in the developing countries about a third of the total expenditure on education. Expenditure
on new building should taper off as the proportion of the population in

TABLE 8.4

DAAD Scholarships for Study in the Federal Republic of Germany and in Nigeria

Year	Medicine		Science Engineering		Others		Total	
	Germany	Nigeria	Germany	Nigeria	Germany	Nigeria	Germany	Nigeria
1957	8	--	--	--	2	--	10	--
1958	2	--	1	--	1	--	4	--
1959	--	--	--	--	1	--	1	--
1960	9	--	1	--	1	--	11	--
1961	13	--	1	--	3	--	17	--
1962	9	--	5	--	2	--	16	--
1963	10	1	2	--	3	5	15	6
1964	12	2	7	3	4	13	23	18
1965	15	2	--	8	--	21	15	31
1966	7	6	2	16	2	37	11	59
1967	5	11	--	12	1	34	6	57
1968	4	18	--	13	1	36	5	67
1969	1	23	--	9	--	24	1	56
1970	1	17	1	20	3	39	5	76
1971	--	19	1	61	--	39	1	119
1972	--	21	--	77	7	45	7	143

Note: DAAD is Deutscher Akademischer Austrauscholienst (German Academic Exchange Service).

Source: Peter Kasprzyk, Die Forderung afrikanischer Studenten durch den DAAD, DAAD-FORUM Studien, Berichte, Materialien Deutscher Akademischer Austauschdienst (Bonn–Bad Godesberg, 1974), p. 15.

TABLE 8.5

DAAD Scholarships for Study in the Federal Republic of Germany and in Ethiopia

Year	Medicine		Science Engineering		Others		Total	
	Germany	Ethiopia	Germany	Ethiopia	Germany	Ethiopia	Germany	Ethiopia
1956	--	--	2	--	2	--	4	--
1957	--	--	2	--	2	--	4	--
1958	--	--	4	--	2	--	6	--
1959	--	--	4	--	2	--	6	--
1960	1	--	3	--	10	--	14	--
1961	--	--	1	--	1	--	2	--
1962	1	--	2	--	5	--	8	--
1963	--	--	--	--	1	--	1	--
1964	--	1	--	2	2	7	2	10
1965	--	--	1	4	1	6	2	10
1966	--	--	--	5	--	5	--	10
1967	1	--	2	6	1	5	4	11
1968	--	3	--	6	2	6	2	15
1969	--	3	1	6	--	6	1	15
1970	--	6	1	7	1	12	2	25
1971	--	10	1	20	2	20	3	50
1972	1	10	--	16	1	20	2	46

Source: Peter Kasprzyk, Die Forderung afrikanischer Studenten durch den DAAD, DAAD–FORUM Studien, Berichte, Materialien Deutscher Akademischer Austauschdienst (Bonn–Bad Godesberg, 1974), p. 15.

schools rises until gradually full enrollment is obtained, although a greatly increased amount of paper, printing machinery, and books is needed annually. On the other hand, important changes that are being made to increase the amount of science teaching and practical training, especially that for technologists and other vocational skills, is leading to a sharp increase in capital costs. The same changes are affecting the movement of educational materials. Developing countries must import increased amounts of scientific equipment, machinery for training purposes, publications, new forms of educational media, and so on.

The growth in the amount of capital lending and credit, especially from the World Bank Group, has been a reaction to increased demand. However, in the case of measures of aid for the regular trade in educational materials, little progress has been made, though a number of bilateral donor countries and nongovernmental bodies have made useful gifts. Educational Ministries often find that articles that cannot be obtained domestically are of key strategic importance to their educational plan. The situation that often arises, unhappily, is that although the educational project has high priority, its foreign exchange costs are given a lower priority when taken under the criteria for the allocation of foreign exchange. Normally the foreign exchange components of educational expenditure of an average developing country are only around 6 to 7 percent, but the items may be of particular importance. Bottlenecks occur, which can be solved only by external cooperation or special foreign exchange allocations by Ministries of Finance.

The major part of educational cooperation is made up of technical assistance or capital loans or grants, and regular official help is not normally given for the recurrent movement of educational materials, though gifts of paper and other materials in kind are made by individual donors. Unicef has an important program for supplying school equipment, especially for science teaching. It has established samples and a guidelist, which can be used for local production purposes as well as for import or supply under cooperation programs. Other agencies such as the UNDP and the bilateral donors also supply equipment, but usually only as part of technical assistance.

Two trade agreements negotiated by Unesco in the late 1940s and early 1950s provide for reduction of import duties on educational materials. Their coverage, however, is small in terms of the range of supplies needed. Bilateral trade agreements also, in some cases, make special provision for the import of scientific and educational materials, with the exporting countries agreeing to accept payment in local currencies. Both the Unesco agreements are somewhat out of date since they were conceived when the main interest was centered on the free communication of information rather than on

development needs. The communication objective should clearly continue to be pursued; nevertheless, the report of the expert meeting
called to review the agreements in May 1968 includes the following
extract:

> "The conclusion would seem to be that these
> agreements are no answer to the basic devel-
> opment needs." This is no doubt what led
> UNCTAD at its first Conference to invite
> Unesco "To continue in consultation with other
> international agencies concerned, its studies
> of the international trade in education and scien-
> tific materials as a factor in accelerating the
> development of the developing countries."

A further aspect of this subject is that Unesco resolutions have
asked that education should participate in supplementary or compensa-
tory finance schemes. These are arrangements under which it is proposed that countries may receive special allotments of foreign exchange when their balance-of-payments situation is depressed by
temporary difficulties such as export fluctuations. Since educational
planning involves long-term expenditure commitments, it is argued
that there is a need for arrangements to iron out fluctuations due to
temporary foreign exchange difficulties.

The necessary studies and international action have not yet
taken place, although the needs have been stressed by the developing
countries. An interesting example of a device, but at present a limited one, to aid the flow of educational materials between countries
by overcoming foreign exchange difficulties is the Unesco Book
Coupon Scheme, which enables institutions and individuals to obtain
publications, educational films, and scientific material from abroad
without foreign exchange drawbacks. Fifty-two countries are participating as purchasers and suppliers; transactions to date are not
far short of $100 million. This type of scheme needs extension to a
wider range of educational materials needing foreign exchange, which
causes bottlenecks and inefficiencies.

Some examples of both the needs and the problems in the supply and local production of materials is contained in the report of a
workshop of Asian countries held in Tokyo in 1972 under the sponsorship of the Japanese National Institute of Educational Research (NIER)
and Unesco. The report contained the following statement from the
Indian participant:

> There is a mushroom growth of producers and
> dealers of audio-visual materials and teaching
> aids in India and at present over 200 such sources

and agencies can be listed. Producers who are
pouring out materials of a fairly good quality
are few. Some time back in our all-India
search for audio-visual materials for an international exhibition at Bangkok, we could select
suitable materials from about a dozen firms in
India. Commendable graphic materials in the
form of charts, maps, auto-didactic playway
materials, models, and allied three-dimensional
materials are being produced. There is a dearth
of good filmstrips and instructional films.

The growth and popular utilization of instructional technology is closely linked up with
the availability of audio-visual equipment and
hardware. The average monthly production of
16 mm sound projectors by two and sometimes
by three firms in India totals up to 160 projectors. Half of these go to educational institutions and are used for direct educational purposes. It is estimated that at present there are
more than 9,000 projectors in educational institutions in the country.

The Indonesian participant said,

The distribution of materials, the lending of
apparatus and materials would be very costly,
due to the great distances in Indonesia, the
possibility of loss and damage, the poor communications and availability of copies. As for
machines and apparatus, like cameras, projectors, tape recorders, films, tapes and books,
since these articles are all imported goods, the
loss or damage of machines and tools would result in insuperable difficulties. To import
machines would need years because of lack of
funds and intricate administrative procedures.
. . . For the same reasons as stated above,
the Government has no government assisted
machinery or agencies. Occasionally an order
is placed for the production of materials, at
local manufacturers of school materials. The
manufacturer stops production as soon as the
order is carried out. . . . There are provinces
outside Java, which could not even buy materials
locally. They have to order everything from Java,

or establish manufacturer plants only for the
period it is needed to meet this demand. These
are mainly workshops, improvised from local
entrepreneurs.
          No local independent machinery can exist
without continuous demand from the public.
Therefore no local entrepreneur would be
easily persuaded to establish any manufacturing enterprise.

The workshop recommended that an international production
system should be established under the auspices of the United Nations or Unesco that would provide techniques on local production
methods and as much international aid as possible should be har-
nessed to this purpose wherever it was clear that the possibilities
of their use were viable and effective.

This whole area of cooperation activity is one that needs review
and improvement with the help of both Unesco and UNCTAD, as well
as bilateral cooperation agencies. Assistance from transnational
corporations could also be valuable. It would not be unreasonable,
since these corporations make considerable profits in the developing
countries, for them to be willing to aid the education sector. This
they could do through helping in the setting up in factories in the developing countries of low-cost production lines, worked out with educators of the developing countries, which because of the international
scope of the demand could avoid the problems of lack of incentive to
local production pointed out above by the Indonesian participant in
the Tokyo workshop.

Paper is also a key educational supply problem in a number of
countries, and gifts in kind have been made by Sweden and Canada.
Possibilities of increasing local production of paper by substitutes for
soft wood are discussed in Chapter 12.

NOTES

1. C. Oehler and H. Pabel, Foreign University Students in the
Federal Republic of Germany (Bonn, 1967).
          2. ED. 74/WS/1 Paris (30 May 1974), p. 16.
          3. Unesco (ED 71 Conf 8/5).
          4. William D. Carter, Study Abroad and Educational Develop-
ment (11EP/Unesco, 1973).
          5. (ED-73/Conf/716/3), Annex IV, p. 7 give reports provided
by Asian countries of the structure and organization of the national
services responsible for training abroad.
          6. See "Education, Manpower and Welfare Policies," Journal
of Human Resources 1, no. 2 (1966).

**PROBLEMS OF PLANNING,
DESIGN OF PROJECTS,
SUPPLY, MANAGEMENT,
AND EVALUATION**

PLANS AND STRATEGIES OF COOPERATION

Each country has to decide for itself its educational objectives and the extent to which they are integrated with overall social, economic, and cultural aspects of national development and how far purely educational and cultural aims should be pursued for their own sake. The great majority of developing countries have by now set up overall plans and educational plans which are so integrated in varying degrees.

It follows that requests for educational assistance under cooperation programs ought to fit in with educational plans. Practice among developing countries varies in this regard. Some, as in the case of Indonesia, have worked out effective procedures for this. Others deal with their cooperation projects in a case-by-case manner, and a useful step on the recipient end of the cooperation process would be for them to review their machinery and methods for participating in educational cooperation to secure more coherence with their national plans.

An exchange of experience between developing countries on methods and machinery for planning the best use of cooperation opportunities might be a valuable step for an international agency, such as Unesco, to initiate, perhaps by means of a conference or seminar organized by the IIEP.

There are, however, certain limitations on the possibilities of better planning of cooperation at both the receiving and the supply end of the process. There are always, in the case of bilateral cooperation, internal and external political factors that affect both parties in the cooperation, and very often at short notice. There is also the inherent dilemma of how to use external assistance in

relation to priorities. On the one hand, it is often stated as a principle that cooperation should relate to priorities. Cooperating countries do not like to see their assistance frittered away on unimportant
projects. On the other hand, cooperation is by definition supplementary to the main national effort, and the country's own resources
should be mobilized to take care of top national priorities. A meeting place between the horns of the dilemma may perhaps be found in
a form of planning at the receiver end that identifies at an earlier
stage than at present those particular items in national educational
priorities requiring external cooperation and that sets time schedules
on the assistance so as not to create enduring dependencies.

On the donor side of cooperation, planning is even more difficult. To some extent long-term planning is inhibited by uncertainties as to the amount of future resources that will be available,
though a number of important bilateral and multilateral agencies
are able to work over longer time spans than previously. Another
difficulty is the plurality of donors and the lack of any assurance
that any particular request for cooperation will fall to one source of
assistance rather than to another. Further, whereas in a national
plan there are clear targets both in quantity and in terms of the different levels of education, targets for educational assistance for the
typical donor-cooperator are made up of potential requests for cooperation from 80 or 90 developing countries. A number of bilateral
agencies, particularly those of the smaller donor countries, have
overcome this problem to some extent by concentrating in advance
upon a limited selection of countries.

The lack of long-term planning of educational cooperation also
limits the capacity of donor agencies to supply suitable assistance.
Donor agencies often need new skills and backstopping arrangements
to be able to meet different kinds of requests. This is so in the
field of new forms of basic education both at the school and nonformal level. Deficiencies in longer-term planning also permit enduring educational dependencies to renew themselves regularly.

Subject to the resolution of the dilemma regarding the use of
internal or external resources for top priorities and to the improvement at both ends of the planning of cooperation needs, cooperation
is likely to be most efficient when it is applied to those parts of the
educational system where development in the form of qualitative
change is most active and resources lag behind the possibilities of
reform.

The criticism in the 1960s was that educational systems were
dysfunctional because they were not sufficiently related to overall
development plans. There is a growing view that the overall plans
themselves were, and still are in many respects, dysfunctional to
the real needs of the developing countries. Emphasis is shifting

from rates of economic growth as indicated in each country's overall
increase in income per head to needed changes in economic and social structure, income distribution, and forms of development that
reduce the various dependencies from which a number of populations
suffer in relation to controlling influences from both outside and
within the country. The implications of such new assessments of
development are reflected in the demand for a greater democratization of education, better educational opportunity, and basic education
for all. At the international level these demands are reflected in
the United Nations resolution regarding a New Economic Order,
quoted at the outset of Chapter 1.

Although these concepts have received approbation by governments when advanced at international conferences and while they
figure in some national plans, they are not yet being widely applied
by the developing countries, and it follows that they have as yet little
impact on cooperation activities. Donor agencies, therefore, have
to steer a careful course between, on the one hand, supporting the
most progressive aims declared by the countries with which they are
cooperating and, on the other, not becoming involved in projects
which are doomed to failure because they are premature in relation
to the possibilities of their absorption into national policy and execution. In the following chapter discussing the cases of Thailand and
Peru, it will be seen how certain projects were unsuccessful because these conditions were not met.

There are, nevertheless, important cases where it is good for
the aid projects to be to an appropriate degree in advance of the local possibilities, provided it is carefully planned as an experiment.
The system of organizing schools in mutually supporting "nuclei,"
which is now a fundamental feature of the far-reaching educational
reform in Peru, was the subject of external aid initiatives combined
with some national support during the 1960s, but it did not at that
time have the possibilities of widespread adoption because of the
prevailing sociopolitical and educational policy.

Similarly, the comprehensive schools set up with a Canadian
initiative in the 1960s in Thailand, which were criticized as being
overexpensive and not fitting into the broader national possibilities
of extension over a wide section of the Thai population, were later
found to have provided valuable indirect impulses to secondary education in Thailand. Adapted forms of the schools assisted under the
project are being spread. These results were due to the efficiency
with which the Thai administration took up these positive factors;
but judged on its direct purpose, the project, it would seem, should
have been geared originally more closely to actual possibilities.

In promoting educational change, care should be taken to distinguish between experiments that have to be developed under research

and development procedures before they can be applied and pilot
projects ready for multiplaction. Failure to make this distinction
has brought the pilot project concept into discredit.

The question of how far external assistance can be an active
influence on educational reform depends, therefore, on each particular case, taking into account both the direct and the indirect impact. But the general principle would appear to be to choose projects that are both at the part of the system where most activity in
favor of change is taking place and where the implementation possibilities are already established by government policy. Some may
believe that this diminishes the activating role of assistance in that
this reduces its impact on the rate of national progress, whereas,
desirably, it should move somewhat ahead of the situation in order
to influence it. This, as discussed earlier, is a belief that is likely
to cause difficulties and in the circumstances of the average developing country is likely to be regarded as outside interference, unless
limited to purely technical matters.

This does not mean that cooperating agencies and the outside
educational world generally cannot influence countries in the direction of educational progress. It means that the best way of doing so
is not by specific projects that go beyond the local possibilities, but
by cooperating in the creation of research and development centers
assisting experimentation and increasing the flow of information between countries to facilitate the spread of innovatory ideas. In
short, the policy in such matters should be educational and stimu-
lative and not interventionist.

We may, therefore, derive as a strategic principle that cooperating programs should, subject to the provisos expressed, be conceived as having the prime purpose of promoting the development,
reform, and renovation of educational systems as a contribution to
raise world educational levels generally. This, however, is not the
whole task. The second principle is that there are also medium-
and short-term needs to be met, as well as assistance in regenerating the educational system itself. Here the criticism is encountered
that short-term assistance to the existing system becomes medium
term, while medium term becomes long term, and in the end the
substitution of external by internal resources is delayed and dependency prolonged. The answer would seem to be to delineate more
closely what is meant by short term and medium term rather than
to reduce this type of cooperation.

As far as short-term aid is really a matter of an emergency
need (for example, to reconstruct schools destroyed by disasters or
for paper or other consumable supplies), the self-perpetuation issue
does not arise. The danger does arise, however, in the case of
forms of equipment that could be made locally after a short initial

period of assistance but which continue to be imported through lack of the necessary initiatives. Part of the strategy of supplying equipment and the consumable materials of education should be to identify and assist in developing local production possibilities and to taper off short-term immediate assistance into medium-term aid for local production.

A similar situation arises with short-term aid in the form of the appointment of expatriate personnel to fill urgent gaps for key personnel--in particular, university faculties and specialties. Once, however, the specialized personnel arrive, the tendency develops to regard them as part of the establishment and to utilize for other purposes people who are trained to replace them. Thus a university may have set up a department of chemistry and recruit some outside teaching staff with the intention of replacing them as nationals acquire the necessary knowledge. It often happens that as soon as the nationals come forward, however, it becomes policy to place them in industry or in government service connected with their specialty --prolonging the foreign expertise in education rather than in business and administration.

This may be wise from the standpoint of the country's overall policy, but educationally it prevents sound medium-term or longer-term national development in the branch of education concerned. The expatriate element may be dynamic and the source of educational change. Nevertheless, the fact it is foreign and not integrated with national policy formation in most cases may result in the discipline in question becoming an enclave rather than a dynamic force within the system. Subject to th: e provisos, a valuable role exists for short-term or stopgap educational assistance, and provision for it should be made in the strategies of donor agencies, even those that tend to stress more the longer term than the short term, since the short term can often be an important leverage to longer-term change.

Medium-term or bridging aid makes up the bulk of educational assistance and consists typically of program aid to provide teachers and experts and grants for study abroad. The expatriate teaching force, while performing their specific teaching duties well, may nevertheless act as a brake on a country's redeployment of its educational resources to meet development needs. Most foreign teachers work at the second level and are recruited to meet growing demands by parents for education at the second level. This demand is not always compatible with development needs or the need to redistribute resources to primary or basic education to satisfy the human right to at least a minimum of education. The presence of expatriate teachers may delay or even prevent the readjustment of the resource allocation between the different levels, which would take place if they were not there and which may be desirable for development purposes. The answer would seem to be not to avoid entirely this form of aid since it obviously can serve very important purposes in the development of an educational system. It is rather that it should be planned more closely (the supply of expatriates should be more flexible) and for shorter terms so that it can vary with changes in the national plan. The provision of career opportunities and arrangements in advance for their replacement should be made part of the educational planning of foreign aid.

Similar considerations apply to study abroad, which is a short-term or in some cases a medium-term measure. Where it is a large item, regular reviews have to be made on a cost-benefit basis of the program's utility as compared with the creation of national or regional facilities to prevent self-perpetuation and continued dependence on foreign sources of training and study.

While cooperating agencies at the donor end, especially the ex-colonial powers, are likely to continue to have to supply teachers (since that often is requested by their partners), the future seems to lie more with project aid closely linked to economic development, except in two important fields. The first is the possible development of massive programs of universal education, either formal or non-formal, though, at present in the absence of overall programs, these are dealt with on a project basis consistent with the current view that the teaching of literacy has to be linked with specific employment outlets. The second is the area of science and technology and its teaching, where there is a considerable backlog of program-type assistance needed.

Institution-building combines the features of both program and project aid when it takes place in countries at a relatively low level of educational development. The overall picture is that institution-building has largely come to an end from the standpoint of aid needs, except in the fields of centers of excellence in certain countries (especially when they can be used regionally) and centers and faculties concerned with research and development and experimentation in education. The strategy, therefore, should be to shift institution-building experience and resources to these two fields and to take particular care not to reproduce some of the cases of the 1950s and 1960s where European and American patterns were assumed to be applicable to circumstances where new types of institutions were, as events showed, really required. Projects for the creation of educational research and development institutions must be tested out by the same kind of research and experimentation and feasibility analysis, which it will be their task to apply to other projects.

The adoption of the strategic principle of linking educational cooperation projects to projects of overall development has implications in the mechanism of educational cooperation at both the donor

and recipient end. At the recipient end, it would be useful to have a
section in the Ministry of Planning with the sole task of examining
all external aid and physical investment, whether public or private,
to derive the educational implications. Provision could then be made
either in the overall aid project itself or by the foreign enterprise
making the investment for the cost of the educational implications to
be carried on the overall aid project itself. Where several foreign
enterprises enter a particular area, they could be expected to pool
their contribution to the educational system to ensure the necessary
supply of literate workers who had sufficient basic education on
which industrial or agricultural training could be built. The same
consideration should apply to internal development programs since
experience shows that, especially in the fields of basic education,
rural education, and creation of literacy, success requires that
there must be some visible or forthcoming economic development to
create the incentive. On the employers' side, the absence of a literate population is likely to conflict with the execution of sound development policy, as well as reduce productivity.

It is clear from the foregoing that the art or science of the
initiation and execution of educational cooperation is not simple.
There are, nevertheless, steady streams of valuable assistance,
which are obviously justified and run without difficulty. Moreover
the larger the number of criteria and caveats, the more difficult it
is to get anything done. A certain degree of risk is necessary in all
enterprise.

CRITERIA OF PROGRAM AND PROJECT CHOICE
AND DESIGN: SUPPLY PROBLEMS

A perfectionist approach is out of order, but it may be useful
to summarize what would appear to be the main criteria to be used
in an educational cooperation program, namely that it should take
place in a genuine spirit of cooperation and not of tutelage and
clearly be requested by the recipient country; that it meet a defined
need in a priority area that cannot be satisfied domestically, quan-
titatively or qualitatively; that it be related to the national development plan and not create enduring dependencies; that it should be the
result of a dialogue between educators from both ends of the cooperation process conducted within the framework of the cooperation policies of both parties; that it should aim to bring in new ideas and be
modernizing and innovatory rather than buttress ineffective traditional systems; that it be carefully related to the recipient country's
resources for its use and maintenance, as well as to its needs, so
that new institutions can survive when the assistance ends; that

capital investment generating recurrent expenditure the national
budget cannot afford be avoided; that loans and credits should not
place an undue debt burden on the recipient country; that experimental and pilot projects, while being forward looking and progressive,
should be of a type that permits their being propagated widely and
that they should not be too far in advance of the absorptive capacity
of the existing institutional framework; that cooperation programs
should not overload either party with excessive administrative work;
that cooperation programs should be planned ahead as far as possible
and not be sporadic; and that there should be the maximum possible
exchange of information at the country level between different cooperating agencies and with the country programing machinery of the
UNDP.

Within the foregoing criteria, careful project choice based on
a thorough diagnosis of the problem is the first rule of operations,
and project preparation is not far behind.

The original design and conception of assistance projects usually receives insufficient attention; and various matters are taken
for granted, although in fact they are dubious and crucial to the success of the enterprise. A study made by the United Nations Research
Institute for Social Development[1] made a detailed survey of the
views of both foreign and national experts and reasons for failure.
The results are telling. The study shows the mistakes most frequently referred to are those in the prior conception and planning of
the project, as is indicated in Table 9.1.

Writing in 1975 in Focus: Technical Cooperation published by
the Society for International Development, Pattabhi Raman, an official of the UNDP, states,[2]

> . . . what is often criticized is not that the
> Agencies "sell," but what they sell. It is my
> observation that, over the years, what they sell,
> by and large, has had the character of "ready-
> made garments" rather than "custom-tailored
> clothes," even though, I should point out, this
> has become less pronounced with some Agencies
> lately. The problem, in other words, is the
> tendency to put forward pro forma projects,
> rather than proposals based on a careful and
> systematic analysis of the particular develop-
> ment objectives, opportunities, resources and
> constraints of particular countries. There is no
> strong evidence of innovative approaches.
>
> The point in reiterating this common criti-
> cism is not to blame the Agencies and absolve

TABLE 9.1

Major Mistakes Made on Informants' Most Recent Projects
(in percent)

	Foreign Experts	National Experts
No major mistakes were made	17	37
Mentions major mistakes	79	58
No opinion, vague replies	2	5
	100	100
Total number of informants[a]	(205)	(93)
Of those who mention major mistakes, percent who refer to the following:[b]	(N = 170)	(N = 59)
Deficiencies in foreign staffing	2	0
Deficiencies in national staffing	8	3
Deficiencies in staffing (type unspecified)	9	10
Subtotal	19	13
Defects within foreign staff	8	3
Defects within national staff	16	5
Defects within staff (type unspecified)	22	27
Subtotal	46	35
Timing too quick or locale too large	18	17
Timing too slow or locale too small	4	3
Subtotal	22	20
Inadequate internationally supplied resources	1	0
Inadequate national supplied resources	6	5
Inadequate resources (type unspecified)	18	17
Lack of coordination among sponsoring agencies	27	20
Subtotal	52	42
Technical mistakes	11	12
Mistakes about motivation or psychology of local population	18	24
Mistakes in planning or conception	52	59

[a]Besides the two informants who could not be classified by project sphere, 24 others are excluded from this table because they did not answer the question on major mistakes.

[b]The percentages in this part of the table total more than 100 percent because informants could refer to more than one kind of error.

Source: U.N. Publication (67.IV.4), p. 152.

others of responsibility for the situation. Rather,
it is to suggest that this tendency can be overcome
to a large extent by a country programming methodology. In my opinion, to the extent that the
methodology encourages and enables the Agencies
to serve as custom tailors rather than as purveyors
of ready-made garments, we are bound to discover
new approaches and new dimensions.

The margin between project identification and preparation is a
thin one, since before the project can be accepted it has to be presented in full. Identification can be combined with preparation in
certain cases where the project is clearly identifiable. At the same
time there is a real difference because the process of identification
springs from a wider form of action, namely diagnosis, than is the
case with preparation. The diagnosis in which identification is a part
has to range over many factors outside the project itself, such as
comparison with alternative uses of the resources, the availability
of local resources to support those imported from abroad, and the
general educational and economic conjuncture.

Preparation, on the other hand, is concerned more with the
detailed elaboration of the costs to be used to implement the work.
Nevertheless, project preparation should not be undertaken entirely
on a narrow, cost-effective basis. The implementation, if it is a
project of any depth and complexity, will involve sociological and
pedagogic factors as well as mechanistic ones. Preparation should
contain assessments of the alternative educational methods and patterns to be used and of how its social impact and acceptability by the
population can be facilitated. It is indeed at the preparation stage
that local difficulties as regards acceptability or feasibility of operating certain methods may be thrown up in such a way that the original
diagnosis has to be changed, or perhaps the project abandoned or
given a different shape.

A number of agencies have given considerable attention to
project preparation, but few have adequate systems for the follow-up
and subsequent amendment of the project while it is in course of
operation if things are not going well. Just as diagnosis and identification, though important, are not sufficient without careful preparation, so execution when the time comes is more than a one-time
effort. The tendency often arises in busy agencies to regard their
task as finished as soon as the implementation stage has begun,
apart from the forward action for the provision of equipment and
personnel within the limits of the original project. Actually what
happens not infrequently is that the project is launched, but after a
while it becomes clear that the project, despite careful identification
and preparation, is not likely to lead to effective results.

This may happen either because the situation becomes much clearer when the first steps of implementation are being taken and latent difficulties come to the fore. Or it may be that the time lag between the diagnosis and preparation and actual implementation has been so long (with many agencies, it is in the area of two years) that the local situation has changed and a rediagnosis and identification are really required. It is rare for agencies to have an automatic system built into them by which, once a project is started, it can be reassessed and reconstructed in a new way or abandoned before it goes too far.

This does not mean that evaluation is not now becoming widespread, but that evaluation usually takes place after the event. The usual practice when someone in charge of a project discovers that it is not going well is to wait until the evaluation period has been completed, at which stage the project director and experts write reports indicating that it was not a success. What is required is a system of evaluating the progress of projects that permits difficulties to be identified at an early stage, so that a "troubleshooting" mission can be sent out to rethink the project before it is too late. It is usually best that such a mission be dissociated from the division actually running the project; otherwise, the correct degree of objectivity cannot always be obtained.

Linked to administration and execution, but with special problems of its own, is the question of supply. Supply normally means either building, equipment, or consumable materials and goods, or specialized personnel in the form of teaching or administrative staff.

As regards building and equipment, although it has long been recognized that it is a mistake to assume that developing countries necessarily need the most modern equipment and buildings, there is an almost irresistible tendency to provide them to a degree well above the standards in the surroundings in which they are placed. This tendency gives projects a special, expensive "donor" character, singling them out from other national projects and frequently causing them to fail to take root as a lasting contribution to the educational system.

Sometimes this will extend to the whole of an institution, even a university or technical institute, which may be excellent technically but beyond the means of the country to maintain in the long term and not fully geared to national aspirations at other than the elitist level. Simpler cases are buildings put up under loans from bilateral and international agencies that are excellently designed but place a burden larger than might be necessary upon the country in the repayment of the loan or using up credits that might otherwise be more widely extended.

Similarly in the case of equipment the danger is to provide typical labor-saving machinery used in the industrialized countries, although in the developing countries the strong demand is for forms of industrial activity that will create employment. The problem here is that the staff concerned with supply of equipment are not necessarily always fully briefed in the broader aspects of the assistance program. The same kind of problem arises when libraries and documentary services are provided. The inevitable tendency seems to be to attempt a certain perfection based on standards in the developed countries, whereas what is required initially for a number of years is something more economical and practical and particularly related to the curricula of the schools and the interest of the country involved.

Local Production Centers for educational materials, though advocated in theory, are not established as frequently as desirable. The administrators dealing with supply and distribution are not necessarily skilled in the development of production possibilities. These require a different range of contacts and skills, and closer links need to be established both on the recipient and donor side between the users and potential suppliers of materials.

As regards the supply of personnel, the situation is somewhat in reverse: namely, the quality of the staff supplied for expert missions in the developing countries has tended to decline over the recent years. This is partly due to increased demand for expert personnel and teaching staff in the donor countries themselves to meet the rapid educational expansion that they have been experiencing. It is also due to salaries no longer being as relatively advantageous as those at home. A further cause is the fact that the educational expertise of the developing countries has greatly increased so that the added value of the foreign expert is reduced.

Several delegations from the developing countries in addressing themselves to the subject of education cooperation at the 1974 Unesco General Conference drew attention to some deficiencies in the level of expertise being provided in the educational field by cooperation agencies. One answer to this problem may be to utilize more short-term missions by top-level experts rather than too many long-term assignments of those of lesser qualifications.

MANAGEMENT

One of the needs of developing countries, which frequently is not sufficiently emphasized, is improved management, particularly at the provincial and district level and also that of the large school. In addition to reducing the effectiveness of the current system, management weaknesses are a constraint on educational development and reform and innovation.

In a number of proposals for reform, district officers and teachers themselves in sizable schools are to be given increased organizational duties. The recommendations of the International Commission on Education regarding the creation of a learning society, or the Peruvian educational reform, which is described in Chapter 10, move in this direction, the teacher becoming a teacher-educator and along with the local administrators and headmasters, a cooperator in the organization of the learning society. Certainly, almost all new types of action, whether conventional or more innovatory, place additional burdens on educational management all down the line.

External cooperation in the form of foreign experts is unlikely to be the right form of cooperation since management problems at the provincial and local level are only partially susceptible of standard solutions applied elsewhere. They arise mostly out of localized circumstances. However, training activities can well involve demands for communication equipment and radio and television programs, for which both supplies and some expert help from abroad are needed. There may also be needs for credits to set up the necessary infrastructure of training facilities and to secure equipment and supplies and, in poor communities, for external agencies to assist by providing funds and transport at the community level to enable seminar and informal gathering activities to be undertaken by local educational administrators and teachers.

The extent of the strain on educational management at the provincial and district level depends on the pace of educational change, though, even where change is slow, improvements in cost-effectiveness from better management may also be important. Where change is needed and desired, the training activities for organizing and managing the new developments benefit from being linked to participation in the initiation of the process of change.

Thus, another point of entry to the management problem is to link it with research, experimentation, and development. External resources can help district educators and administrators work out and try out new methods, within the degree of flexibility accorded by the national curriculum, since national and local funds are normally earmarked for other purposes. There is no better training for people who have to administer a system than to take part themselves in the process of reflection and experimentation involved in correcting faults in the system and adjusting it to more modern and effective lines.

Educational management may be one of the most useful fields of cooperation among the developing countries themselves. Some developing countries have already attained a major level of educational development; others are still struggling and could benefit from advice and assistance from other developing countries. This may be a valuable area of assistance from donor agencies. There is already a certain amount of bilateral educational cooperation between the developing countries, and the UNDP has a section concerned with this, but its amount is small.

Sooner or later there should be some kind of general forum or even administrative machinery in which developing countries could utilize their ever growing capacities to deal with their own educational problems with encouragement and support from the international community.

In the field of actual management of cooperation programs themselves a constraint affecting both aid-giving and aid-receiving countries is the strain that the volume of aid for education places on the administrations concerned. The problems experienced by the UN development system described in the Jackson Report exist also in the bilateral aid agencies. It is not easy to assist projects quickly and with the right professional skills. Sometimes the problem is that the criteria are unduly rigid or that the process of checking and rechecking is over-bureaucratized and unnecessarily detailed.

According to the Peterson Commission, which reviewed U.S. aid programs in 1970, the USAID had then a checklist of 68 statutory criteria, only a small number of which relate to the purposes of the particular project. The Peterson Commission Report stated, "In the views of the Commission the present . . . administration of US foreign aid is excessively cumbersome; . . . the equivalent of 700 full time officials is now required to see that the regulations are followed."[3]

At the aid-receiving end, bureaucratic obstacles are also rife, for example, equipment provided sometimes cannot be brought through customs and out of storage without long delays and formalities, or it is delivered and kept locked up instead of being used owing to archaic laws or practices regarding responsibility for government property.

In some cases, lack of adequate information for the identification, appraisal, and preparation of projects is a major constraint, and aid-suppliers hesitate to face the task of collecting new data through expensive survey missions. This tends to reflect itself in statements by aid-giving agencies that there are not enough good projects, which often means there are not enough "ready-made" projects. That good projects that cannot be adopted for lack of funds exist is shown in many of the unmet requests made to Unesco, as well as to bilateral agencies. This obstacle is accentuated by insufficiencies of coordination of effort among the suppliers of aid, since they do not as a matter of standard practice pass on to other sources of aid projects they have appraised but cannot aid from their own funds.

The obstacle of insufficient coordination or harmonization of aid goes beyond the question of the will to exchange information and avoid waste of effort. There is a financial and administrative difficulty in that bilateral aid works on an annual program and multilateral aid is planned biennially. Neither, however, are planned on criteria that permit quick "rescue" or "pump-priming" operations. Yet this could be one of the important roles of aid. Greater flexibility seems required to permit allocations for short-term operations of special urgency which can resolve bottlenecks.

Flexibility means longer-term as well as shorter-term commitments. Hesitations about the length of commitment on both sides can lead to a "stop-go" process among aid givers and receivers, which destroys the balance of aid projects. There are obvious limits to an aid-supplier's ability to foresee future resources he will have available. But is it not possible to increase the proportion of long-term commitments within total commitments? There are often serious obstacles to long-term commitments also on the aid-receiving side due to changes of ministers and staff, which hinder continuity.[4]

Long delays in taking decisions after projects have been prepared are also damaging to continuity. Examples are to be found of serious gaps left in educational systems in the expectation of cooperation that was not finally accorded. The average aid request takes about two years to reach the operation stage, but often longer delays are involved during which time imbalances may have occurred that may change the priorities.

Since priorities depend on intimate political as well as purely educational factors, recipients tend to prefer multilateral to bilateral assistance where they require it for an overview of their educational systems and the assessment of their priorities. Once priorities for external cooperation are established, they can usefully be made known by the government to all of the various interested cooperation agencies, though there are not often regular procedures for doing this.

Special difficulties arise for smaller cooperation agencies. Since the impact they expect to make is limited, it is uneconomic for them to spend a lot of time on project identification and diagnosing needs, and some do not have the local specialized staff available. The outcome may be to adopt "pet" projects, or to specialize in particular types of aid, or to pick up smaller items in coordinated aid projects. The UNDP country programing should be able to help them as should coordination of effort with other donors.

The overall management problems of cooperation agencies themselves has had attention from the Development Assistance Committee of the OECD and by some other organizations, but there has been little exchange of experience between donors and recipients specifically in the educational sector. The initiation of some seminars for the exchange of experience could well be profitable.

Procedural obstacles to improved management, other than those of a broader and more policy-oriented nature already mentioned (such as program versus project aid, tied aid, length of period of financial commitment, and capacity to respond sufficiently quickly to new needs), are mainly the following. Individual donor agencies have different criteria for the acceptance of projects, and usually there is considerable variation between them in the type of justification and data they require and the form in which the request must be presented. At the recipient end of the cooperation network, it is difficult to be informed of all these variations; and not all of the questions are the most relevant as to whether the cooperation project is the most suitable. Thus, when a project has not been accepted by one donor agency, valuable time may be lost in having to recast its presentation to submit it to other donors. It would seem desirable to establish among the donors themselves, in consultation with the recipients, a standard form of data required, not for particular agencies' special requirements and criteria but for finding an answer to the basic question whether the project has been sufficiently well diagnosed and identified for educational development purposes. Another difficulty is the lack of memory systems and means of finding and exchanging previous reports on similar projects, both at the donor and recipient level.

Further problems stem from insufficient delegation of responsibility to regional and country representatives by donor agencies. This will sometimes mean the upgrading and strengthening of the regional and country posts. Yet another problem is the tendency to "sell prefabricated projects" to recipient countries, which means the insufficient use of country programing procedures that relate the particular educational project to overall development.

Another more technical issue concerns procurement practices for supplies, which are often unnecessarily time consuming due to overelaborate technical specifications or difficulties of import because of customs and poor distribution facilities.

Finally there are some useful operational features that are apparently fortuitous but that greatly influence the success or failure of projects and that should be sought after in the actual operation of projects. Most of these are derivable from the practical experience of people working in the field and seldom appear among the required procedures, though they may as a matter of practice be crucial. One of these is that it is usually necessary that there should be at least one highly placed official in the recipient government possessing the necessary continuity of office and influence, who is personally committed to the project and will help to push it along. Otherwise a project can become easily bogged down at middle and lower levels of operational administration, especially when items involving local cost and effort to support the project have to be provided.

Another requirement is that there should be a sufficient amount
of support in the educational establishment itself, which should have
explained to it the advantages that will accrue so that opposition
based on fears of loss of prestige or fields of interest where change
is involved will be reduced. Finally, there is the requirement, often
the most difficult of all since it requires considerable administrative
skill, of synchronizing the various inputs of staff, equipment, teaching, student time, and so on so that long gaps do not appear. It is
not uncommon for the equipment to arrive long after the teachers
and students are ready, and sometimes the reverse takes place, and
institutions are set up before a sufficient flow of qualified teachers
and students are available to enter them.

Thus, when referring earlier to educational cooperation as an
art as well as a system of management, we had in mind especially
the role of the personnel in the field who have to help to turn proposals and projects into realities. A special kind of capacity is required, covering personal qualities such as ability to be both liked
and respected by colleagues and counterparts who are being advised
and also the ability to cut through or circumvent red tape, which
often will tie the project up too much at both ends of the cooperation
network. For this reason, the selection and briefing of cooperation
personnel is an exceptionally important factor in the whole process.
The qualities required contain a substantial element of personal devotion, which frequently makes an individual project a success but
makes it not susceptible of generalization, since the same degree of
devotion cannot be assumed on a generalized scale. This is the
weakness of the pilot project approach, which has been discussed
already. This element, however, has to be counterbalanced by a
capacity to see the particular activities undertaken in the framework
of acceptability by and absorption into the policy and practices of the
recipient country. Both selection and briefing procedures are fruitful areas for improvement in order to make educational cooperation
more effective. There are very considerable variations between
donor agencies as to the time spent and methods used in recruiting
and briefing experts or institutions being used in cooperation programs; Unesco provides a briefing period of two weeks, a substantial
portion of which is given to administrative matters. The German
technical cooperation administration provides in some cases up to
three months, including instruction in the language of the country to
be assisted. Much depends on the previous experience of the expert
to be briefed. This field, too, forms a promising area for greater
exchange of experience through seminars, visits, and other forms of
cooperation within educational cooperation as a whole.

Although good recruiting, briefing of experts, and staff training of administrations all play an important role in educational

cooperation, they are part of the total problem of management and involve two other key factors. The first is ensuring close and reliable relations between headquarters and the field. Headquarters needs briefing from the field as much or more than the other way around. Distance from operations is sometimes an advantage that enables a project to be seen steadily and whole, but it is disadvantageous in respect of what are often decisive and detailed points of operation, which make all the difference between success and failure. Further, in a difficult area of work where many institutional forces and human factors as well as technical considerations operate, it is necessary to have the "feel" of a project, which is frequently only possible for field personnel with long experience of the country and of the day-to-day operational issues.

The balance between the influence of headquarters and the field varies between agencies. Some such as Unicef give more delegated authority to their regional and country officers than Unesco. However, the new trend in Unesco as elsewhere is in favor of more intensive delegation of responsibility to the field, though this does not diminish the art of the headquarters administrator of creatively stimulating, coordinating, analyzing, and evaluating cooperation programs and guiding them with a light rein.

At the higher policy level there is also an insufficiency of exchange of information as to policies and procedures among donor agencies. The Development Assistance Committee of the OECD has, from time to time, held meetings on educational cooperation problems, and the Secretariat has proposed and the Committee accepted various measures of coordination--usually of an informal nature. There is, however, no continuing attempt made to bring together both donor and recipient countries for exchanges at the purely technical level that would improve cooperation procedures and keep the various donors and recipients informed of the results of projects after they have been adopted, even if it is too much to expect that they should be informed beforehand. Here there well may be a fruitful field for action by an international agency (for example, Unesco or the IIEP), which will meet the desire frequently expressed by agency officials to know more about the way in which other agencies operate and the successes and failures they encounter.

The need for coordination is apparent at both the donor and recipient end of the cooperation network since there have been examples of countries setting up, as a result of uncoordinated cooperation programs, institutions that produce an output that is beyond the capacity of the country to absorb. A number of agencies from different social systems created in one important country rival institutes of technology, which produced higher-level engineers than the economy could absorb; at the same time industry was being held up for lack of middle-level technicians. Neither of the cooperating partners is, in principle, favorable to coordination despite what they frequently say, since recipients often play off one donor against the other to obtain better terms; and on the donor side, there is competition to secure the best use of cooperation funds allotted to them. Nevertheless, owing to the apparent difficulties that have arisen through lack of coordination, steps are being taken increasingly at the local or national level to secure an exchange of information, if not before the event at least after the necessary bidding has been done and projects approved. Thus, a number of "donor clubs," which are informal groups of major donors called together by the recipient government, are in operation; and they do serve as an informal system of checking the worst excesses of a lack of coordination among aid projects. Too much cannot be expected from this system, and the final answer must lie with the recipient country, which should take special steps to incorporate its proposed requests for assistance in its educational plan and to make them widely known.

There has been considerable interest in evaluation, and useful steps have been taken in a number of cooperation programs. But there is still much to be done. The tendency is to undertake over-elaborate evaluations after the event and not to give sufficient attention to before-the-fact evaluation of the feasibility of projects and the requirements needed for success. There has also been insufficient attention to "built-in" evaluation.

Built-in evaluation may take a procedural form by which benchmarks are made at the time the project starts and progress is ticked off according to a preconceived schedule. This method is useful particularly for research purposes, but, from the standpoint of management, it is not wholly sufficient and has to be watched since it can lead to an excessive use of time on study rather than action and create much clerical work. More useful for managerial purposes are procedures under which both the field office and headquarters can keep projects under regular review in terms of key issues, ensuring that the results of this reporting can be acted upon in time.

A useful measure, in addition to promoting closer and franker exchanges between headquarters and the field, is by having a small "trouble-shooting" unit with the function of being available to try to solve problems in the early stages. This kind of flexible, built-in evaluation could well be located both at headquarters and in the regions but, in principle, should be under different control than that of the actual project administration. The German technical cooperation administration operates a system of this kind. Something like this is also provided for in the joint inspection unit that Unesco and the UNDP operate together, but the results of its activities too often

come after the events. Since most agencies have a substantial turnover of personnel and poor documentation memory systems, evaluation after the project has been completed is less reliable as a form
of improving the design, management, and operation of projects
than are procedures based on built-in forms of management control
and evaluation of a flexible but effective kind as described.

NOTES

1. Herbert H. Hyman, Gene N. Levine, and Charles R.
Wright, Inducing Social Change in Developing Communities: An
International Survey of Expert Advice (New York: UNRISD, 1967).

2. Focus: Technical Cooperation, 1975/2, published quarterly in International Development Review, by the Society for International Development, Washington, D.C., p. 23.

3. Peter G. Peterson, "A Foreign Economic Aid Perspective"
(Washington, D.C.: Government Printing Office, December 1971),
p. 22.

4. See Director General's Statement to Executive Board
(EX/IN 55), p. 9, "When examining an educational project the other
day I found that, since its commencement, there had been a succession of six ministers of education over a period of five years."

10

SOME COUNTRY CASES: PERU, THAILAND, AND THE LEAST DEVELOPED COUNTRIES

Before drawing final conclusions and suggestions from the preceding analysis of cooperation policies, trends, and action at the different levels, it is desirable to consider some cases and problems at the level of individual countries. Three countries (Peru, Thailand, and Indonesia) have been selected to illustrate different types of problems and cases. Some discussion also follows of the special problem of the "least developed countries" as defined by the United Nations.

Peru has been chosen because it is the country where a far-reaching program of educational reform is in progress, perhaps the greatest single educational change at present being attempted in any country. It provides material to answer the question whether external assistance can contribute to fundamental educational reform in countries anxious to reduce dependencies on the more developed countries.

Some individual cases in Thailand are discussed because it has had rather an intensive experience of educational assistance programs over the last two decades. The projects analyzed are earlier cases, which give an illustration of the range of difficulties that easily can accompany seemingly well-conceived projects.

Indonesia is a classic example of educational cooperation playing an important role in a country's educational development. Frank Method has set out in Chapter 11 in some detail both the progress and the vicissitudes of educational assistance over the last 20 years. Items of particular interest include the considerable size of the volume of educational aid over the years and the problems and successes revealed in the timing of the various stages and types of assistance: the initial concentration upon assisting through study abroad the creation of a group of educational leaders followed by aid in the establishment of a sophisticated organization of educational planning;

and the procedures for incorporating external assistance into the national plan and the "donors' club," which meets at the initiative of the Indonesian planning authorities, and are also especially interesting features.

The least developed countries are discussed because of their special problems, which may call for fundamentally new approaches both to the educational problems of many of them and to the type and volume of cooperation required.

PERU

Peru has had considerable experience of educational cooperation, especially with the United States. It is a case of particular interest because the country is engaged in a large-scale educational reform, which is placing new needs both on its own educational resources and the possibilities of cooperation from external sources of assistance.

The educational reform is part of a program for a major transformation of the social and economic structure of the country and poses the question of what role educational cooperation, which is often assailed as "buttressing the status quo" (to quote the Pearson Report), can play in such a situation.

In what follows it will be shown that, while attaching themselves rigorously so far as concerns policy objectives and implementation to the implementation of a strictly Peruvian oriented and guided program of profound educational change, the Peruvian Government is utilizing the cooperation of a wide variety of providers of aid, which would disprove the "buttressing" charge in the case of the circumstances of Peru.

The Peruvian situation also does not fit in with Tibor Mende's adverse assessment of the utility of educational assistance, criticized in Chapter 2. Whether it is a question of the financial aid for Peruvian education from the World Bank and the Government of Hungary or the contributions in expertise and equipment of the eight other bilateral and multilateral educational cooperation agreements, it is clear that the current type of educational cooperation in Peru lends no support to his assertion that foreign aid has "practically nothing to offer in the field of education." Nevertheless, the path to effective cooperation is not always smooth, and this was the case with Peru.

To put the matter in perspective, some account of past efforts of cooperation is required. Bilateral aid from the United States began in 1909--inauspiciously, in terms of modern theory and practice of educational cooperation. By arrangement between the two Presidents, a U.S. team of 24 educators were sent to Lima. None were Spanish-speaking, and all were Protestants, and their attempts to introduce the type of education prevalent in the United States received no support below the presidential level. They were attacked by the educational establishment, the Church, and public opinion through the press; and their mission came to an end leaving little trace.

In 1944 Peru and the United States tried a different method and set up a joint cooperative program, the Servicio Cooperativo Peruano Norte-Americano de Educacion (SECPANE). This service was based, on the U.S. side, on the Institute of Inter-American Affairs, which was in close relation with the Department of State and influenced by the policy of hemispheric defense and opposition to communism.

It constituted a more sophisticated attempt with more active governmental involvement on both sides than the previous effort. This service remained in existence for 18 years and was supported successively by the U.S. Point Four Program and the Technical Assistance Program of the International Cooperation Administration.

Robert G. Myers has written on the work of this service (SECPANE) in U.S. Foreign Policy in Peru,[1] a study sponsored by the Institute of Latin American Studies. It is the source drawn heavily upon in the historical part of what follows. He points out that there were many interesting initiatives. One of these, which was later to prove very significant, was the setting up of nuclear schools that grouped eight or ten incomplete rural primary schools under a six-year course in the nearest town. Curriculum reform also was introduced relating education in the rural schools more closely to agriculture and health. SECPANE also contributed to the setting up of comprehensive schools (Grandes Unidades Escolares--GUE).

SECPANE had other advanced ideas and a program aiming at the educational betterment of marginal groups. Moreover the nuclear schools had attached to them special training programs for teachers and suitable teaching material.

According to Myers's analysis, however, their projects, though interesting and valuable in themselves, did not take root at the time. The nuclear schools presented a threat to the current social stratification system under which the educational system was organized in the interests of the urban-mestizo class. The technical streams in the comprehensive schools produced few pupils who found employment in industry (as few as 11 percent according to a 1961 study) because the teaching had little relation to actual job requirements. In practice little impact was made.

Myers's explanation of this, which seems the right one, is that the program was in advance of the political will for educational change in the country and that the Peruvians who cooperated lacked fundamental support from the educational establishment. Although

the Peruvian Government controlled two-thirds of the SECPANE
budget, it was the U.S. advisers who pressed the programs through.
He writes, "Peruvian counterparts seldom initiated projects and
tended to rubber stamp American suggestions."[2] SECPANE was
phased out in 1962, when a military coup took place, and the various
projects including the nuclear schools became neglected in the years
that followed as they had not taken root.

Thus, although the SECPANE initiative had many valuable
characteristics and was clearly much more workable than the previous effort, it never succeeded in solving the fundamental problem
referred to elsewhere--especially in the case of Thailand--of putting
proposals forward that were ripe for execution in light of the political and managerial possibilities and of the wishes of the educational
establishment and the administration. Although SECPANE was independent of the Ministry of Education, the Ministry, in practice, was
able to block initiatives and even programs. The example is quoted
of textbooks that were supplied but remained in the warehouse because the Ministry would not approve their issue.

Shortly after the cessation of SECPANE, educational aid from
the United States was renewed when a new Peruvian Government
came into office. This time a further new method was tried--name-
ly, to contract the work out to a team of educational advisers from
Columbia University. This method operated until 1968, when the
present military revolutionary government took office. The team
had a purely advisory role and exercised less direct influence than
had been the case with the two previous initiatives. A wide variety
of educational advice was given on such matters as teacher education, vocational training, rural education, educational materials,
and research; and help was given on institution-building at the higher
levels. Short-term advisers were brought in to assist the permanent
team. School meals were provided also to the extent of $12 million
between 1965 and 1968. The Peace Corps helped in school construction, food distribution, and English teaching.

Myers's evaluation of the work of the U.S. team during the
1960s is that the performance was varied, the main continuing weakness being that projects were too often pressed before the society
was in a position to accept them. Sometimes this was due to the absorptive capacity not being sufficient in terms of the capacity of poli-
ticians and administrators to take up and implement these suggestions. In other cases it was because the project identification and
preparation had not been related sufficiently to felt national and local
needs.

Difficulties were sometimes due to lack of adequate lines of
communication with the government officials and educators most
affected by the changes recommended, and the problem of the

"foreignness" of the group, as in the case of previous efforts, remained. Ideas put forward sprang mostly from the U.S. team rather than the active efforts of Peruvians supported by the group.

During the same period the Social Progress Trust Fund provided to the OAS by the United States was used through the IDB to establish engineering and agricultural faculties in universities. The Rockefeller and Ford Foundations also helped some of the key faculties. Some European aid agencies and universities gave some smaller-scale assistance, as did Unesco, which had assisted in the 1950s through the Major Project for Primary Education in Latin America. The United Nations/Unesco/ILO Andean Indian project, also started in the 1950s, had some important activities in Peru and was one of the sources of experimentation and ideas that have been taken up since. Toward the end of the period, the OAS increased its educational work leading to the setting up of its Inter-American Council for Education, Science, and Culture. The IDB gave education loans at easy rates mainly for quality improvement in education. The FAO and ILO were also active, in cooperation with Unesco, in the fields of agricultural and industrial education, extension work, and education in rural areas linked to community development.

Another form of assistance was institution-building--for example, the setting up with U.S. assistance of ESAN (Escuela Superior de Administracion y Negocios--a graduate business school aided by Stanford University). This particular center, however, though well conceived technically and receiving valuable professional help, like some of the other projects discussed, did not gear fully into the actual needs of Peruvian society and succeed in placing the requisite number of their output in key positions. Yet another form of aid was for study abroad mostly in the United States; there was also university-to-university assistance.

The sum total of the educational cooperation effort of the 1960s from all sources did not contribute greatly to educational development in the sense of growth plus change meaning reform. Nor did it have, on the other hand, a significant role in buttressing the existing system. On the whole, it associated itself with progressive educators in Peru and propagated educational methods and ideas and assisted catalytic projects that were later to prove useful when the time came for the reform.

In the late 1960s there arose the dispute between the United States and the Peruvian Government over the expropriation of the International Petroleum Company, an American concern exploiting Peruvian oil resources. Around the same time the Peruvian Government switched from the purchase of U.S. military aircraft to French. The dispute led, unfortunately, to an educational loan for $9 million, which had already been approved, being withheld as part of the bargaining over the expropriation. The withholding of the loan was not purely an educational step but was part of a freezing of all U.S. technical assistance pending the oil negotiations. About the same time a World Bank loan for regional teacher training colleges, which had been prepared and apparently approved, was also withdrawn.

The new military revolutionary government came into power in 1968, and the USAID mission left, leaving only a single representative remaining to maintain some continuity with possible future efforts. The new government took a strong independent line about external assistance and laid it down that cooperation should be purely advisory and technical. It should not operate on the margin of decision-making or be concerned with taking initiatives for new programs. Despite the withdrawal of the USAID mission, cooperation from the United States continued to a large extent in the form of assistance from foundations, nongovernmental organizations, and business groups. Study abroad mainly in the United States continued to remain on the same pattern and level as before. Moreover, as will be seen below, U.S. official aid was resumed in the 1970s, though with a less predominant role in Peru's overall cooperation with external providers of aid.

As the new Peruvian regime became increasingly established and sure of its stability and paths of policy, its attitude to external cooperation mellowed. Mutual confidence led to the use of a wide range of cooperation agreements on new patterns (both diplomatic and technical), which fitted in with the new approach to cooperation and the objectives of the reform.

As regards the educational planning required to implement the reform, Unesco and its IIEP made available their technical advice, and a Unesco consultant assisted with financial estimates. However, the overall work of planning and implementing the reform was essentially Peruvian and carried out the sociopolitical philosophy of the military revolutionary government that had taken power, as well as some ideas that had been latent for a number of years in Peru.

Indeed, one of the major objectives of the revolutionary policy into which educational reform was integrated was the reduction of dependence--dependence of the nation on external political economic and cultural forces and ideas and dependence of the less favored population groups on the more favored.

The new educational system was suggested in detail by the Commission on Educational Reform, a group of Peruvian educators whose report issued in 1970 (Reforme de la Educacion Peruana: Informe General) paralleled many of the ideas and suggestions for educational development that appeared later in 1971 in the report of the International Commission on Educational Development set up by Unesco (the Faure Commission).

Many trends of experience among Peruvian educators in innovatory forms of education, such as the nonformal educational activities of SENATI (the employers organization that worked with the
state in supplementing the formal educational system by training and
nonformal education) and educational organizations at the community
level, found a favorable climate for wider application in the light of
the new governmental policy.

The educational reform was to be accomplished through a
large-scale delegation of authority to local district or nuclear educational centers utilizing the total educational resources of the area
and relating them primarily to work and life rather than to academic
attainment. Education was to be recurrent rather than related to
fixed periods of childhood and youth, and an adult educational stream
leading to the professions and the university was designed to operate
interlocking with and becoming part of the regular system.

The major innovations in the reform in addition to the creation
of the nuclear system are (1) two streams of basic education (one for
the regular system and the other for adults) are interlocked at all
educational levels and chronological subdivisions of the structure
are ended; (2) what was before the upper secondary level is now absorbed into the higher education level, and lower secondary becomes
part of basic education; (3) science and technology and preschool education are stressed, and the role of women is to be "revalued";
(4) indigenous languages and cultures are to be preserved, and self-
education is to be emphasized; (5) the teacher is to become a "teacher
educator," a manager of the learning resources in the community,
and a catalytic agent in awakening abilities of children, adolescents,
and adults and stimulating in them a permanent process of self-
development; (6) teachers and parents are given the responsibility of
participating in the management of the community "nucleos"; (7) all
existing teachers are to be retrained and must learn a vernacular
tongue; (8) promotion of teachers is to be based on an evaluation of
their performance in these new roles; and (9) the universities now
have closer links with the government, and the university teachers
have become civil servants. Students who receive scholarships or
study abroad have to give certain services to the nation as a condition of receiving their degrees.

The National Institute of Research and Educational Development
(INIDE) was created in 1971 to assist the development of the reform,
to provide and circulate documentary material, and to undertake in-
service training. Its subjects of special studies are the social role
of rural teachers; mathematics in the curriculum of elementary
schools; the psychological effects of marginality (that is, being members of population groups on the border of the national economy and
society as a whole); the rise in educational costs; the relation between

higher education and the labor market; and the development of the child's vocabulary.

The INIDE has received assistance from the UNDP, Unesco, Unicef, the OAS, the USAID, the German Federal Republic, France, and the Ford Foundation in the form of direct grants for research (and for some short-term studies) and of fellowships for training abroad. The Ford Foundation also gives support to the Institute of Peruvian Studies, which has made a number of studies of rural areas and educational development.

To assess the role external cooperation is playing in the Peruvian reform, the first step is to look at the cooperation projects to be initiated in 1974, which are set out in the Peruvian Educational Plan[3] for that year. Educational loans and credits from abroad not included in the list are a loan agreement of $24 million by the World Bank Group concluded in 1973, which is about to be implemented, and a Hungarian credit amounting to $2 million. In the autumn of 1974 after the publication of the plan, France concluded a $1 million cooperation agreement with Peru for a center for the training of instructors in vocational training.

Apart from these amounts and excluding earthquake relief funds, the largest sums are funded by Canada, the German Federal Republic, the USAID, France, Unicef, the Netherlands, and the OAS. Unesco is administering $1 million from German church organizations for the earthquake disaster zone under the Funds-in-Trust procedure as well as cooperating in the projects funded by the UNDP and Unicef. It is playing a leading role in the cooperation for science teaching and is associated with the World Bank loan under its cooperation agreement with the Bank.

It will be seen that the sum for U.S. assistance is around $400,000 apart from $2,540,000 for reconstruction of schools after the earthquake disaster. The cooperation covers a series of key technical services and materials. Relations between Peru and the United States improved during 1974, and the volume of assistance provided by educational cooperation may increase henceforth.

The Federal Republic of Germany has concentrated its cooperation on assisting the production of educational materials, the modernization of equipment for printing and documentation in the Ministry of Education, and the training of specialists in bilingual education; the OAS on the production of educational materials, teacher training, and educational administration; Unesco on science teaching and some elements of help (involving small sums) to basic education, literacy, and adult education. France is concentrating on the modern teaching of instructors of vocational training. The Netherlands are helping with electronic equipment and technical assistance for a technical institute.

The largest amounts of educational cooperation are concentrated on the construction and equipment of the Higher Schools of Professional Education (ESEP--previously upper secondary level but now the first cycle of higher education); on the upper grades of the basic nine-year educational cycle; on the INIDE; and as regards content upon science teaching and the production of educational materials.

There is no doubt because of the strategic place of these items in the reform of the educational system, which is being implemented from both a human resources or manpower standpoint and a social one. Effective functioning at this level is vital to the whole conception of opening up professional and higher education to wider population groups and of instituting work experience as a standard educational qualification. Moreover, an additional consideration may well have been that considerable experience already exists among providers of cooperation at the second or higher level.

Cooperation at the level of grades 1 to 6 of the basic cycle and for literacy (with the Program of Integral Literacy--ALFIN) is very small and follows the general pattern of the distribution at the world level of educational aid between levels discussed in Chapter 2. The reason may be that despite the new interest aid agencies have shown in cooperation at this level,[4] as part of the problem of universalizing minimum basic education, experience in successful design and operation of projects and programs remains small.

Assistance, though related to reform, seems to be running on the established lines of such items as techniques of educational planning (the USAID is helping with the provision of a simulation model), improvement of the teaching of science and mathematics and building construction and the provision of equipment.

A less usual type of cooperation related closely to the objectives of the reform is the assistance given by the German Federal Republic to training specialists in bilingual education, since under the new decree all teachers must speak one of the Indian languages in use in Peru and education is to be bilingual in the regions affected. The work of U.S. specialists has also rendered valuable assistance on language problems. The Summer Institute of Linguistics (SIL) aided by the Ford Foundation has experimented with bilingual teaching and written down dialects previously only spoken. There has also been an important series of anthropological and social studies in Peru funded from outside by agencies such as Unesco and U.S. universities and useful now to the implementation of the educational reform.

Another area of interest is preschool or initial education. Assistance has hitherto been small at this level and largely provided by Unicef. Governments of countries with a considerable number of

school-age children not receiving a minimum basic education normally feel they must give priority to the first grades of primary
rather than preprimary education. The Peruvian plan gives importance to preprimary education as part of its total or lifelong approach to education.

The greatest single need for developing countries undertaking
reform is for aid to finance the new expenditure that educational
change involves, and the World Bank loan is an example of this.
The Peruvian GNP per head as at 1971 was $480 with an average
annual percentage population growth rate of 3.1 between 1960 and
1971. The corresponding growth rate of GNP per head was 2 percent a year over the same period. Educational expenditure grew
from 1.6 percent of GNP in 1950 to 4.5 percent in 1973, rising to
over 5 percent in 1975 according to the development plan, and to
21.4 percent of national revenue. It is planned to remain at about
that figure, which means considerable growth since the national
budget itself is increasing in size and the proportion of local resources in total educational expenditure is becoming increased under
the reform.

Thus, Peru has a large part of its resources already devoted
to education and a resilient economy. This does not, however,
mean that there is no need for financial assistance for educational
reform. The process of large-scale reform, like the introduction
of a new model in an automobile factory, involves additional finance
for "retooling." The cost cannot entirely be met by switching funds
from the old output to the new, because in education it is necessary
to maintain the old output while the new is being generated.

Thus the $24 million loan from the World Bank for the capital
equipment needed for the reformed system was very timely. The
$24 million is for two educational levels. Firstly, it covers the
third cycle of basic education (grades 7 to 9) of the new Basic Education Centers, which are to serve as a nucleus around which will revolve the various teaching and learning resources in each district or
community. Secondly, it will lead to the establishment of 16 new
ESEPs (Higher Schools of Professional Education), which under reform constitute the first cycle of higher education. The loan is a
valuable external contribution to a capital outlay of $390 million,
which is estimated to be needed over the period 1971-80 to finance
the reform.

It will be noted that the list of aid projects in the 1974 plan already cited includes little help to the second and third cycles of
higher education, and what there is is in science teaching and study
abroad. When the military government came into power in 1968, it
had problems with the universities and introduced drastic changes--
notably asserting the government's final authority to close down

particular universities if it considered this necessary. University teachers were made into civil servants, which usually involved a reduction of salaries. Many professors left the universities to take up work in the government service or in industry. Autonomy of the universities was proclaimed, but these developments reduced in fact the independence and tendency to unplanned expansion of the previous decades. An agency, the Peruvian National University Council (CONUP), was set up to assist and coordinate the university system.

The reduction of external assistance to the universities (though international cooperation continues to take place at the nongovernmental and interuniversity level) is due partly to the past uncontrolled overexpansion of the universities in relation to career possibilities and to the changed attitude toward higher education in the reform. When the reform and reorganization of the universities have had full effect, no doubt there will be a strong demand for quality improvement in which external assistance may have much to offer. Libraries lack modern texts, and deficiencies in the standard of teaching leads to large-scale study abroad. Thus the longer term may see important aid demands for equipment, particularly in specialized faculties, and for assistance in creating more managerial and administrative skills in university administration. There may therefore be a future field of cooperation in the replanning and restructuring of the universities and in the field of university administration.

Another field where further changes may be expected that will have an effect on educational aid is the area of study abroad, which has continued much on previous lines. A study by Robert G. Myers[5] shows that the number of Peruvian students studying abroad has remained at the same level (between 20,000 and 30,000) during the last decade, although with the increase in enrollment in Peruvian universities the percentage has fallen. While study abroad is not hampered by government restrictions on immigration and currency flows out of Peru, changes may be considered necessary if this policy leads to brain drain and losses of needed foreign currency.

From a study of Peruvian students in the United States in 1966 and a follow-up one in 1970, it was estimated that only 12 percent intended to remain abroad (when combined with those undecided, the percentage rose to 32) in 1966, but by 1970, 8 percent still intended to remain (with the undecided, the figure remained 32 percent). Most of the nonreturnees were undergraduates, unsponsored, of a lower-middle socioeconomic status, who had obtained immigrant visas before leaving to study in the United States and whose job assurance on their return to Peru was not predictable. The loss they implied when evaluated in terms of potential utilization of their talents was minimal.

However, of the small percentage of doctoral candidates studying abroad, a relatively high number intended to emigrate. Here the
loss was more significant than with that of the undergraduates because the need in Peru for doctors in science, medicine, and engineering, for example, is great, although the demand in terms of
job assurance and remuneration is often not as high as in other countries.

In terms of the financial loss to Peru of what has been spent
on the student's education abroad, the fact that most expenses were
met by private means, international associations, or a combination
of the two with the student's part-time work makes the loss small
when compared with the potential cost of building similar facilities
in Peru. Nevertheless since the reduction of dependency is one of
the reform's objectives, and in view of the transformation of Peruvian society that is envisaged, a greater "Peruvianization" of the
higher educational system has to be envisaged. Since the universities appear overexpanded in relation to career possibilities and resources, a process of rationalization with the system might reduce
the need for foreign study. The IDB is assisting a manpower study
related to higher-level personnel.

The report prepared by the IIEP called Planning Universities
for Change contains many useful suggestions on techniques of planning and rationalization of higher education. International agencies
such as the OAS and IDB and foundations such as Ford and Rockefeller would also have useful experience in this field to contribute at
the technical level.

In the areas of teacher training and educational management
there seems to be another important possibility of cooperation as the
reform proceeds. Obviously the carrying out of the reform is going
to place heavy demands on managerial capacity in the educational
system, notably at the provincial, district, and community levels as
part of the devolution of responsibility. The Peruvian General Education Law of March 1972, which sets up the reform, states,

> It is thus not the teacher's role to simply teach
> his courses even if this is done exceptionally
> well. The teacher's work must be all embracing
> and exercised in various areas: in the search for
> knowledge, the acquisition of skills and further-
> more, in the guidance of the student and in his
> cooperation in the complementary activities en-
> tailed in the administrative aspects. The image
> of the teacher as such is substituted by that of
> the teacher educator who fully shares in the work
> of the educational teacher. Based on this concept

the teacher must assume more responsibilities
than those traditionally assigned him and recognized. This implies that he reassumes his
fundamental mission as the educator and educational guide of the community. In this spirit,
the Decree Law further sanctions the direct
participation of teachers through the Teaching
Communities, in the management of the educational centers and nuclei. [6]

The training of the necessary managerial capacity at these
levels is essentially a Peruvian matter, but this area of activity is
so vital for the implementation of educational reform that the international educational community could profit from following the progress made. Moreover, printing equipment for the issuing of manuals and the supply of simple calculating instruments to help in district and local planning and administration may be a needed area of
assistance, as well as the financing of expenses for travel and the
organization of seminars at which rural teachers and educational
administrators can exchange views.

Of equal importance to the managerial requirements is the
major program of retraining teachers, which has already commenced.
So much is being attempted at the same time that heavy demands are
being made on the capacity to train teachers in the changes being
made. The changes range from the introduction of new methods of
teaching mathematics and science to the teacher having to play a
managerial role in the educational process.

Thus support for teacher training would be another important
area of educational cooperation, for example, the additional capital
expenditure required for buildings and extensions at teacher training
colleges and the setting up of experimental schools attached to them.
Possible contributions could take the form of hardware such as
closed-circuit television and recording instruments or software such
as research and experimentation at the teacher training colleges
themselves for methods that will increase the efficiency and speed
by which the different educational levels can be attained.

A further area of useful assistance, therefore, might be in
research and development. The existing work of the INIDE could
well be extended from its present scope to set up in the field facilities for experimentation. In order to create a teaching and managerial force spread over the whole country that fully understands and
implements the reform, it is important that the training given and
instruction in the new methods and content should be linked as far as
possible to actual practical work and experimentation. For a considerable time to come, a major part of the teaching force will be

imbued with the old methods and approaches, and it is necessary to motivate them to change by greater participation on their part in the design of the changes themselves.

Finally, there is the whole educational experiment itself, especially its effort to create greater equity of education between social groups and to meet at least the minimum educational needs of all in a society still substantially short of universal primary education, while providing new channels of opportunity to rise up the educational ladder. While the Peruvian reform is essentially built around the school, as the projected links with the world of work are increased and the regular basic cycle and the basic work cycle begin to interlock, new types of educational situations may develop in which the division between formal and nonformal education will break down. Some ECLA*/UNDP/Unesco/ILO/FAO cooperation in this field would be of mutual advantage.

Thus Peru presents a most interesting case, both of existing educational assistance and for the development of possible new lines that can be used in other less well-placed countries. Peru itself is only just below the limit of $500 per-capita income, which has been used in United Nations circles to define the category of developing countries, and at its present rate of progress should soon move above that limit. This would be a reason not for discontinuing cooperation in the form of aid but rather for making it more selective, of greater mutual benefit to both partners, and of use to other developing countries through the experience gained by Peruvians as a source of expertise for the consideration of other countries contemplating embarking on fundamental educational reform. In this way educational assistance becomes a more genuine form of worldwide cooperation, and an additional step is taken to break down the division of the world into so-called developed donors and developing recipients.

In particular some mechanism may be required going beyond the documentary reporting service on innovation recently established at the International Bureau of Education, in order to spread on a worldwide scale information on the Peruvian reform. Many countries and agencies are much interested in this nationwide effort to relate education more closely to actual living and working conditions, along the lines of the Faure Report, Learning to Be. It might, for instance, be worth considering having an international specialist located in Peru with no other task than to report in conjunction with the Peruvian Ministry of Education on the progress of what is currently the most ambitious attempt of any country at large-scale educational reform.

---

*Economic Commission for Latin America.

The Peruvian Government is attempting to develop a new system of society, which follows neither the free enterprise nor the socialist type of system and which, though not itself a free parliamentary system, is nonetheless proceeding in a process (sometimes harsh, sometimes conciliatory) of testing out its proposals before implementation against the main interests concerned. This has led to a description of it as a nonparliamentary government using parliamentary methods. However this may be, from the standpoint of educational reform and cooperation, the country presents an important microcosm of experience.

THAILAND

Thailand has had a wide variety of experience of educational assistance, both international and bilateral. From the early 1950s, when educational aid first started to gain momentum on a world scale, Thailand presented attractive features to aid agencies. The country contained a largely homogeneous population (apart from some hill tribes and some border groups), with a single language and an ancient culture integrated into all phases of life including education. Thailand had never experienced colonization and seemed ready for forms of modernization and of structural change not overly deflected already toward European models of educational development.

Although a low-income country with poor material levels of living, its location at the crossroads of Southeast Asia, where it had become host to a number of international organizations, its valuable agricultural output, and other economic possibilities seemed to provide a sound basis for further development, together with its relatively strong foreign exchange position owing to its former role as a leading base for U.S. forces in Southeast Asia.

In what follows, two major efforts of educational assistance will be discussed--one affecting general secondary education and the other basic education. It is now possible to evaluate them and to elicit both warnings and lessons for the planning and operation of educational aid.

When the need for modernization of the educational system with external aid was taken up in 1949, an area clearly needing action was secondary education. It was overacademic in subject matter and teaching methods, and insufficient attention was given to vocational needs and the prospects of pupils who would terminate their studies without going on to higher education. Pupils were poorly prepared either with knowledge or psychologically to take part in efforts to raise the country's living levels through development.

A project was launched under Unesco sponsorship in 1951, when a pilot school, in which the academic and vocational streams were combined, was set up at Cha Cheong Sao, which was later extended to Cholburi in 1954. This project was a total failure, and both schools reverted to their academic status within a few years despite a large input of advice and external aid through Unesco involving many foreign experts. Attempts to diffuse what results had been obtained were abandoned in 1959 when the aid ceased. An evaluation committee appointed by the Thai Ministry of Education in 1957 had urged that the foreign experts should be withdrawn.

The reason for the failure was that the operation had been conceived too much in purely pedagogic terms, without realizing the nature of the administrative and social process required in the country as a whole for the innovation to take root. The aim had been to produce better-than-average schools, which would be imitated elsewhere, but neither in the pilot areas themselves nor elsewhere did the valuable pedagogic work have an impact because it was not geared to possibilities of implementation and the steps needed for that purpose.

The Cha Cheong Sao project was replaced by a much broader activity aided by the United States in which action was spread from the start over 12 educational regions, thereby reducing the problem of diffusion. This project had the wider objective of improving education at all levels, undertaking in-service and preservice training of teachers, and establishing local supervisory centers and a devolution of centralized control. Thus, instead of attempting to create a model for the country as a whole, the new project was based on regional differences and attempted to mobilize the efforts of local authorities from the start.

If one reviews the results of the Cha Cheong Sao project, the judgment that it was a failure is tempered if the indirect effects are taken into account. These mainly concerned the educational techniques and methods introduced by the individual experts, particularly the greater freedom introduced into the classroom in terms of exchanges between the teacher and the pupils. The Thai system of teaching had been and still is to a considerable extent largely autocratic, with a good deal of rote learning and unchallenging respect for the teacher's viewpoint.

The same was true of curriculum organization and the layout of classrooms. Through the in-service training given to teachers, a number of new practices, which were within the authority of the teacher himself in the class, were spread throughout the country. Moreover, the fundamental pedagogic concepts in the project had received a good deal of ventilation in Thai educational circles. The fundamental difficulty was that they went beyond what the Thais themselves were able to absorb in practice and organize into the system at that time, and that the foreign experts themselves had too abstract a conception of what could be done by new techniques and methods in Thai circumstances, unless they were accompanied by action on a much wider front.

Another project that was also doomed to failure was in operation over about the same period, though it did not come to an end until 1961. This was the project in the field of fundamental education, known as TUFEC (Thai-Unesco Fundamental Education Center), which attempted to try out on a large scale the concepts of community development that had emerged in the United Nations and Unesco, part of which was the introduction of fundamental education in the sense of inculcation of community and civic values associated with adult education and local development possibilities.

Despite the fact that 71 teams were trained at TUFEC and sent to various parts of the country and some short courses for local district officials were given, the Department of National Community Development did not include provision to continue TUFEC in the national plan. The reason, as in the case of the Cha Cheong Sao project, was that the project was unable to maintain itself and accordingly could scarcely be expected to provide for the widespread diffusion of itself. Once again, the problem seems to have been the absence of recognition by the organizers at the early stages of the preconditions necessary for the grafting of fundamental education onto the Thai system of education.

One of the difficulties, for instance, was that since fundamental education implied instruction to work on practical problems, agricultural training was introduced. However, it was not accepted in the villages as useful, since the peasants themselves often knew better from experience than the instructors, and the community doctrine that was used did not fit in with local traditions and motivations to change them.

Nor were the experts themselves free from blame. One of the comments made by the report by the Chief of Mission during the project's operation was,

> The Pilot Project has not been particularly well
> served in the experts furnished by Unesco. Few
> have left any real mark and some have lacked the
> professional qualifications and experience to be
> expected of consultants in a project of this sort.
> Their contribution has been diminished by poor
> living conditions and isolation, which have borne
> heavily on wives and families; by difficulties of
> communication with their Thai colleagues; by

> lack of opportunities to travel within Thailand;
> by blood clots within the administrative blood
> stream.

Part of the problem was lack of sufficient preparation of the experts and lack of clear definition of their tasks, and this became apparent to the Thais working with them.

These difficulties from the past are worth recalling because they still appear among aid experts working on rural projects. Moreover, although there has been an immense improvement in the Thai administration, one of the recurrent problems in all developing countries is what was called above the "administrative blood clots." Thus, in the section on Thailand in the Annual Review of the Canadian International Development Agency for 1970-71, it is stated, "Loan funds allocated to Thailand have not been disbursed as quickly as might have been hoped."[7]

The lesson emerges clearly. The belief that it is possible to change the education system through a general message from outside or by foreign technical expertise is a fundamental misunderstanding in a mature culture like the Thai. The educational system is interwoven with the administrative, political, and cultural structures, and local motivations of various kinds, which are only changed by national actions, which are more of an internal engineering--a social engineering--character than one that is pedagogic or technical.

For a thorough analysis of the Cha Cheong Sao and TUFEC projects, the reader should see the book by J. S. Nairns, International Aid to Thailand,[8] which, as well as Unesco and Thai documents, sets out the events in detail. In the foregoing, these have been drawn on, as have the author's own observations as a member of Unesco's Social Science Department at the time. Two quotations from Nairns's book, which indicate some of the administrative problems, follow:*

> Students feared that by becoming FEO's [Funda-
> mental Education officers] they had in fact be-
> come orphaned as far as a parent organisation
> was concerned. What was the channel of promo-
> tion for a TUFEC worker, and where would pro-
> motion lead? Would the young teacher who be-
> came an FEO have the same opportunity to be-
> come, say, a headmaster as would a fellow teacher
> who stayed within the Ministry's normal school
> system? In the end, it was this sort of question
> which led to the mass exodus of FEO's sometime
> between early 1959 and 1963. Again the lesson

---

*Reprinted with permission of Yale University Press.

seems obvious. So basic an issue as the career
prospects of personnel can only be solved, and
some assurance given, within the framework of
a known and viable institution.

Nairns suggests the following schema and commentary, showing the
main elements and typologies of action involved:[9]

Distinction	Typologies Used in Aid Projects in Thailand	Notes on Typologies	Reemphasis Reemphasis Required
Operational method	Persuasion	No legal, economic, or political powers.	No change.
Resources	Only personnel skills and techniques of communication	Initially skills and communications were the only resources required.	Ultimately material resources would be an important determinant (that is, if diffusion became a reality), and this would call for further contractual commitments by participating governments or organizations.
Experience	Highly specialized	Experience relative to an appropriate skill, but little relative to the local milieu.	A buildup of a cadre of experienced personnel at the field level through creation of career service and renewal of tenures.
Cultural values	Western or non-indigenous	The majority of personnel were ethnically Western, and those who were not had been inculcated with Western skills and values.	A major reemphasis of personnel selection and training with provision of (1) orientation courses, (2) more perceptive use of fellowship programs to provide indigenous UN personnel and training for specific posts.

He concludes that "most indications are that the search for wide-ranging solutions continues. Ultimately such solutions may yet be found; meanwhile, failure to capitalize on experience may betray other projects into going the way of TUFEC and Cha Cheong Sao. "[10]

The moral from the experiences described, which accounts for the subtitle The New Colonialism? of his book (which refers to international agencies and not the ex-colonial powers), is that it is extremely difficult to bring about from external sources substantial changes in societies such as that of Thailand with strong cultural traditions, even on the basis that outside influence be desirable to promote United Nations conceptions of development. The best results appear to be obtained when there are precise objectives that link in with an already maturing national motivation and mobilization of initial resources.

Thus, Unesco has in operation at present in Thailand a project to assist the government in establishing their Institute for the Promotion of Science Teaching and Technology, due to become in 1977 a unit in the Ministry of Education. Its purpose is to change the curricula and methods in Thai schools and colleges in these specific fields, and the need is one that is clearly felt by the Thai Government and educational opinion. This project, the first phase of which started in 1970, is producing and trying out in pilot schools and textbooks in the sciences and engineering and also is working on the production of low-cost equipment. Locally produced materials are used, the extent being as high as 75 percent in physics equipment. A team of five international staff and eight short-term consultants work closely with Thai counterparts, and few difficulties have arisen to inhibit what appears to be developing as a successful project.

A teacher training project for technical education at the King Mongkut Institute of Technology, Thombouri, also sponsored by Unesco, has been developing on well-planned technical lines but has encountered some problems in getting the teaching staff to accept the modern conceptions and methods of teaching and learning that the project is designed to promote in this important institute. No doubt, time will overcome these difficulties, but there is again a certain risk in going to considerable expense to introduce new methods before the motivations in the profession are as well developed as they are in the case of the Institute for the Promotion of Science Teaching and Technology. That is to be a new departure springing out of felt needs and with a scope wide enough to overcome traditional attitudes on the part of individual teachers already in post.

Another project that is based on the principle, which appears to be a rewarding one, of establishing an institute, is the National Curriculum Development Center to be established with the assistance

of a long-term IDA credit. Its task is to make the educational system more relevant to needs, especially in the rural areas. It also
will be concerned with problems of diversifying second-level education and preparing new programs for primary teacher training. It
will be amalgamated with the Institute for the Promotion of Science
Teaching and Technology under the framework of a single institution
by 1977.

These projects for establishing institutes, which will later be
absorbed into the Ministry of Education, represent an approach designed to draw out from within the country itself its motivations and
resources and thereby rely less on the importation of expert advice
and ideas, however good, from abroad. Some years must elapse before it can be seen how well this approach works, but there is already a good example in operation in Thailand in the form of the
Asian Institute of Technology, which serves the region as well as
Thailand itself.

Other projects that follow the same principle of acting through
local resources and avoiding the failures at Cha Cheong Sao and
TUFEC are assistance given by the Ford Foundation for a three-
year period starting in 1973 to stimulate educational planning and research focused on primary and nonformal education, especially the
problems of the rural areas. The Asia Foundation, also operating
on the same principle, is contributing to adult and nonformal educational development in rural areas through assistance to the Buddhist
ecclesiastical authorities for integrated community services at the
village level, in which education is included.

A further example, illustrating the principle of helping to build
up local capacity to innovate rather than sending in teams of foreign
experts, is the Maeklong Integrated Rural Development Program of
the Thai Government operated through the three universities of
Kasetsart, Mahidol, and Thammasat, and assisted by the Rockefeller
Foundation. Adult education teams from the University of Thammasat
live in the villages and serve as teachers and then train local teachers
to replace them, the emphasis being on vocational training linked with
functional literacy and local agricultural needs. This project also
illustrates the policy of the Rockefeller Foundation of assisting universities to extend their role of promoting economic and social development.

Unesco itself, through its own expert in educational planning,
is helping Thai education with much interesting and novel advice on
educational innovation, particularly directed at basic education and
the needs of the rural areas. Further, Unicef has an innovatory
project for the preparation of rural teachers as change agents in the
community and is aiding the establishment of pilot curricula for community schools, including young adults as well as adolescents, and

providing for the in-service training of officials in this area of educational development. The results are yet to be evaluated.

One of the curious things about aid operations is the way in
which mistakes become repeated even after the reasons for them in
similar cases have been identified. It is interesting to note that in
the conference convened by the UN and Unesco in 1954 on social aspects of technical assistance, a great deal of advice was given as a
result of the experience of the nongovernmental organizations (they
put in a paper with the title "One Hundred Years of Technical Assistance"), by the colonial powers that also had experience of developing education in their former colonies, and by social scientists famil-
iar with local problems and social structures. The concepts and
recommendations, which were published and widely aired, have not
prevented errors then criticized from being repeated.

One of the points stressed then and often since is that the externally inspired project should not be too expensive or overdesigned
in relation to the country's capacity to continue the effort, or in the
case of pilot projects to extend the good results widely throughout
the country. A case that arose in Thailand, which had some of these
characteristics though it had certain other advantages, was the project for comprehensive schools at the second level, which was aided
by a $3 million Canadian loan. Around 1960, "comprehensive"
schools, which covered both academic and vocationally oriented
streams, had recently been introduced in the United Kingdom, and
Thai observers were impressed with them. A move began to use
them as a sort of model, adjusted to Thai conditions. An experimental comprehensive school was set up in Korat in 1960 by the Thai
Ministry of Education, but since it was experimental it was not included in the educational plan. This school was successful: Dropout
was reduced, and attitudes to vocational work became more positive
owing to the flexibility of the curriculum.

In 1965, the Thai Ministry of Education established a Committee for Comprehensive Secondary Schools, and contact was made
with the Canadian authorities for a possible loan for the purpose.
After studies conducted by the Canadians and by the National Economic Development Board of the Government of Thailand, a long-
term interest-free loan was agreed for the purchase of equipment in
Canada and grants for the training of Thai teachers and supervisors
in a Canadian university. * The Canadian Government also agreed

---

*The project was summarized in the Annual Review of the CIDA
as follows: "The aim was to transform 20 Thai secondary schools
into comprehensives, to avoid an early and total separation of academic from vocational streams. Of the $3.6 million Canadian

to provide a team of five advisers to work with the project in Thailand for two years.

The project involved extensive revision of the curriculum offered in the participating schools, which, according to the Final Report on the project issued by the Thai Ministry of Education in 1971, was "intended to meet the needs of those who will not be continuing their education in a college or university, as well as those who aspire to such higher education."[11] The revised curriculum was to provide a more flexible curriculum with a wide range of elective courses (40 to 50), including vocational and prevocational subjects, so that students in lower secondary grades could explore and follow their individual interests, talents, needs, and occupational possibilities. The comprehensive school curriculum was to cover seven broad study areas: academics, physical education, fine arts, home economics, agriculture, industrial arts, and business education. The number of elective courses offered to the students was to increase as the students progressed through the grades.

However, a high proportion of students continued to opt for academic studies leading to entrance into university, though "dropout problems decreased steadily as more students pursued courses suited to their own aptitudes and inclinations" and "attitudes towards vocational education or blue-collar occupations have been more positive. . . ."[12] A very small proportion of comprehensive school graduates entered directly into the labor force. Most continued their education either in the general secondary schools or in vocational schools.

Emphasis was laid on the training of teachers (especially practical arts teachers) and staff. In-service training facilities were set up. Included as part of the in-service education program were various seminars held for teachers throughout the year and orientation for new teachers and new students and parents. Another area emphasized was that of guidance. Efforts were made to define guidance and to make this a full-time occupation instead of a part-time function of teachers.

Thai staff members were sent to Canada to be instructed in and observe the comprehensive approach. However, recommendations were made for the transfer of the training of comprehensive school personnel from Canada to Thailand, and this step was taken.

---

assistance, $1 million was used to purchase technical educational equipment from Canada. The first of 110 Thai teachers and administrators began taking one-year courses at the University of Alberta in 1966. The last of that University's field staff in Thailand will leave in 1972." [Annual Review of the Canadian International Development Agency for 1970-71 (Ottawa: CIDA, 1972).]

The project was originally designed to run for three years, from 1966 to 1969. Delays, mostly financial (the Bank of Thailand loan for purchase of equipment had not yet come through), resulted in the project being extended in 1970 for an additional two years in order to consolidate the gains made, successfully complete the project, and provide for a Thai training program for personnel. The Secondary Education Department noted "its determination to extend the comprehensive form of education."[13]

Enrollments steadily increased in the comprehensive schools. All 20 of the project schools were expected to be at least partially utilizing the comprehensive approach by the end of 1972. Maximum class size was raised from 35 students to 45, and some schools enrolled 2,000 students. This created problems of teachers' loads and lack of space.

The largest single problem was that of finance (delays in financing as well as lack of funds). Equipment and laboratories for practical arts courses are expensive and need maintenance and special installations in buildings. Most of the Canadian assistance was devoted to the supply of such equipment and its installation. The buildings were provided by the Thais. It emerged that further foreign assistance was necessary for the provision of equipment if the comprehensive school program was to continue.

As regards internal financing, the Canadian team recommended maximum use of local resources (self-help, increased school fees, and so on), though this would be limited in consideration of the special and expensive equipment required for good practical arts courses, business and industrial arts being especially costly. This recommendation was not realistic as it was scarcely feasible to expect special regulations to be developed for what was in national terms not a large project. On the provincial level, the involvement of provincial authorities was recommended, as was coordination to avoid duplication of facilities in districts. Thus, the high cost of the comprehensive program was recognized early on, pointing to the need to reduce its scope to a minimum and for the Secondary Education Department to plan ahead for the procurement of equipment.

Another problem that was apparent was the lack of direction and coordination of curriculum planning. As of 1971 there was a great variety of agencies, committees, and individuals, outside as well as within the Secondary Education Department, who were concerned with curriculum development. The Canadian team recommended the establishment of a curriculum branch in the Department of Secondary Education "to serve as the executive arm of the Department in curriculum matters."[14] This recommendation was in contradiction to the organizational structure of the Ministry as a whole, in which curriculum development activities are the responsibility of the Department of

Educational Techniques. It had little chance of adoption, springing as it did from an aid project concerned with only a small part of the education system. The team also saw the need for coordination between the Department of Secondary Education and that of Vocational Education.

They urged that the examination system continue to be revised, with more emphasis on progress made than on level of achievement, especially as many of the courses were of an exploratory nature. It was therefore required in the comprehensive schools that account be taken of the work done during the year as well as of examination scores.

The project as a whole, however, has not achieved the success hoped for because of the reasons set out in CIDA's Annual Review (1970-72).

> One striking success has been seen in the way
> some other Thai schools have adopted the cur-
> riculum developed for these comprehensives.
> Against that has to be set the fact that not all
> the 20 schools will become comprehensive as
> soon as originally planned. More serious is the
> capital cost factor: costs per pupil are running
> more than three times as high in the 20 schools
> as they are in other secondary schools which
> the Thais themselves are converting to compre-
> hensives; the gap may increase to five times as
> high. The differences will show in the quality
> of equipment and teachers, and in class sizes.
> The Canadian programme may be a success in-
> side the 20 schools, but it can hardly be re-
> peated in many other schools in Thailand. [15]

Nevertheless, the Canadian-aided comprehensive school project produced three interesting second-generation effects. Firstly, many secondary schools outside the project requested to be allowed to enter the project, and as of 1971, six secondary schools had been granted permission to use the comprehensive curriculum. The Thai Government Final Report, however, stated that "apart from receiving permission to use the curriculum these schools have as yet received little help to assist them in implementing it, and are in serious need of such help." [16]

Secondly, the project has had the effect of delineating for the Thais the real possibilities for the national development of comprehensive schools. They are in the process of working out a model of a less expensive nature adapted to the impulsion for greater democratization of education now current.

Perhaps the most positive aspect of the Canadian comprehensive school project has been the development of "Type II" comprehensive schools, of which some have been supplied equipment by Unicef, while 32 are being partly financed with an IDA credit from the World Bank Group. These are schools with fewer options, though still maintaining a diversified curriculum, and have costs far more in line with the costs of existing ordinary secondary schools.

Thirdly, many Asian countries showed interest in Thailand's comprehensive project; and visitors came to study the project from Laos, Indonesia, India, Malaysia, as well as delegates of SEAMEO, resulting in a valuable exchange of ideas.

The present comprehensive schools set up under the project are likely to become "centers of excellence," like the grammar schools in Europe, and thus be an important contribution to the total educational system, even though the original idea of extending them largely throughout the country in their present form is no longer viable.

A more recent cooperation agreement, which has been of considerable dimension and affects diversified secondary schools, rural teacher training colleges, and higher-level science education is that now being financed from IDA credits of the World Bank Group.

The new IDA project covers 10 rural teacher training colleges, 32 diversified secondary schools, the National Curriculum Development Center, and a Preinvestment Study for teaching by television and the expansion of the faculty of Science at Songkhla University. Before the new IDA project was adopted there had been a project identification mission from Unesco in 1970, which had made a different set of proposals. Their proposals had been oriented to the purpose of securing greater equity in the distribution of educational opportunity by expanding education in the northeastern part of the country. Their proposals had been for the establishment of 125 new upper-primary schools to cover about 50,000 pupils in the villages. This was to be followed later by an expansion of lower secondary enrollments of 35,000 pupils in the comprehensive schools. Included also was a project for an Agricultural Teacher Training College for 200 additional students by expanding one of the existing agricultural vocational schools in the northeast. This was to help to convert the present heavy imbalance between urban and rural enrollment and to increase the number of farmers' children going up the educational pyramid, since lower primary enrollment is practically universal. It also included a project that was a venture in the field of nonformal education for rural adolescents who terminate after the lower primary course of four years. The objective was to develop and expand rural youth clubs, which will assure the retention of literacy acquired at school, and to give some practical training in productive agricultural

activities. This would involve establishing three schools for the
training of 400 youth workers aged 18 to 20, who will organize and
animate the clubs' activities. The project involved a number of
special features such as the publication of pamphlets and such of a
simple nature and the provision of supervised credit and savings
facilities for the club members.

This ambitious project, although excellent in its intent, did
not receive the necessary degree of support from the Thai Government agencies or from the World Bank itself and was dropped in
favor of the one already described of concentrating on diversified
secondary schools and rural teacher training colleges. This was an
instance, which sometimes occurs, of a group of outside experts
making recommendations that presuppose policies and possibilities
of adoption within countries, which do not correspond with what the
countries themselves desire or consider feasible. This illustrates
the discussion in Chapter 9 of the importance in project identification
of keeping proposals in close relation with the feasible, as well as
the desirable, by very close contacts with national administrations.

It will be seen from the foregoing that Thailand presents many
interesting features of educational aid, that the impact has been on
the whole favorable, and that both sides of the aid partnership have
learned something in the process. A particularly valuable feature of
aid for Thailand has been the existence of a DAC group, which has
had the task since 1962 of coordinating the aid effort. The chairmanship is taken by the leading donor countries in rotation, but the meetings at the working level are chaired by the UNDP representative.
This makes an important contribution to the planning and oversight
of aid for education as well as for assistance of all kinds.

A recent innovation by the group has been to set up a committee
at the working level on technical and vocational education. Its task
is not only to survey and exchange information and results of the
various aid projects in these fields but also to review the whole Thai
situation as regards needs, in cooperation with the Thai authorities.
This is expected to lead to schedules of needs and, in due course,
identification of specific projects that members of the group may
wish to take up. This type of more or less formal machinery for
the coordination of aid from the different donors is extremely rare
and in most countries takes the form of informal "donors' clubs"
or ad hoc meetings, which are called by the recipient government.
Informal arrangements also exist for close contact between the
agencies working on educational aid, and the Thai Government is
to be congratulated on the effectiveness and flexibility, and at the
same time the degree of coordination on its own side, that it exercises in its dealings with the donor agencies.

LEAST DEVELOPED COUNTRIES

It was usual in the 1960s to regard the least developed countries as cases no different in kind, but only in degree, from that of
other less developed countries. The Second UNCTAD Conference in
1968 took the first step to identify them as a group,[17] and the UN
General Assemblies in December 1969 and October 1970[18] asked the
Secretary General to recommend special measures and to include a
separate section on them in the International Strategy for the Second
Development Decade.

As a result of studies made by both UNCTAD and the UN Economic and Social Council (ECOSOC) Committee for Development
Planning a list of 25 countries was established.[19] The basic indica-
tor were countries that have a per-capita GNP of $100 or less, a
share of 10 percent or less of manufacturing in GNP, and a literacy
rate of 20 percent or less.

The major special measures recommended are that these countries should be given special treatment and be the subject of concerted
action by development assistance agencies. In 1973 the ECOSOC[20]
stated that "the organisations of the United Nations system should
take further concentrated efforts including the adaptation of their operational rules, the terms and conditions under which assistance is
provided and their institutional arrangements for according priority
and coordinated attention to the particular problems and needs of the
LDC [least developed country]."

Further, the Fourth Conference of Heads of States of Governments of Nonaligned Countries in Algiers in September 1973 recommended that[21] "in international economic action, top priority should
be given to the urgent implementation of the programme adopted by
UNCTAD III and other specialised international institutions of special
measures in favour of the LDC" and that "efforts should be exerted
towards formulating and implementing new measures in all fields
. . . so as to enable the LDC to derive equitable benefits from general measures undertaken in favour of all the developing countries."

The main result has been an overall increase in development
assistance allocations to the countries taken as a group and more
flexible and softer financial provisions. There is also a growing
questioning of previous assumptions that these countries, many of
them landlocked and not well endowed with natural resources, fitted
into the usual types of development model. This has been particularly true of the educational sector. In the least educationally developed
of the countries in this category, it appears that new types of educational systems may be required.

There is the further difficulty in the educational sector that the
25 countries in the UN-designated group do not fully correspond to

the countries that are least developed educationally, though of course there is a considerable consistency. A number of the countries that are least developed under these criteria have higher enrollment ratios and a more effective educational system than some with higher income levels. The decision to include the illiteracy rate as one of the criteria is a reflection on past rather than present educational performance.

Within the UN category of the least developed countries, there are three types of countries in terms of educational development. First there are those with enrollment ratios over 50 percent for children aged 6 to 11. Lesotho, for instance, has an enrollment ratio (according to the Unesco figures) of 69.2 percent (see Table 10.1). Rwanda has 63 percent, Uganda 51, Botswana 55.7, and Laos 50.3. These compare favorably with enrollment ratios in a number of higher-income countries. The reason is usually that the founders of the educational system, often missionaries, built the system on a simple local basis responding to needs without the heavy centralized structure that characterizes some of the other ex-colonies. The second group consists of a middle range of countries with primary enrollment ratios of between 25 and 40 percent (Malawi, Chad, Dahomey, Burundi, Tanzania, Sudan, and Nepal). The third group contains the countries where the enrollment ratio is between 10 and 25 percent, with Somalia at 5.9 percent.

These great variations between countries on a similar income level are explainable both by the reasons given above and by the amount of teachers' salaries in relation to per-capita income. Extension of educational systems in the third category to cover the mass of the population, together with a reasonable access to the second and higher levels, clearly would be beyond the country's resources if projected on the present basis. The solution must lie for these countries either in the continuance of a form of educational dualism, in which an overexpensive system exists parallel with educational poverty, or the devising of new teaching and learning patterns, formal and nonformal, which are within the country's economic and educational resource possibilities.

According to estimates of the Unesco Secretariat,[22] official technical assistance to education amounted to $135.7 million or 30 percent of total official aid, averaged for the years 1970 and 1972. This percentage of educational assistance is much higher than for the developing countries as a whole, owing mostly to the large number of expatriate secondary-level schoolteachers provided under cooperation agreements. This is illustrated by Table 10.2. In the case of Tanzania, there has been considerable change in the figures since the date given, which is 1966 for that country.

TABLE 10.1

Enrollment Ratios in Least Developed Countries by Age Groups and Years, Both Sexes

Country	6 to 11 Years						12 to 17 Years						18 to 29 Years					
	1960	1965	1970	1975	1980	1985	1960	1965	1970	1975	1980	1985	1960	1965	1970	1975	1980	1985
Total	13.4	18.2	21.9	24.6	26.0	26.5	8.7	11.5	14.3	16.5	18.3	19.1	0.4	0.6	0.9	1.3	1.7	2.0
Asian countries																		
Afghanistan	5.3	10.1	14.2	15.7	16.6	17.8	4.0	7.6	11.7	15.6	17.6	18.4	0.3	0.6	1.3	2.1	2.8	3.4
Nepal	13.5	17.7	23.4	26.7	28.8	30.8	5.8	7.2	8.9	12.2	14.0	15.0	0.9	1.3	1.6	2.1	2.8	3.1
Yemen Arab Republic	4.7	5.7	6.5	12.2	13.9	14.6	3.4	3.4	3.0	4.2	9.0	11.0	0.0	0.1	0.1	0.2	0.4	1.1
Laos	21.1	33.9	44.2	50.3	54.7	56.6	5.8	7.5	11.2	14.8	18.2	18.8	0.2	0.3	0.4	0.7	1.0	1.3
Bhutan	1.3	7.1	9.2	12.5	14.2	16.1	0.7	3.2	4.2	5.8	7.7	8.7	0.0	0.2	0.4	0.4	0.6	0.8
Maldives	1.8	6.0	8.7	13.2	15.3	17.5	0.8	2.0	3.4	6.8	8.4	9.4	0.1	0.1	0.3	0.4	0.7	0.8
African countries	14.6	19.4	23.0	26.2	27.2	27.5	9.6	12.9	15.8	17.6	19.3	20.0	0.3	0.5	0.9	1.3	1.5	1.8
Ethiopia	3.7	6.1	10.0	11.5	12.9	13.7	4.7	7.3	11.7	13.9	15.5	16.4	0.2	0.4	0.9	1.4	1.8	2.1
Sudan	13.5	15.4	23.4	28.0	31.1	32.1	7.5	9.4	15.5	19.3	20.5	20.6	0.3	0.5	1.0	1.4	2.3	2.6
Tanzania	14.4	22.7	23.3	26.7	27.5	27.1	16.7	23.0	21.7	23.2	25.3	24.9	0.3	0.4	0.6	0.7	0.9	1.0

Uganda	34.3	40.5	49.5	51.8	53.6	53.0	24.5	27.4	31.0	36.0	38.3	41.2	0.4	0.8	1.7	2.0	2.4	3.0
Upper Volta	7.1	9.7	9.9	10.8	10.9	10.7	1.9	3.8	4.5	4.7	5.2	5.2	0.0	0.1	0.2	0.3	0.3	0.3
Mali	8.3	15.3	16.0	18.0	18.7	19.0	2.5	8.5	14.8	15.3	17.0	17.3	0.1	0.5	1.2	1.9	1.8	1.8
Malawi	40.3	39.7	36.2	40.7	41.9	41.1	12.3	15.8	16.1	15.8	19.0	22.0	0.1	0.3	0.4	0.5	0.5	0.7
Guinea	13.9	22.1	24.1	23.8	23.7	23.3	8.9	14.4	19.8	18.2	18.6	18.2	0.1	0.4	1.3	1.6	1.8	2.2
Chad	9.9	21.3	21.8	26.1	28.4	29.2	5.7	11.0	10.6	9.6	12.4	13.7	0.3	0.5	0.4	0.4	0.5	0.5
Niger	4.6	8.7	10.4	11.9	12.4	12.4	1.3	3.6	5.1	6.3	7.2	7.5	0.0	0.1	0.1	0.2	0.3	0.4
Rwanda	47.0	53.9	60.9	63.0	62.7	61.5	16.1	15.1	14.6	14.9	15.4	15.3	0.2	0.2	0.3	0.4	0.5	0.6
Burundi	17.3	24.2	25.7	28.6	29.7	30.2	4.0	6.9	9.4	11.0	11.9	12.6	0.1	0.2	0.3	0.5	0.5	0.6
Dahomey	20.0	25.8	31.2	32.7	33.6	33.6	8.1	11.9	13.7	15.1	17.1	17.7	0.3	0.6	1.1	1.2	1.6	2.0
Somalia	3.4	3.9	4.2	5.9	6.6	6.4	3.8	5.4	7.2	8.0	9.8	10.9	0.3	0.8	1.5	2.4	2.6	3.1
Lesotho	50.8	63.3	66.5	69.2	71.1	70.0	61.8	65.5	65.9	63.5	66.2	65.9	4.2	3.5	2.5	2.7	2.9	3.1
Botswana	16.8	37.8	50.5	55.7	58.7	58.9	33.2	42.5	44.4	46.5	45.9	47.1	2.3	3.1	2.4	2.0	1.8	1.8
Latin America																		
Haiti	20.7	25.4	23.7	24.9	24.8	24.1	20.0	17.6	18.6	21.1	21.6	21.7	1.5	0.5	0.4	0.5	0.7	0.7
Oceania																		
Western Samoa	96.0	94.3	88.9	95.5	95.5	95.5	67.4	55.5	54.1	51.1	54.3	56.3	1.6	2.3	3.2	3.7	4.3	4.7

Source: Unesco Document (ED-74/Conf/601/Ref 2), May 1974.

TABLE 10.2

Expatriate Teachers by Level and Type of Education
in Selected Number of the 25 LDCs
(teaching posts held by foreigners as percentage of total teaching staff)

Country	First Level	Second Level			Teacher Training	Third Level
		General Education	Technical/Vocational Education			
Botswana (1972)	--	83.0	41.2		81.1	--
Chad (1967)	--	89.8	60.4		94.3	--
Mali (1970)	3.9	50.3	44.3		50.0	--
Niger (1972)	14.5	77.8	79.3		61.5	--
Rwanda (1972)	--	24.3	85.5		n.a.	64.9
Somalia (1971)	19.6	40.7	65.5		100.0	72.6
Tanzania (1966)	--	67.5	70.6		62.8	51.2
Laos (1972)	0.2	40.6	49.2		39.9	--
Average	--	59.3	62.0		70.0	--

Source: Unesco Office of Statistics, LDC/Ref 1, Paris, April 1974.

Most projects were for higher education, followed by the second level; primary education was far behind. Teacher training and fellowships took a substantial part of the assistance, and educational planning and curriculum development had little.

Aid from the USSR was for fellowships and for education and training projects (11 are mentioned by Unesco) related to agricultural colleges, technical institutes, and training centers, usually as part of development loans at low rates of interest. China had only two projects, one for science equipment for schools in Guinea and one for the construction of a technical school in the Yemen Arab Republic.

Multilateral educational aid was $150 million a year on the average for the 1969-72 period according to the Unesco estimates already cited. This was about a third of the total bilateral aid to education of all kinds (technical assistance, capital, fellowships, and so on). Multilateral aid for education was increasing more slowly over that period compared with bilateral aid, and the action taken by UNCTAD and the UN, which has led to a considerable rate of increase of educational assistance since, was very timely.

Most of the multilateral assistance for education for the least developed countries went to teacher training, followed by literacy projects. There was little for educational planning and research and development. Funds are needed for the latter activities since the creation of teaching and learning patterns related more closely to local needs and financial possibilities is a crucial need in many of the least developed countries. Disappointing, too, is the small amount going to rural education and women's education--apart from some Unicef activities--in view of their great importance to food production and raising living levels in the rural areas.

Unesco sent out a questionnaire to the 25 countries to make use of the replies at an expert meeting of senior officials of those countries held in July 1974 at Unesco. The majority of the countries replying (13) gave clearly the first priority to that kind of education that provided information and training for people to enable them to participate consciously and actively in rural development. The second priority was given to literacy training. These items were followed by scientific and technological education and the training of senior and middle-level personnel for industry, agriculture, and health services.

The same priority was shown in the answers relating to desirable reforms. The majority of the replies selected "extending a minimum of education to the largest possible number of people." This is linked with the introduction into curricula of material related to work needs and development.

The replies also showed that governments felt that measures should be introduced to promote faster action by Unesco, a simplifi-

cation of procedures, and an improvement of the effectiveness of
aid by reorganizing "the whole mechanism" and procedures of aid
[the study of which was proposed in UNCTAD Resolution 62 (III)].
The priority area for cooperation was given as concerted action "in
the field of rural education for promoting the production by the countries themselves of basic educational supply, teaching materials,
and agricultural implements. "

In general it may be said that both at the level of the replies to
the questionnaire and that of the expert discussion by officials of the
countries concerned, most emphasis was placed upon aid in the form
of actual resources and finance from abroad and facilities to develop
domestic production of supplies, rather than upon the supply of expertise or teachers. This flows from the nature of the priority
selected, since for basic education and literacy, as was seen in
Chapter 6, the form of assistance under cooperation programs is
different from that which prevailed heavily in the 1960s, when secondary technical and higher education were the priorities.

The difficulties of increasing enrollment ratios in the average
least developed country on the basis of the existing system can be
seen from Table 10.1, which projects up to 1984 the rates of enrollment increase of the 1960s together with estimated population increases up to 1970-85. The table illustrates at the same time the
great differences of educational progress between countries within
the group as a whole.

The conclusion to be drawn is that whereas there has been a
welcome increase in the allocation, both bilateral and multilateral,
to educational assistance to the least developed countries, there is,
however, at present little sign of the concerted action recommended
by the UN. On the other hand, cooperation is beginning, in some
valuable instances, to assist in generating new teaching and learning
patterns.

Five of the African countries (Upper Volta, Dahomey, Uganda,
Guinea, and Tanzania) have introduced some innovations of structure,
with varying degrees of success, and outside cooperation--the Tan-
zanian reform, linked to overall social change, and the Ujaama system
of cooperative self-reliance in rural areas being the most complete
and far reaching. Ethiopia established a plan for fundamental reform
in 1972, with the assistance of a World Bank Sector Review, which has
still to be implemented. Nepal has a new plan to restructure primary
education on the basis of a three-year cycle adapted to local needs,
and a number of the other countries are studying or have in hand measures of partial reform of their system.

Cooperation with external agencies has been a feature of these
activities, but usually at the stage of advice and pilot projects for
which experts and equipment are supplied. The new question to be

faced is whether financial assistance can now be given to the educational sector as a whole in the least educationally developed of the 25 countries, to accompany reform of the structure and the cost effectiveness of their educational systems.

A Unesco conference for the least developed countries is being held later in 1975, and perhaps as a result some activities may be recommended and be implemented by bilateral and multilateral agencies acting in concert, though the predominant note is likely to be the need for resources rather than advice.

Since the designation of the 25 least developed countries, a number of events have altered the situation in different countries. Although none of the 25 least developed countries has climbed into a higher category, some have had their present and prospective positions worsened. Unicef, for instance, has added Bangladesh, Burma, and the Democratic Yemen Republic to countries to be assisted on a similar basis. Further, following the oil crisis, the Secretary General of the United Nations listed a number of developing countries as "most seriously affected." These are Bangladesh, the Central African Republic, Chad, Dahomey, Democratic Yemen, El Salvador, Ethiopia, Ghana, Guinea, Guyana, Haiti, Honduras, India, the Ivory Coast, Kenya, the Khmer Republic, Laos, Lesotho, Madagascar, Mali, Mauritania, Niger, Pakistan, Rwanda, Senegal, Sierra Leone, Somalia, Sri Lanka, the Sudan, the United Republic of Cameroon, the United Republic of Tanzania, Upper Volta, and the Yemen Arab Republic.

The possibilities of education playing its role in concerted or integrated action programs for development has never been tested fully since there have been few if any such development initiatives under cooperation programs. There have been cases where assistance has been heavily concentrated on particular countries, but scarcely in an integrated way involving all the different sectors. In Chapter 9 on the planning and operation of cooperation programs, attention was drawn to this approach. One of the suggestions was that a project bureau should be established in such countries with the specific task of drawing attention to the educational implications of measures in other sectors and to secure an adequate allotment to education from all forms of capital investment--whether official or private, internal or external sources.

This change is particularly needed where the countries have resources of raw materials, such as Indonesia or Mauritania, and foreign enterprises enter and draw a profit from their development. It is reasonable--since those enterprises, often several in competition with each other, draw upon the local reserves of educated labor to be trained for specific tasks--that these firms should help to fill the general reservoir by means of levies to be allotted to the educational system. This could be an interesting contribution to the developing countries that are least developed and to others with some special claim to international cooperation owing to their low income levels, for which concerted external assistance is required.

This change should accompany the steps already suggested, which the governments of these countries should take themselves to redesign their educational systems, so that they are less modeled on those inherited from earlier regimes and are more adjusted to work and living needs and economic possibilities and opportunities.

This matter will be discussed again in Chapter 13 on reform and innovation, since it is in those countries that an impasse is being reached between the expansion of education on existing lines and the realities of development needs and perspectives.

NOTES

1. Daniel Sharp, ed. , U.S. Foreign Policy in Peru (Austin: Texas Press, 1972), pp. 330ff.

2. Ibid. , p. 343.

3. Ministerio de Educacion, Oficina Sectorial de Planificacion, Plan Operativo 1974, May 1974.

4. See Philip H. Coombs with Ray C. Prosser and Manzoor Ahmed, New Paths to Learning for Rural Children and Youth (New York: ICED, 1973); and Philip H. Coombs and Manzoor Ahmed, Attacking Rural Poverty (Baltimore: Johns Hopkins Press, 1974).

5. Robert G. Myers, "International Education, Emigration, and National Policy: A Longitudinal Case Study of Peruvians Trained in the United States," Cooperative Education Review, no. 3, 1972.

6. Peruvian General Education Law, Decree 19326, March 1972, p. xix.

7. Annual Review of the Canadian International Development Agency for 1970-71 (Ottawa: CIDA, 1972), p. 26.

8. (New Haven, Conn.: Yale University Press, 1966).

9. Ibid. , p. 260.

10. Ibid. , p. 280.

11. "Final Report." Comprehensive School Project, Department of Secondary Education (Bangkok: Ministry of Education, 1971).

12. Ibid.

13. Ibid.

14. Ibid.

15. CIDA, op. cit.

16. Ibid.

17. UNCTAD Resolution 24(11).

18. UN Resolution 2564 (XXIV); UN Resolution 2626 (XXV).

19. The UN Statement (TAD/426), April 4, 1972, lists the following as the least developed countries: Afghanistan, Bhutan, Botswana, Burundi, Chad, Dahomey, Ethiopia, Guinea, Haiti, Laos, Lesotho, Malawi, the Maldives, Mali, Nepal, Niger, Rwanda, Sikkim, Somalia, the Sudan, Uganda, Tanzania, Upper Volta, Western Samoa, the Yemen.

20. UN Resolution 1975 (LIV).

21. Resolution no. 5.

22. (LDC/Ref 1), Paris, April 1974.

EXTERNAL ASSISTANCE TO
EDUCATION IN INDONESIA
Francis J. Method

Indonesia is the fifth largest country in the world. Though that fact alone should draw attention, one's attention is drawn mainly because of the remarkable progress that has been made in expanding and transforming education in Indonesia in the 25 years since Independence. External assistance has played an important part in this progress. In this chapter emphasis is placed on those aspects that illustrate general patterns of assistance, which may provide some lessons from the Indonesian experience that can be applied beneficially elsewhere. No attempt has been made to be comprehensive or to describe current programs, priorities, and structures in Indonesia.

On securing its independence, Indonesia severed most of its colonial links with the Netherlands and since 1949 has had a diversity of educational assistance sources and educational influences, including a new and more cooperative relationship with the Netherlands. The educational system of today is almost entirely post-Independence; and, to the degree to which its development has been shaped by external influences, these influences have been postcolonial, international, and perhaps more technocratic (that is, less a defense of an old system than an attempt to build a new system) than they have been in most countries. The process of nation-building has been paralleled by the evolution of assistance programs, and by looking carefully at the evolution of assistance to education one can see a process of mutual learning and maturation. It is worth remembering that the history of assistance to education as we know it today starts in the same postwar period and atmosphere as it started in Indonesia; and many of the priorities, limitations, and lessons waiting to be learned were shared by both donor and recipient alike.

FROM 1942 TO 1949

During the colonial period the Indonesian educational system developed in two streams, one a rather small and closely controlled system designed to train the basic manpower required by the colonial government and the other a rapidly growing set of loosely controlled private initiatives, some with a strongly nationalistic orientation. For a population estimated at 70 million in 1942 there were about 2.4 million students in elementary schools--most poorly staffed and locally (village) financed--offering a three-year education; less than 50,000 students in secondary schools, mostly primary teachers and a small number preparing for higher education; and 1,800 students in tertiary education, including those overseas. Ninety-three percent of the population was estimated to be illiterate.

From 1942 to 1949 Indonesia was occupied in fighting for her independence, first under the Japanese occupation and then under the threat of being recolonized by the Netherlands. Though Indonesian leaders during the years of the struggle for independence made heroic efforts to salvage and maintain as much of their meager educational facilities as possible, by 1949 little had changed for the better. The years of fighting had left the system badly disrupted and the universities dispersed. Many of the Dutch staff had left, and the new republic faced the formidable tasks of both expanding and nationalizing a system, which hardly could be said to exist as a system, and of meeting both their urgent manpower requirements and the popular expectations of mass education. On the positive side, the educational system was now under at least nominal Indonesian control and was seen as both a tool and an important goal of development.

Much criticism of external assistance to education seems to assume, retrospectively, that all options were open. It gives little weight to the contemporary pressures and practical problems that confront a planner/decision-maker at any particular time. In looking at the Indonesian educational situation in 1949, a number of factors stand out as substantially determining the educational development priorities. Though it remains quite true that much has been learned from the mistakes of this period, and better trained and more experienced administrators and analysts might not make the same mistakes if confronted with the same situation (though that is not at all certain), it also should be recalled that neither Indonesia nor any of the assistance agencies had, in 1949, personnel with experience in planning educational development in developing countries. The following are only some of the characteristics that bore on later educational developments.

The existing system, though clearly too small for Indonesia's needs and needing rapid expansion, was also bottom-heavy, with a relatively large enrollment at the primary level topped by a highly selective set of institutions offering higher training and with an unusually small middle-level sector. Expansion at the first level had to compete for resources with the more urgent needs for training the middle and higher-level manpower that the young republic required. External assistance began with work at these higher levels and had only begun to work down by the beginning of the 1960s.

The limited numbers getting advanced training prior to 1949 had been concentrated in medicine, law, technology, and a small program for administrators. Most advanced work had been conducted overseas, mainly in the Netherlands. As an Indonesianized higher education system grew, these same disciplines dominated and shaped the system. As assistance grew, its early emphases were also on medicine, technology, and public administration. Economics and language education were early additions, combined with overseas graduate fellowship training in these same disciplines.

Most of the education prior to 1949 had been in the Dutch language, with some attempts to use Indonesian in the private schools and at the lower levels. Language problems (the transition to English and then to Indonesian) were to be both a priority task of the educators and a major limitation on the use of external assistance personnel. English became emphasized as the new language of wider communication, thus biasing assistance toward English-speaking sources and, since Bahasa Indonesian was stressed at lower levels, concentrating it at the higher levels.

Most of the teaching staff, particularly at the higher levels, were Dutch or Eurasian, with only a handful of Indonesians, mostly Javanese. The student bodies were similarly composed. The system had to be expanded rapidly and extended geographically while replacing Dutch professors and training Indonesian professors. Thus, despite a strong current of nationalism and independence, expansion of higher education required external assistance.

In 1942 most of the education system had been concentrated in Jakarta and West Central Java, but during the period 1942-49, Indonesia was forced to disperse facilities and make various ad hoc arrangements, which continued after 1949. Two new universities coalesced in Jogjakarta in Eastern Java, what is now Gajah Mada University and the Islamic University (IAIN Sunan Kalijaga Yogyakarta). This early concentration of education, particularly higher education, in Java meant that assistance to higher education also concentrated in Java.

The necessities of using whatever facilities could be found furthered the process by which the universities that developed were amalgams of dispersed faculties and part-time professors and students. Though there was, after 1949, a strong emphasis on higher education, there were only a few higher education institutions that could be assisted as institutions.

Higher education was run in faculties, small and scattered, with a minimum of curriculum planning, a lecture and self-study approach with a single examination after a specified number of years, and little requirement of attendance on the part of either the students or the faculty. University planning and the planning of high-level manpower were not possible with such a system. Though assistance at higher levels was the first priority, until major changes could be made in university structure and practice, external assistance was effectively limited to teaching faculty, books, and fellowships.

A number of Indonesian intellectuals emerged as professors and education leaders, many of them trained in medicine or law, and a pattern of part-time professor/part-time government official emerged that continues today. Though numbers were inadequate and lines of authority often confused, external experts seemed to find "counterpart" relationships somewhat more easily in Indonesia than in other countries, where the civil servant/professor roles were more distinct.

Finally, a distinction must be drawn between the capacity of the government to arrive at a decision regarding its developmental priorities and the capacities to plan, implement, and administer the resulting programs. At Independence, Indonesia had virtually no administrative capacity. In fact, one of the first priorities for Indonesia was the training of administrative personnel. Throughout the 1950s there is a general pattern of Ministry responsibility for programs administered by project development offices outside the Ministry, with substantial administrative responsibility on the part of the respective donors. This appears to have been a necessary structure for expediting development work in priority areas, which was the primary task of the Ministry. However, it was not until the late 1960s that serious attention was given to developing the planning and administrative capacities of the Ministry itself, and there continue to be project implementation offices outside the Ministry in 1974.

FROM 1949 TO 1964

The range of donors grew more diverse as the assistance program grew. Whereas in the early years most of the non-Dutch assistance was from the United States, by 1958-59, of 1,556 scholars/trainees overseas, 526 were in the United States, 382 in Colombo Plan countries, and 417 in the Netherlands; and by 1963-64 of 2,784 scholars/trainees, there were 800 in the United States, 656 in the USSR, about 400 in Eastern Europe, 369 in Japan, 284 in Germany (Federal Republic), and 165 in Egypt. Some were on Indonesian Government fellowships, but the majority were financed from outside Indonesia. Much of this assistance was new and provided contact by Indonesians with new information centers and systems. In addition to the Netherlands and Japan, an important old contact was with Egypt, where Islamic students had been sent in significant numbers since the nineteenth century--and where several pre-Independence leaders had been educated.

There seems to have been a similar diversity of sources for non-Indonesian teachers, limited mainly by the requirement that they be able to teach in English, though Dutch continued in practice until the late 1950s. Indonesian was also used.

Indonesia probably had a greater diversity of assistance, particularly for fellowships and for personnel, during the 1950s than any other country at that time, providing an unusual diversity of training opportunities and exposure to a variety of contrasting systems. In part, this reflected the general interest in Indonesia of almost all the major countries, and in part it was a deliberate policy of Indonesia to check external influence by diversifying it.

After 1949 there was considerable suspicion of offers of assistance to education from the Great Power nations, and, when significant assistance began in the early 1950s, it was both proffered and received cautiously. Indonesia took care that assistance was supportive of the educational priorities of the new republic. Expansion, indigenization, and the training of badly needed technicians were the priorities. There was no time to worry about the fine points of planning, administration, and organization.

The first assistance priorities reflected this and emphasized the supply of overseas fellowships, classroom teachers, and some finance for equipment, concentrated in technical training and medicine. This seems to have been a convenient starting point for both Indonesia and its initial sources of assistance. Though in retrospect it seems unimaginative, with rather conventional inputs to an expanding system and little attention to curriculum reform and planning, these were the areas for which assistance was most desired by the Indonesians and were the types of assistance most easily provided by donors. Priorities would shift as the republic grew and matured and gained time to think and plan. One can see some shifts by considering the period 1949-50 to 1964-65 in three periods of about five years each.

During the first five or six years, the focus was on immediate manpower problems (particularly the consolidating of higher education faculties into recognizable universities--the University of Indonesia, Gajah Mada University, and the Institute of Technology at Bandung), and external assistance was mainly in the form of teaching faculty and overseas fellowships. This was generally program support, combining a supply of faculty with a number of fellowships, not closely linked to particular institutions or faculties. Ford Foundation support to SGBT*/Bandung is a major exception.

The last half of the 1950s, from about 1955 to 1959, was a period of rapid expansion and diversification for the Indonesian system and there was a related expansion and diversification of external assistance, both in terms of sources and in terms of attention to other educational sectors and educational problems.

The earlier expansion of higher education and of overseas fellowships was beginning to show results in increased production and in the alleviation of the shortages of teaching staff left by the exodus of Dutch teachers. Attention began to shift to the secondary level, particularly to problems of teacher supply for the academic high schools and for the vocational/technical schools.

While the program support flows of external teaching staff to universities and of overseas fellowships continued, assistance now began to flow into the IKIPs (teacher training institutes for secondary schools), toward project support for individual faculties and toward technical assistance with qualitative problems of language. Increasingly, external assistance took a project form, focusing on a particular institution or faculty of an institution and providing not only faculty and overseas fellowships but also advisory-management personnel and some equipment and capital costs. "Affiliations" with similar developed-country institutions became a favored mode of assistance.

The cautious and low-profile stance of the first few years gave way to an attitude on the part of the Indonesians that they needed all the help they could get, and a willingness on the part of the donors to involve themselves much more directly in the implementation. Indonesia began to be looked upon as a possible "success story," and there was a general interest in being part of it. It should, however, be understood that until the 1960s, Indonesia attracted major interest partly because there were only a few other large independent nations being assisted (India, Pakistan, and Turkey), and the enthusiastic expectations of "success" were not yet tempered by much comparative experience.

Through the 1950s there had been little planning of education, as the term is now understood, but there had been reasonable

---

*Technical Teacher Training School.

consensus on the priority tasks, namely the rapid expansion of the
system as a whole and the diversification of institutions--particular-
ly technical ones--to provide the needed manpower for the new republic. Government higher-education institutions grew from two in
1949 to 53 in 1959, and private, from two in 1950 to 80 in 1959. Enrollments grew tenfold, from 6,000 to about 60,000.

There was further rapid expansion during the period 1959-65,
but there were now attempts to plan the expansion, to gain some influence over the quality and growth of private institutions, and to
diversify the system geographically. A policy decision was made
to establish a state university and a teacher education institute in
each of the 26 provinces.

This rapid expansion placed further pressure on the already
strained academic resources, and such attempts at planning as
there were seem to have resulted in little more than determination
of the sectors and areas in which expansion was desired. In fact,
some of the attempts to gain some influence over the private institutions seem mainly to have stimulated their expansion--through being classified under the 1961 law they gained recognition and an increased legitimacy and, through the attempt to induce cooperation
through government subsidy, an incentive and means of expansion
were provided.

Between 1960 and 1963, 19 new government institutions were
started, mainly in the provinces without universities, and private
institutions grew from 80 in 1959 to 228 by 1965. Total enrollments
in state and private institutions grew from about 60,000 in 1959 to
278,000 in 1965.

Initially, Indonesia's efforts to plan and rationalize its higher
education system were welcomed by assistance agencies, and further
plans were made for assistance to this sector. However, as rapid
expansion continued without adequate administrative control or effective planning, the educational situation became increasingly chaotic, and the attempts to assist in selected areas or institutions became almost impossible. During this same period the political scene
in Indonesia was highly charged, both internally and in Indonesia's
external relations with many countries and with the UN. Though it
is beyond the scope of this study to attempt an explanation of the intense and complex politics of this period, the situation affected external assistance in at least three ways.

After 1961 there were no significant new programs, though existing programs continued until late 1964 or early 1965, when it had
become difficult to work in Indonesia and diplomatic relationships
were broken with most donor nations.

Though few new projects were begun in Indonesia after 1961-62, the fellowship programs were continued and some were even increased. In some respects this brought external assistance back to the stance it had had in the early 1950s, when the priorities had been general expansion and the main way by which assistance could emphasize quality was to concentrate on people rather than on projects or institutions. A similar situation arose in Peru after 1968, when political disputes with the United States and others made many forms of assistance temporarily impossible, but fellowships continued with little change. The Indonesian experience is one of the clearest examples illustrating the lesson that, though political problems may at various times make conventional technical assistance programs unworkable, unacceptable, or otherwise unadvisable in a given country, there is usually little technical reason not to support fellowship programs as needed. Put another way, in any situation where either donor or recipient is reluctant to use external assistance for direct support of local institutions and programs, external assistance may still have a mutually acceptable and productive role in facilitating study abroad.

The disruption of assistance coincided with a period of dissension and unrest within Indonesia, and the general momentum of educational expansion and reform was lost. Many of the projects were terminated in midstream, and much of the experience was left unassessed and inadequately recorded. Perhaps more serious than the loss of momentum was the loss of the experience. It is difficult to reconstruct this period and draw lessons from it even now; it must have been even more impossible to see objectively during the period of turmoil that followed. Though in later years Indonesia seems to have done surprisingly well in avoiding the repetition of earlier mistakes, it is doubtful whether other educational development situations benefited as much as they might have from Indonesia's experience, representing one of the major concentrations of the first 15 years of international development efforts.

Though the period 1964-66 was a serious setback for education in Indonesia and for Indonesia as a whole, the interruption of external assistance for three years provides a unique opportunity to ask whether the assistance had any lasting effects. Was assistance directed to those sectors that were critical to the system, or was much of it of low priority, frills to the system, and likely not to have been undertaken except for the availability of assistance? Was a structure of institutions being built or only a set of programs?

Probably the single most important influence of external assistance was in the restructuring of the university model away from the "laissez-faire" or free-study Dutch model, which existed prior to

1954, toward the "guided-study" model of U.S. universities, which prevails today. The change was to a model intermediate between the Dutch and the U.S. models, not a copy. External assistance (primarily U.S.) enabled some adaptations of both, which fundamentally changed the pattern and efficiency of higher education in Indonesia.

One of the priorities was medical personnel. A pattern of medical training existed that apparently produced well-trained doctors. However, the numbers were small, and since students studied and took their exams at their own leisurely pace, it was difficult to predict the output and plan an expansion program.

In 1951-52 a team of Indonesian educators was sent to look at institutions in the United States, Czechoslovakia, and the Soviet Union. In 1954 the University of Indonesia medical faculty was affiliated with the Medical School at the University of California-Berkeley. Assistance took the form of a three-year contract (later extended to six) financed by the International Cooperation Agency (ICA, forerunner of USAID) providing about 14 American professors annually, some $2 million in equipment, books, and supplies, and a large number of overseas scholarships for study at Berkeley. This had two main effects, in addition to its assistance to the growth of medical training.

First, it brought a more efficient model, in the sense of higher and more predictable outputs. The medical school had admitted hundreds of students each year but had produced only 19 doctors in 1950, 15 in 1951, 21 in 1952, and 22 in 1953. In 1954 the medical school began selecting students by achievement, adopted the semester system, imposed some attendance requirements--particularly in laboratory courses--required exams at the end of each semester, blocked advancement until earlier course work had been successfully completed, and made other changes intended to build an institution that would train doctors rapidly and at predictable rates rather than just provide opportunity for the relaxed study of medicine. Though there continued to be serious scholars who preferred the old system, these changes began to unclog the system of perennial students, and by 1959 the numbers graduated annually had risen to 157.

The apparent success of this reform, at least in raising the numbers and making the output predictable enough to allow projections of trained personnel, led to its being rapidly adopted (actually before its effects had been fully demonstrated) in other institutions of higher education. The U.S. model was not completely adopted anywhere (mainly because teaching faculties don't change their work habits as quickly as university models are changed), but elements of these reforms were to be found in most institutions by the early 1960s.

The second significant aspect of this early medical contract was that it established a pattern for the delivery of technical assistance to

higher education, which continued until 1964. Shortly after the affiliation contract with Berkeley, other affiliations were developed. In
1954 Berkeley received Ford Foundation support to help the economics faculty, and Cornell received a grant to develop the Institute for
Social and Economic Research at the University of Indonesia. The
University of Kentucky received ICA support for an affiliation with
the Institute of Technology at Bandung in 1956. A Ford Foundation
contract in 1957 with Kentucky assisted the Faculty of Agriculture at
Bogor, which lasted until 1964. In 1956, ICA provided help to Gajah
Mada with a contract in engineering to the University of California-
Los Angeles and in economics to the University of Wisconsin. Johns
Hopkins also formed an affiliation with Gajah Mada's Faculty of Social and Political Science. A Ford contract with the State University
of New York provided help to several of the teachers colleges. The
last in this series of affiliations (1961-64) was financed by ICA between the University of Indiana and the Institute of Public Administration. A similar assistance effort was started (but not completed) by
the Soviet Union, committing about $5 million in equipment, scholar-
ships, and staff to establish a technical faculty at Ambon.

The affiliations had advantages of relatively uncluttered communication between the contracting and the receiving institution,
which both facilitated planning and administration and established a
commitment of the contracting institution's professional reputation
to the success of the project. An important disadvantage was that
these arrangements resulted in project implementation offices functioning in addition to Ministry channels. This may have been necessary in the absence of effective Ministry planning and administrative
capacity, but it also contributed to the fragmented responsibilities,
put the Ministry into a coordinating rather than a planning and leading
role, and delayed the development of an effective planning capacity.
When a planning capacity began to be developed after 1967-68, it was
as much to plan and channel assistance as to plan endogenous development. Assistance agencies gave support at least partly because
they were no longer prepared to plan, implement, or justify their
programs through project offices.

The assistance by the Ford Foundation in the area of technical
teacher training is an early example of concentrated assistance to a
sector and appears to have had lasting impact even though support
was discontinued in 1960-61. In 1951 ICA granted almost $1 million
in equipment for technical education. This was needed assistance in
a priority area, but Indonesia was still cautious in accepting personnel and the grant was limited to equipment. In any case, there were
not yet many institutions that could be assisted. In 1952, the Ford
Foundation made a grant to the William Hood Dunwoody Industrial
Institute (the leading technical training institute in the United States)

to assist the development of SGBT/Bandung. This combined capital assistance with buildings, advisory and instructional personnel, and fellowships for study at Dunwoody. There have since been a variety of other efforts in technical and vocational education, but the basis for most of the system is traceable to the work done at the SGBT in the 1950s. The factors that made this work effective seem to have been as follows:

    1. Technical and vocational education was clearly a high priority, and to some extent a system was being created from a vacuum;

    2. The concentration was on the training of teacher trainers and on the development of a teacher training institution--most of the other efforts to establish technical training institutions during the 1950s were frustrated due to lack of teaching staff;

    3. There was a close relationship with an overseas institution capable of training trainers, and the early emphasis was on fellow-ship training--usually one to one and one-half years and resulting in certificates rather than degrees;

    4. The project was patient enough to spend its first several years building an institution and training staff (though it had only be-gun to produce a second generation of technical teachers when sup-port was ended in the early 1960s, the personnel who had been trained carried on and were the basis for the expansion of the technical train-ing system in later years); and

    5. This effort was one of the few during the 1950s to include a sectoral planning effort. Assistance was provided to the Ministry of Education, Information, and Culture for a Special Study Committee on Technical Education. Between 1958 and 1960, acting with the au-thority of a ministerial decree, it carried out a thorough study of the existing state of technical education and prepared detailed recommen-dations for its improvement. Most of the work was carried out by Indonesian staff with only consultant help, and all materials were pub-lished in a two-volume study/report to the Ministry. Thus, the study contributed to immediate planning and also left a body of material and of personnel who had experience with the planning exercise. In a meeting in December 1973 with the project Implementation Staff of the IDA Technical Education Project, it was striking that all the staff were products of the earlier fellowship program, and most of them had worked on the survey.

    The Indonesians had been faced with critical high-level man-power shortages and had welcomed help. Assistance agencies had sought ways of assisting with the solution of long-term manpower problems of development and had attempted to do this by fellowship

training and developing key faculties. Both were more or less convinced that what was being done was what should be done.

However, by the early 1960s it was clear that though large
numbers of economists were being trained, the economics faculties
were losing their best people to government so fast that they were
ceasing to be good faculties. The training schools for technical
teachers were losing their graduates to industry. The teacher training colleges were producing better teachers than the economy was
ready to support, and the faculties were continually being broken up
and dispersed to create new IKIPs. Medical graduates were working
in ministries instead of as doctors, and the faculties continued heavily expatriate. The overall result was a growing pool of well-educated
manpower, most of it being well utilized by Indonesia, but a continuing heavy and expensive dependence on expatriate faculty and frus-
tratingly slow progress in establishing Indonesian training faculties
and facilities of high quality, which would continue to provide needed
skills over the long term.

Were the institutional and sectoral assistance efforts of the
1950s successes or failures? Perhaps they were both, and perhaps
the question is moot in any case. The facts are not in dispute--
larger and more productive institutions were built, largely due to
external assistance. Critical manpower shortages were being al-
leviated. In terms of whose objectives does one assess the question?
Whose objectives determined the original assistance goals?

The lesson here seems to be that though both Indonesia and the
donors had approximately the same objectives, they had almost the
reverse priorities. Indonesia was achieving its first priority (increased supplies of critical manpower) but not its second priority of
obtaining a training capacity that could be sustained within their own
human and financial resources. The donors had not achieved their
first priority of establishing high-quality, long-term training capacity but had, as a second priority, contributed importantly to alleviat-
ing high-level manpower shortages.

There may also be a second lesson here. The policy of concentrating resources and attention on building a few key feeder faculties
or "centers of excellence," as they came to be called, seems not to
have worked, at least in the short term. The primary reason seems
to have been that while new faculties were being built (and understaffed
Ministries being strengthened), the best faculty members would be
difficult to keep concentrated in one or two places, and the "critical
mass" necessary for a truly excellent faculty would tend more toward
fission than to fusion. There is some evidence that a few faculties
are beginning to distinguish themselves in the 1970s, but this is more
than a decade after the period of most rapid expansion and dispersal
of universities. Assistance agencies seem to have been slow in

understanding the dynamics and the length of time by which excellent
university faculties would evolve and mature. On the Indonesian side,
higher education policy is still, at least officially, built around centers of excellence. Fortunately, though policy still recognizes a set
of centers of excellence as being the most prestigious, both the donors
and the Indonesian Ministry are now taking a more balanced approach
to the development of higher education and are trying to strengthen
provincial faculties and help them relate to provincial needs rather
than just be poor cousins of the more favored universities.

Before proceeding further in analyzing the priorities and operational practice of assistance agencies, it is necessary to comment
on the Indonesian administrative structure within which the agencies
worked.

Neither the Basic Law in Education (1954) nor Law 22 of 1961
on University Education gave the fundamental structure of administration and organization of education. There was no directive of educational management. There was no clear distinction between technical (educational) functions and administrative functions, so that
both functions were very often in the hands of the same person--
often grossly overloaded and unable to perform either function adequately. Few positions had clear job descriptions, other than those
inferred from ad hoc practice, and it was often difficult to determine
precisely who was responsible for deciding. Other than two sets of
administrative instructions of the Minister (No. 1/BPP/1962 of September 12, 1962, which sets forth the Minister's preferences on university faculty organization, and No. 016/P/PNK/69 of May 30, 1969,
which suggests three alternative systems), as late as 1970 there were
no regulations on the organization of basic, higher, and university
education. This general lack of clear guidance on policy or clear
distinction and specification of administrative roles resulted in a system very much based on personalities, with ad hoc policies subject to
periodic, unpredictable interpretation.

The choice for assistance agencies was often to assist despite
their reservations about sectoral planning and administratio nor not
to assist at all. When agencies did agree to assist, it often meant
doing the planning and administration themselves. It was fine in
theory to wait for the Ministry to consider and agree in detail with
the project plans, but when this meant that no decision would be made
or that it would not be made in time to be included in the current
budget year, it was often preferable to both the agency and the relevant Indonesian officials for the project to go forward with only informal approval. This was particularly the case with approvals for
personnel and equipment--decisions had to be made relatively quickly or the opportunity would be lost, for example, an academic might
need to know within 30 or 60 days whether the appointment was

approved, or an equipment tender might have to be accepted or rejected within a contractually fixed period. Much of the disagreement one finds in later years as to the rationale or precise goals of assistance efforts may be explained by such administrative shortcuts in earlier years.

Prior to 1968, most donors worked sectorally either with programs attempting to supply and train needed categories of specialized manpower or with technical assistance projects directed to the support and development of particular institutions or faculties. In part this was a reflection of the Indonesian separation of educational responsibilities--and hence of priorities for manpower development-- among several coequal ministries, without much effective coordination. However, it is notable that none of the donors seems to have planned their own efforts as part of a system; instead, they seem to have fixed on a manpower sector that seemed to be of high priority for training and to have concentrated on improving medical training, technical training, social science training, public administration training, and so on. The comment here is not a criticism of the manpower sectors that were given priority; they were clearly of priority, and most observers agree that assistance has made major contributions to the supply of specialized manpower. Nevertheless, the set of high-priority assistance projects did not add up to assistance with the development of a system of higher education.

There was almost no assistance with educational management and planning. In part this is explained by the fact that the fields of educational planning and educational economics were still in their infancy during the 1950s, and in part it is explained by the fragmentation of responsibilities among the departments and Ministries. The Ministry of Education was not really set up to plan and determine policy as much as to coordinate and execute the expansion program. Policy was "planned" mainly by the allocation of development funds, with little of the necessary supply and demand analysis by the Ministry of Education. It is impossible to say with certainty, looking back over two decades, whether better planning could have been undertaken. However, the degree to which programs did get out of control and the system expanded beyond its financial and administrative capacity points up a danger of sectoral projects, however needed and expertly implemented, in the absence of adequate coordination mechanisms and overall planning.

A third observation is that the problems of the education system during the early 1960s stemmed perhaps as much from the success of the expansion program as from failures of leadership and mistaken priorities. Even without the other domestic and external political strains that contributed to the growing crisis, it is difficult to see how some degree of crisis could have been avoided in the

education system. Starting with a severe shortage of trained people
and almost no institutional structure, there was more than a forty-
fold increase in higher education (6,000 in 1949 to 278,000 in 1965);
primary enrollment grew from about 800,000 in 1940 in three-year
schools run by the Dutch to about 9 million in 1960 in six-year schools;
lower secondary education grew from about 180,000 in 1951 to about
600,000 in 1961; and senior secondary went from about 33,000 in 1951
to 191,000 in 1961. Though no two sources seem to agree on the enrollment figures, the general pattern of explosive growth seems clear.
Further, the difficulty in getting accurate enrollment figures is itself
evidence of the managerial and administrative problems of this period.

As important as the growth in numbers was the diversification
of types of schools and the extension of primary and secondary education to six years each. There was at first no period of consolidation
and rationalization--though this came later, involuntarily. There
must have been extraordinary effort on the part of all concerned, but
the executive and management burden must have been almost overwhelming. The rapidly expanding system may well have been "needed"
in the sense of being publicly demanded and in accord with government
policy. However, the lesson might be that assistance agencies should
have paid more attention to the administrative and management capacity and the rates at which new initiatives could be absorbed and integrated. It may not be contradictory to suggest that assistance was
needed and properly applied in the right sectors while at the same
time to suggest that the scale and catalytic role of assistance was inappropriate, considering the lack of adequate planning, coordinating,
and administrative capacities in the Ministry and the lack of any significant assistance toward strengthening those capacities.

THE PLANNING OF ASSISTANCE

The range of bilateral donors providing assistance to education
after 1967 was much the same as during the 1950s. The main difference was that assistance from Eastern Europe, the People's Republic of China, and the USSR was not renewed. The Netherlands and
USAID continued as the largest bilateral donors and the Ford Foundation as the largest private donor. The UN agencies became of growing importance, particularly Unesco/UNDP and Unicef, and more
recently there has been expanding assistance from Commonwealth
countries (particularly Australia, Canada, New Zealand, and the
United Kingdom) and from Japan. IBRD/IDA agreed to its first educational loan (for technical training) in 1970, and with subsequent
loans (agricultural training in 1972 and primary school materials
and teacher upgrading in 1973) is now the most important source of
capital assistance.

In 1966-67 the New Order government of General Suharto re-
stored diplomatic relations with most countries and cautious explora-
tions of a renewed assistance program were begun. The new government was faced with urgent and massive tasks of restoring and re-
directing a highly politicized and rather chaotic educational system
and of resuscitating and giving new direction to a badly shattered and
debt-ridden economy. They were looking for help, but they were
also greatly concerned with regaining and retaining administrative
control and policy direction.

On the donor side, there was considerable willingness to re-
start an assistance program as soon as possible, but there was also
uncertainty due to the previous chaos and to having been out of touch
for several years. Most donors were reluctant to begin major new
programs until steps had been taken toward an overall development
assistance policy, which both gave some guidance on internal priorities and took account of Indonesia's difficult economic circumstances,
particularly the huge debt overhang.

Due to Indonesia's low level of reserves and huge debt burden,
the World Bank convened in 1967 an Inter-Governmental Group for
Indonesia (IGGI) to consider new external investment and capital assistance. Though the IGGI was initially a rather ad hoc mechanism
with a limited concern for monetary matters, it drew on other experience of the previous few years with consortia concerned with
India, Pakistan, and Turkey and has evolved into a coordinating body,
which now meets yearly in the Hague to consider Indonesia's overall
needs for external investment and assistance--which sectors, what
types of assistance, what forms of investment. The meetings in the
Hague are attended by, in addition to the Indonesian delegation (usually headed by the Minister of State for Planning), Australia, Belgium, Canada, France, Germany, Italy, Japan, the Netherlands,
New Zealand, the United Kingdom, the United States, Austria, Norway, and Switzerland and the OECD, IMF (International Monetary
Fund), IBRD, and UNDP.

The IGGI, having been established because of concern with Indonesia's solvency and stability, was initially dominated by the donors/
investors. Some countries--for example, the Netherlands--opposed
it on that basis at first. However, as the new Indonesian Government
stabilized and began to plan and to assert its own priorities, it became
more able to negotiate on a cooperative basis. When, in 1968, the
first five-year plan was developed, Indonesia began projecting its
assistance needs, and in each succeeding year the government has
been more able to conduct its annual negotiations with assurance as
to the amounts needed and with effective control over the priorities.
Since about 1971, Indonesia's delegation has essentially presented its
estimates of what assistance was needed, and the IGGI meetings have
been more concerned with matters of coordination, prevention of

duplication, and technical terms. As the IGGI continues now that the
conditions that made it necessary in 1967/68 no longer obtain, it
must be assumed that the IGGI forum serves Indonesia's needs for
coordination as well as it does those of the donors.

Though the IGGI as such has been concerned with capital investment and loan funds, these meetings and the ongoing government
planning in the context of the Pelita (five-year plan) have made it
necessary to plan technical assistance needs on a more systematic
basis than previously. Prior to 1967 requests for assistance had
grown up as needs arose, and attempts had not been made to foresee
educational aid fitting into educational development as projected or
planned over a longer period. This was a common feature of educational aid throughout the developing countries at this time, and Indonesia was in fact one of the first to set up a system of incorporating
requests for educational aid in the national educational plan.

Though from 1968 the Indonesians systematically incorporated
requests for assistance in its national plan, the planning of educational aid requests also required the planning of educational aid at
the donor end. The providers of aid are different political entities
with independent objectives, and, while able to exchange information
and to a certain extent coordinate their efforts, they can only plan in
terms of a response to actions taken at the recipient end to establish
priorities and modes of development. Much of the impetus for planning came from the donor side. However, Indonesia, in taking effective steps to plan its own needs, made possible steps to prevent overlap and duplication and to stimulate exchange of information among
the donors.

The Development Assistance Committee of the OECD, which
contained most of the major donor countries, had been concerned for
some time about the lack of practices among its members for the exchange of information on aid programs at the country level. It was
not possible to find formal and complete solutions owing to the fact
that government-to-government negotiations are considered an essential and mutually useful characteristic of bilateral aid, but a process
developed of encouraging informal meetings of donor agencies wherever this proved possible at the country level. In the case of Indonesia, this initiative, together with action by Unesco/UNDP, led to
the establishment of an informal "donors' club." Starting at first
with very informal meetings of donor-country representatives, it
was later put on a more formal basis both in practice and in principle
by an arrangement under which the Indonesian planning authorities
themselves call and provide the Chairman for the meetings.

The "donors' club" is an unfortunate term, reeking of self-
protective decisions made in back rooms presented to the Indonesians
as a fait accompli. In fact, there is no "club," the meetings are

generally rather informal, and the initiative for convening a meeting is with the Ministry. Most donors participate in the meetings, though those having permanent representation in Jakarta are most prominent, especially Unesco/UNDP. The only important donors to education not participating formally in these meetings are the private organizations, notably the Ford Foundation, though there is considerable informal byplay and Ford now participates on the invitation of the Ministry. The Foundation appears to have been wary of participating in a "donors' club," but, as Indonesian planning capacities have improved and as coordination initiative has been assumed by the Ministry, there is now little concern over participating. In the meantime, country programing coordinated by UNDP has also obviated some of the need for such a donor forum. There seem to be two general lessons in this experience.

First, while acknowledging the proper concern about one-sided and predetermined negotiations, the need for a planning or coordinating mechanism cannot be evaluated with hindsight. Where such a mechanism is perceived to be necessary, the cautious approach is to see that it does not become overly formal and institutionalized and to work to see that the initiative and responsibility are properly lodged with the Ministry as soon as possible, as they have been in the case of Indonesia.

Second, it may be that such coordination mechanisms and careful planning are at least as necessary when there is extensive assistance as when assistance is limited and careful priorities must be set. When resources are scarce, internal pressures in the Ministry to allocate carefully generally suffice to assure most donors that assistance is being used for priority projects. However, in the case of Indonesia after 1968, there was little question about the desirability of assisting more in the field of education. In fact, there seems to have been more resources available than there were clarified needs and fundable proposals. The "donors' club" was started partly because the donors found it difficult to plan in the absence of a planning capacity in the Ministry itself, partly because donors were no longer as willing to plan independently--which sometimes meant being played off one against another--and partly because donors wished to have better assurance than they had had in earlier years that the project desired was fully supported by the responsible officials and in line with the Ministry's own plans and strategy. In those few countries, such as the least developed countries of Africa, where technical assistance is likely to be sharply expanded and derived from more diverse sources, the lessons of Indonesia's coordination efforts may be valuable to the recipients as well as to the diverse donors.

Beginning in 1971, Bappenas (the National Planning and Development Agency) has drawn up an annual list of projects, the Blue Book for Technical Assistance, within all sectors that need external technical assistance. The listing does not include projects already under way. Potential donors for some of the desired projects are indicated either because Indonesia considers those donors to be the most appropriate source or because there has already been an expression of interest in the project on the part of the donor.

If a project is of interest to a donor agency, this interest is usually indicated at the initial donors' club meetings, or "earmarked." Discussions then follow with the Director General of the responsible directorate, the Secretary General, the Office of Educational Development (BPP), Bappenas, or the State Secretariat. If the project is agreed, it is then approved by the donor agency, the Secretary General, and the Cabinet Secretariat, after which it is assigned to a directorate for implementation.

Formally, discussions should proceed in the above order. However, in practice detailed discussion is held usually either with BPP or with Bappenas, and the other bodies are informed of the progress but not directly involved in the planning. This situation seems satisfactory to virtually nobody. The other Indonesian bodies feel inadequately informed about matters that are part of their responsibility, and the donors feel that discussions often are too far removed from the bodies eventually responsible for implementation. Except for the 20 to 30 percent of projects on which discussions have begun, detailed planning only begins after the Blue Book is presented. If careful planning is to be done and if all the formal steps of project approval are to be followed, it can often take two to three years before the project is actually funded. Shortcuts are therefore taken on both sides, particularly when the project is considered of high priority.

First, there is a tendency to negotiate the details on a semiformal basis, often involving the relevant directorate, before proceeding with the more formal process. Second, both the agencies and the Ministry are engaged in various surveys and discussions independent of the Blue Book exercise, so that when a project is indicated there already may have been internal discussion of its feasibility. Third, some projects in the Blue Book are deliberately general and broad enough to include a variety of smaller efforts that may become desirable over the year. This is particularly true of fellowship programs and of projects supplying specialists and advisors to the central ministry. Fourth, some agencies are able to respond more quickly than others (for example, Ford and Unicef) or, as with UNDP/Unesco, are able to give a prior indication of the approximate level of assistance to be allocated to education. This allows planning to proceed more quickly, being that assistance commitments can be made at an earlier stage and areas for which additional assistance must be sought can be identified.

It should be noted, of course, that not all the apparent shortcuts are attempts to circumvent rigid processes. Some agencies are reluctant to be coordinated because, due to some combination of agency ego and mandate, they wish to be sure that their assistance is used for projects of the highest priority and/or for projects of high visibility and prestige. A certain amount of such competition among donors is probably useful from the Indonesian point of view, but if it were to become sufficiently general to negate effectively their attempts to coordinate and to channel assistance to needed but low prestige or visibility projects, they can quickly lose control. Such problems can be particularly serious with regard to any project touching on curriculum reform, the application of technology, the supply of materials or equipment, training for a key economic sector, major experimentation, or the extension of services to new population groups.

A second caveat on the apparent shortcuts is that in many cases both agency personnel and Indonesian officials simply do not know the proper procedures--because they have not bothered to inform themselves, as is often the case with key staff new to their position, or because the procedures are unclear, as they may be when the project does not fall neatly within an obvious department, or because the idea for the project arose from a personal contact and matured before anybody thought to put it into the right channels, or for other reasons having more to do with the limitations of a complex approval process than with the efforts of inventive bureaucrats to circumvent it. It is difficult to judge the net effect of such shortcuts in terms of whether Indonesia eventually gets the assistance it desires, but it seems probable that those projects that Indonesia truly considers of high priority eventually get approved, either by being put back on the right track or by overriding parts of the process. But some projects, however attractive they may seem to their proponents, do not have general approval or consensus as to their priority and tend to get stuck along the way in a form of bureaucratic pocket veto. It is for this reason that those advocating reform are particularly well advised to inform themselves of the appropriate processes, as it is on these projects that there are likely to be differences of opinion and conflicts of interest.

A planning unit in the Ministry's BPP is now able to maintain flow charts for forward planning of up to three years of technical assistance commitments and remaining needs. The donors' club forum and the work of the BPP combined with the country programing exercises conducted by UNDP for mid- and long-term needs, enable a continuing dialogue to anticipate needs and probable assistance. Though sufficiently flexible to enable unanticipated needs to be considered, the process works well enough that virtually all

multilateral and bilateral assistance is anticipated and included in
the planning documents.

The significant contribution of these mechanisms is not that
they have brought about the most appropriate assistance priorities.
It would be inaccurate to suggest that there has been full agreement,
especially about the desirability of mechanisms such as IGGI and the
"donors' club," and the <u>Blue Book</u> priorities have not necessarily
been reflected in the actual assistance programs. The important
contributions to the planning of assistance to education are that these
coordination exercises have accelerated <u>Indonesian</u> planning, that
they have provided a base for the planning of technical assistance,
and that they have created a forum in which matters of program coordination can be discussed and in which the desirability of program
coordination is accepted, at least in principle. Planning capacity in
the Ministry has increased considerably since 1967, and most of the
donors, while they may have educational personnel assigned to projects, no longer have resident education advisors. In short, what
initially was primarily a need of the donors for coordination and planning help has evolved into what is now an increasingly effective Indonesian process for setting priorities and planning external assistance.

In evaluating the effectiveness with which assistance was planned,
at least general answers to two additional questions must be sought:
To what extent was the availability of assistance a determining factor
in Indonesia's plans, and, thus, is an apparent congruence between
Indonesia's development priorities and those of the assistance agencies a result of the agencies having heard their own echo or a result
of effective translation of local priorities into assistance programs?
It is not necessary, and perhaps not possible, to be judgmental as to
the influence of assistance on local priorities, since the assistance
demonstrably was acceptable to local authorities. In any case, assistance is only part of the interaction of Indonesia with external influences, which affect local planning in very indirect ways, such as the
influence of doctors and economists trained overseas in the 1950s on
the development of higher education in the 1960s. However, it is at
all points necessary to keep in mind the fact that external assistance
is often influential far beyond its relatively modest contribution to
educational resources and that, even as local planning and administrative control matures, the possibilities for further development
are greatly influenced by past development. When assistance becomes the main source of development funds, its influence begins to
extend far beyond the projects immediately assisted. This may be the
most important lesson demonstrated by the Indonesian experience.

It is not so much the seductive amounts or interventionist weight
of assistance, as is rather simplistically charged by some critics,
but the budgetary segregation of most assistance as resources to be

used mainly for new developments that has given external assistance
a degree of influence disproportionate to the actual amount of externally supplied resources. One of the most common mistakes
made in international discussions of the role of external assistance
to education, whether in estimating the changes in magnitude implied by current demands that assistance support major reforms or
in bemoaning the small amounts devoted to educational assistance,
is the failure to distinguish between the subvention of resources in
support of educational expansion, administration, and recurrent
maintenance, which are the largest costs of any educational system,
and the supply of resources in support of educational experimentation and research and development, including pilot projects, in which
case even a relatively small flow of resources can have a determining influence on new developments. This is particularly the case
when a country, as had Indonesia through most of this period, has
so many other pressing demands on its scarce resources that it does
not feel able to allocate significant amounts to development budgets.
External development funds gave Indonesian educational planners a
degree of administrative flexibility and an ability to plan new developments that they probably would not have had had new projects been
forced to compete with recurrent claims on resources. Interestingly,
as Indonesia has become more able to finance new developments out
of its own resources, Indonesian planners, especially in the Ministry's Office of Educational Development, have had to give more attention to problems of mainstream expansion. The relative priorities of
assistance agencies are best summarized by Table 11.1, which gives
the number of education projects assisted from 1967 to 1971 by level.

In Table 11.2, the project emphases (note particularly the emphasis on improvement of higher education and vocational and technical education) can be compared with the development budgets for the
first five-year plan, the internal emphases of which are an indication
of the Ministry's development priorities and thus of the areas where
assistance would be considered useful.

There are two budgets to be considered, the recurrent budgets
and the development budgets, both of which include capital costs as
well as recurrent expenditures, a terminology problem that is a
source of some confusion.

External assistance to education (including most program aid,
all project aid, and some commodity aid) is included in the development budgets. These are essentially planning budgets, new monies
for new or expanded activities. They contain elements of both capital
and recurrent expenditure, the distinction from the recurrent budget
being that the recurrent budget absorbs projects after the development phase. This distinction is what has given external assistance
much of its "leverage" value--a "value" not entirely appreciated by

some Indonesian planners, who considered that it made new educational development too dependent on assistance.

TABLE 11.1

Number of Education Projects Assisted 1967-71, by Level

Tertiary education	97
Vocational and technical training at tertiary and secondary level	33
Assistance to research institutes	23
Secondary education	15
Primary education	9
Out-of-school education	4
Assistance to Ministry of Education not specified by level	30
Assistance to other Ministries, not specified by level	15
Total	226 projects

Source: Charles Aamenson, "External Assistance in the Field of Education," 1973 draft, Table 6, p. 46, prepared for Indonesian Ministry of Education as part of National Assessment of Education.

Most of the Indonesian educational expenditure was in the regular recurrent budget--mostly for salaries, with only a small proportion, approximately 5 percent, going for capital costs such as buildings. Further, most of the expenditure for secondary and primary schools was either raised from local sources or was included in local recurrent budgets at the provincial or subprovincial level by the Ministry of the Interior, which was administratively responsible for education at these levels in the provinces. In other words, very little of the recurrent or capital expenditure at the primary level and only a little more at the secondary level was within the budgetary control of the Ministry of Education. For instance, Ruth Daroesman estimated[1] that only about one-fifth of the secondary schools had been built with Ministry of Education funds and few of the primary schools. Thus, since the Ministry of Education was the receiver of most of what donors provided as assistance to education, added to the restrictions created by the allocation of most assistance to the development budgets were the limitations on Ministry of Education involvement at lower levels, which result from financing and administrative practices

TABLE 11.2

Indonesian Ministry of Education and Culture Development Budgets, 1969/70–1972/73
(in millions of rupees)

	1969/70 Budgeted	1969/70 Realized	1970/71 Budgeted	1970/71 Realized	1971/72 Budgeted	1971/72 Realized	1972/73 Budgeted	1972/73 Realized	Five-Year Plan Estimated 1969/1974
1. Education subsector									
a. Quality improvement in primary schools	380	272	423	382	423	--	450	--	3,348
b. Increase in vocational education in secondary schools	309	168	442	285	442	--	1,400	--	2,500
c. Improvement of technical and vocational education	2,495	1,949	2,165	1,636	2,173	--	2,250	--	21,373
d. Improvement in teachers' education	345	224	233	206	233	--	325	--	2,621
e. Development of higher education	1,726	1,537	1,739	1,332	2,539	--	3,000	--	15,500
f. Expansion of community and adult education	160	128	156	136	156	--	200	--	1,742
g. Development of education	--	--	155	133	155	--	230	--	6,645
Subtotal	5,415	4,278	5,312	4,109	6,121	--	7,855	--	53,729
2. Culture subsector									
a. Development of art culture	196	147	206	164	206	--	300	--	4,305
b. Intensification of sports activities	99	93	124	113	124	--	145	--	966
Subtotal	295	240	330	277	330	--	445	--	5,271
3. General	--	--	200	162	200	--	500	--	--
4. Total (1 + 2 + 3)	5,710	4,518	5,842	4,386	6,651	--	8,800	--	59,000

Source: Compiled by IBRD from development budgets, Ministry of Education and Culture, for various years.

completely internal to Indonesia. This has restricted external assistance, until quite recently when the Ministry itself obtained a more substantial planning role at the provincial level, to higher education, the Ministry itself, and those secondary/tertiary institutions, for example, vocational/technical and teacher training institutes, which were part of the Ministry's responsibilities.

The government budget for the Ministry of Education and Culture showed an absolute upward trend during the five-year plan 1968-73, even though it indicated a downward trend compared with the total budget, especially in relation to the development budget, about 8 percent of which was allocated to education in 1971-72, compared with 10 percent in 1970-71. The Ministry's development and recurrent budgets, not including foreign assistance, increased as follows: 1969-70: 18.2 billion rupees (5.5 percent); 1970-71: 23.2 billion rupees (5.06 percent); 1971-72: 27.5 billion rupees (5.30 percent); 1972-73: 38.2 billion rupees (4.86 percent). Total expenditure was estimated at four times these figures. Public expenditure on education during the first five-year plan was estimated at about 3 percent of gross domestic product. The development budget for education is approximately one-third of the recurrent budget, and perhaps one-fourth of all educational expenditure was directly expended by the Ministry of Education and Culture. H. W. Arndt's figures indicate that roughly three-fourths of the development budgets derived from external sources. The development budget of the Ministry of Education thus represents about one-sixteenth of educational expenditure, and about three-fourths of that has derived from external assistance.[2]

The data are very incomplete and often contradictory. However, two aspects should be stressed--first, that the portion of the development budget allocated to education and controlled by the Ministry of Education and Culture was quite small during the first five-year plan period and, second, that the impact of external assistance to education has been in its contribution to the Ministry's development budget, which has received most of its funds from external sources. Increasing proportions of the development budgets are now coming from Indonesian sources, and this may be mainly Indonesian in the second five-year plan. In part this is due to increasing Indonesian contributions (itself part of a rapidly expanding total budget), and in part it is due to a leveling off of external technical assistance.

Considering that assistance to education has been mostly technical assistance and concentrated in the development budget (itself determined by the development plan), it seems more useful to ask questions of its emphasis and influence than of its monetary value. Which sectors have been emphasized? Has it enabled the Indonesian education system to grow in ways it could not have? Has it led the system in directions it would not have gone; has it distorted planning, or helped implement it?

ASSISTANCE TO PLANNING

Though the first programs started in 1967-68 were largely con-
tinuations of the old, this was also a period of considerable rethinking and planning of future programs. Most of the agencies undertook
consultative and project identification missions during this period.
Recalling the lack of systematic planning and program coordination,
which seemed missing from the previous decade, it is striking that
a major emphasis since 1967-68 has been on the development of
planning capacities.

By the late 1960s the concept of educational planning had taken
a wide hold on the international community, and interested governments and international bodies such as Unesco and the International
Institute of Educational Planning began to produce substantial case
studies and works of guidance. The case of Indonesia was seen both
by the Indonesian authorities themselves and by Unesco as a good opportunity for applying the knowledge and methods acquired to one of
the largest developing countries, and one which had developed so far
in a rather unplanned manner.

As a result of a visit to Indonesia sponsored by Unesco of
Edgar Faure (previously French Prime Minister and Minister of
Education, who was later to become the Chairman of the International Commission on Educational Development set up by Unesco),
a number of steps to assist the planning of education in Indonesia
were initiated.

Beginning in 1968, Unesco/UNDP began to provide advisory
and planning personnel to the Ministry of Education and Culture in
the fields of educational planning, technical education, rural education, and higher education. Another expert was provided for development of education for children by Unicef. This was very modest
assistance, one expert and some equipment for each area, but it
marked a change in operating practice from earlier "mission teams"
running their projects with the blessing of the Ministry (but rather
autonomously administered with little direct Ministry involvement
in program design and only informal coordination with other projects
in the same field) to assistance directly to the Ministry and project
development through the Ministry. This also marks the point at
which the UNDP began to be involved directly in country programing
and to attempt a coordinating role among the external bodies assisting education in Indonesia. The provision of advisory personnel by
Unesco/UNDP and other donors would grow steadily in following years.

These first advisory and planning personnel were assigned to
specific fields, for example, technical education, rural education,
and higher education. This was soon recognized as inadequate stop-
gap assistance, focused on short-term capacities and working with

the parts of the system rather than with the system itself. A more systematic approach to planning was clearly needed, probably requiring some institutional capacity in the Ministry.

Unesco and UNDP followed up with assistance for the development of an Office of Educational Development (BPP) in the Ministry, which, though established on paper by the Ministry in 1968, was still little more than an intention in 1970. The situation appeared favorable to the establishment of BPP, owing to the presence of several highly qualified Indonesians, most of whom had received support under earlier fellowship programs for training abroad. However, there was an almost complete absence of middle-level analytical personnel to carry out the actual work of BPP. As a first phase, Unesco/UNDP enabled BPP to contract with AIR-Rand (American Institute for Research and the Rand Corporation) to develop system analyses and to prepare manuals and training materials for the training of Indonesian planners. UNDP contracted separately with two consulting groups (BCEOM in Paris and APT Associates in New York) for consultant help on developing a systematic approach to preinvestment programing.

Ford Foundation and Unicef also began programs designed to assist the development of educational planning capacities in Nigeria, but their approaches differed from those of Unesco and UNDP. Ford began planning a series of studies of the Indonesian education system, which, by 1970, had matured into a program of support to BPP for the carrying out of a National Assessment of Education. Included in the planning was an expectation that the training of Indonesian planners would be accelerated by the practical and introspective experience of working with both Indonesian colleagues and external specialists in designing and carrying out these surveys. Unicef, on the other hand, began looking for ways to improve the planning inputs from the provinces, beginning with West Sumatra and Central Java, and between 1970 and 1972 provided both advisers and materials to provincial planning and materials development efforts.

These efforts (Unesco, UNDP, Unicef, Ford Foundation), plus less programmatic assistance from other bilateral bodies and the World Bank working more on a project basis, began at about the same time, were concerned with the general problem of inadequate planning capacity, and were reasonably compatible. Yet it is striking that they do not appear to have been coordinated formally and, in fact, had some elements of competition. This situation arose partly because of the lack of the very capacity the efforts were attempting to build--namely, the ability of the Ministry to forward-plan and to coordinate its assistance needs. However, this also seems partly a matter of the agencies having somewhat different mandates, which, though not exclusive of other interests, gave emphasis to planning aspects of particular interest--UNDP having a primary concern with country programing; Unesco seeing its primary role as providing technical assistance to current Ministry efforts; Unicef attempting to identify areas where innovations and extensions of opportunity were possible; and the Ford Foundation having taken a primary interest in applying the social sciences to public management.

There seem to have been two general problems stemming from such differences in mandate and from the proliferation of uncoordinated planning activities. First, in a number of small ways these projects duplicated work (for example, at least three analyses of BPP's structure and purpose) leading to some avoidable inefficiency and wasted resources. More seriously, there was concern that agencies would allow unfortunate proprietary interests in the development of BPP to erode needed coordination and collaboration. A related argument, stemming from these same differences, was of whether support for planning should be provided mainly to the executive departments of the Ministry, to Bappenas or to the new planning office of the Ministry.

The second general problem is that none of the agencies seem to have conceived of an improved planning capacity as an end in itself. In most cases the planning capacity was viewed as a piece of the administrative machinery that was needed if the necessary resources and professional attention were to be mobilized and delivered in an efficient manner to new educational developments. In other cases the planning exercises were justified as leading to the identification of the sectors and strategies that should be emphasized during the 1970s. There is nothing wrong with viewing the need for planning capacities in such ways; clearly the effort to develop planning capacities must itself be planned and justified on the expectation that it is going to lead to and make possible various improvements. The difficulty lies in the fact that there were often unspoken assumptions that the sectors and strategies for improvement were already known, at least in general terms. Most agencies at this time were engaged in major reviews of their assistance policies, and there was some tendency to confuse the establishment of Indonesian planning with the preparation of new projects and the carrying out of needed research/surveys.

Care must be taken to ensure that the planning capacity that results is primarily a means for the country's planning and articulation of its own ends and that it is not primarily determined by the sectoral and programmatic interests of the donors. Technical education, for instance, was not emphasized in BPP or in the national assessments, though the World Bank supported a major technical education project in 1970, with a separate planning and implementation office. None of the agencies has limited itself to assisting educational planning. Even Unesco, which has been most directly concerned with the effort to develop BPP, has had difficulty striking the appropriate balance between its other programmatic interests and its desire to strengthen Indonesian planning.

The educational planning situation in 1974 seems to have benefited from all these efforts, but it also seems apparent that, had there been better coordination and/or cooperation from 1969-70, rather more might have been accomplished with less clash of egos and probably less wasted and duplicated effort. Further, though planning capacities are much improved, much of the most technical tasks remain dependent on expatriate specialists. It cannot yet be said that an Indonesian planning capacity has been fully established. In looking at the specific planning efforts in somewhat greater detail (see following section) one finds examples of both very sophisticated planning and of some fairly typical problems of externally assisted planning.

Chief among the early difficulties of BPP was a premature reliance on the more technical, mechanical aspects of systems analysis. The organizations contracted by Unesco/UNDP (AIR-Rand, BCEOM, and APT Associates) carried out their assignments and undoubtedly have made a contribution to the development of educational planning in Indonesia. However, the real issue is not whether these organizations performed their tasks well, but whether the task and the terms of reference had been defined adequately in terms of Indonesian conditions and of what was feasible. Some felt at the time that the technical progress in international circles on the scientific aspects of educational planning was being pressed beyond absorptive capacity at the actual planning and implementation level in Indonesia and that the right step would have been to have favored educational designing with a broader brush until such time as programs for the training of staff and for the improvement of statistics and other necessary data had matured. The result has been some uneven but occasionally impressive planning and analysis, but continuing glaring gaps remain in essential data and middle-level staff.

A second general problem stems from the initial desire to have, as soon as possible, a planning capacity of international standard. The initial support was prestigious and associated with IIEP and Unesco/Paris, which were attempting to provide leadership and to define the methodologies and standards of educational planning. Thus there was a reluctance to consider anything but the best and latest in techniques and to have results as soon as possible. As noted earlier, at least part of the external interest in an improved Indonesian planning capacity was to improve their own capacity to anticipate and coordinate assistance needs. A first priority was, therefore, given to the establishment of central capacities and to

links more with Bappenas than with the other parts of the Ministry of
Education. Further, the attempt to match external experts with local
counterparts meant that both external and local expertise was concentrated in one place--Jakarta. All these factors combined to develop
an educational planning office with an early capacity to plan long-
range educational development but with almost no capacity to assist
the Ministry with planning and implementation problems of a more
immediate nature.

The early experience of the BPP illustrates several general
principles. First, that the enthusiasm from outside sources to apply
the latest techniques known to them (many of which are not practiced
in their own countries) leads to overexpenditure of effort on sophisticated approaches when simpler ones may be both effective and less
costly. Second, a delicate balance must be struck between the desire of assistance agencies to support innovations and accelerate reforms and the ability and willingness of the Ministry and other authority structures to provide the necessary leadership and make the structural changes implied. Where, as with Unicef's attempts to assist
provincial planning, the assistance is too far out of phase with the
Ministry's plans (in this case, being attempted before the government was able or willing to devolve substantial authority to the
provinces), the assistance effort will be frustrated, however technically expert it may be. More generally, if a collision with absorptive capacity is to be avoided, it is necessary to emphasize the creation of an institutional base and trained staff before the major effort
is launched. This is required down the administrative line and at the
periphery, as well as at the top and center. It is dangerous to be
misled by the fact that there are very highly qualified personnel at
the top level into thinking that an educational system is ready to implement measures that require considerable administrative and analytical skills and authority to innovate at the local level.

The most important innovation resulting from the BCEOM/APT
recommendations was the systematic approach to planning and the
isolation of task patterns within the total system and the treatment
of these as separable task clusters. These clusters were (1) development of a new planning methodology; (2) strategies for the introduction of educational technology; (3) systematic preparation of development project proposals; (4) identification of goals, objectives, and
educational targets; (5) measuring the output of Indonesian education;
(6) preparing a cost manual for estimating costs of inputs into projects; (7) developing a quantitative model of the formal education system; (8) specifying a PPBS (program planning and budgeting system)
system and applying it to development projects; (9) developing methodology for evaluating development projects; and (10) setting up management control systems.

The approach was called Total Systems Programing (TSP) because the project was aimed not at certain aspects of education as separate undertakings such as educational planning, administrator/supervisor training, teacher training, curriculum development, or technical assistance programing, but at the integration of the formal education system so as to diversify outputs in response to societal and individual goals. The different aspects are developed or improved to the extent that they contribute effectively to this integration.

The Ford Foundation-assisted National Assessment of Education and the Unesco/Indonesian contract with AIR-Rand also covered many of these same clusters, and an informal division of labor developed between them. The National Assessment Task Forces were organized by sectors and levels--that is, higher education, primary education, financing, administration, and so on--while the AIR-Rand project of assessment and planning was organized as four clusters, each with a task force: (1) the systematic preparation of project proposals and statements of goals and objectives; (2) identifying goals, objectives, and targets; (3) identifying and selecting innovation inputs and processes; and (4) BPP organization, function, and procedures.

The AIR-Rand project seems to have had three outcomes: (1) the collection and correlation of basic statistics and information on organization, curricula, finances, and manpower requirements; (2) the learning obtained from participation in the process of assessing the system by a number of then inexperienced Indonesian staff of BPP; and (3) the preparation of the cluster materials in such a way that they could be used for subsequent training of Indonesian planners and administrative staff. This seems likely to be the most lasting impact of the work, for the nature of the four clusters is such that the work could not (and was not intended to) result in a final model or a set of specified proposals. Rather, the background data and statements of objectives were collected and organized in such a way that they illustrated the possible application of appropriate analytic and decision-making processes. The four sets or clusters of manuals that resulted thus are tools or guidelines for future planning exercises, rather than a planning exercise in themselves.

The sectoral task forces of the national assessment were more planning exercises in themselves. However, they also concentrated on the analytical processes, that is, on assessing and suggesting implications rather than on drawing final conclusions to be set forth as a recommended plan. These task forces had much the same outcomes as in the AIR-Rand work. In addition, three characteristics of these exercises seem worth noting.

1. The task forces did not work steadily toward a final report but proceeded by "levels" of assessment, with the first level being

little more than fact-finding and opinion-gathering, the second being more of an assessment of what the issues seemed to be, and the third being an attempt to set out the areas of policy choice and the implications for future decision-making. This had the advantage of providing a maximum of opportunities for participation in the process by a wide range of Indonesians; it emphasized the process over the product; and it provided a continuing flow of assessment help to decision-makers without preempting their final responsibility.

2. Related to (1), all the reports were presented in draft form, with areas clearly marked in which there might be disagreement over facts or implications, and with recommendations that these areas be checked or analyzed further. This presentation in draft form seems to have resulted mainly from lack of time to complete the exercise, but it does not now seem likely that the assessment will be finalized, and it may be wise not to do so. From conversation with various officials, it seems clear that such tentative and speculative reports provided officials with welcome flexibility and discretion, which they would not have had had the reports been more final or declarative.

3. Several of the studies concentrated on the social demand for education (see especially Hal Carpenter, Social Demand for Education, and Pearse, Demand for Higher Education). This was a needed antidote to the earlier emphasis on supply, financing, and administrative problems and is one of the few examples of a systemic study that has given a prominent and early place to social demand studies.

In addition to the comments above, four comments are offered for both parts of the assessment effort.

1. One of the strengths of these efforts was that they were done for BPP, not for the agencies. They were not academic exercises or studies but were part of the process of planning and part of the process of developing a planning office. At the beginning, BPP did not exist, except on paper; but by the "end" of the process, BPP was functioning and itself giving leadership to ongoing assessment and planning exercises. BPP is still evolving; it is not yet playing as strong or effective a role as many people would like to see. But it does exist; it has added a planning and project development capacity, which the Ministry did not possess previously; and it is unlikely that it would have developed as quickly or had the opportunity for its personnel to acquire practical skills had not these assessment efforts been supported.

2. The use of expatriate specialists as consultants and advisers was generally confined to those areas requiring technical expertise and experience, and there was a conscious effort to leave as

much of the field work and analysis as possible to Indonesians.
There was major expatriate involvement at all stages, and it may
even be argued that there was too much. However, the important
aspect is that it seems to have been provided reasonably sensitively
and discreetly, without the expatriate "experts" appearing to have
done the work for their counterparts. The Indonesian coordinator of
the assessment was careful to keep control of the actual assessing
even though, as in the case of C. E. Beeby, the consultant's prestige and credibility may have been adequate for his recommendations
to stand by themselves. In contrast, the AIR-Rand work, though
done for BPP, is unfortunately recognized too generally as non-
Indonesian work. It was, after all, a technical consulting contract
expected to provide a finished product, which it did, but a point
should still be noted of some loss of Indonesian identification and
therefore use.

        3. Most of the reports, manuals, and draft assessments, how-
ever well done as technical writing, are very dense and technically
written. As such, they are unlikely to be read by people other than
those actually involved in the assessment. In fact, it is doubtful
whether any but a handful have read all or most of the assessments.
Their circulation is further limited by most of them remaining in-
timidatingly stamped "Draft: Not for Quotation." Some of the
assessments are too complete for use by any but the most specialized, and there is an apparent need for rather journalistic extrac-
tions and summaries for use by a wider audience. Many of the documents were written in English (though some are in Bahasa Indonesian),
and it would be useful to have summary documents written in both
languages. This is a good example of the fact, commonly overlooked,
that the use and utility of a study or piece of research is often as
much determined by its form and forum as by its substance.

        4. The language problems encountered in Indonesia may con-
tain some lessons for application of consultant help in other countries.
Most of the senior professional Indonesians functioned capably in
English, and most of the long-term consultants or technical assistance
personnel obtained some capacity in Bahasa Indonesian. However,
most short-term consultants and many junior Indonesian professionals
did not have more than minimal second-language capability, and, even
when they had some speaking ability, they were rarely able to write
easily in the second language. It is impossible to calculate the loss
in professional dialogue that resulted, but it seems worth considering
that a small investment in a capable translation unit might have more
than justified its cost.

        The UNDP/Unesco Phase I of institution-building for the Office
of Educational Development began in 1970. In June 1971, this was

superseded by Phase II, based on the recommendations of BCEOM/ APT Associates, and the same consultants were contracted to spend the summer running training seminars for the staff of BPP. The program recommended as Phase II was the total systems preinvestment programing approach. This National Educational Development Program Project is essentially an attempt to integrate all the UNDP/ Unesco technical assistance to education into a systematic approach. In addition to this "system" project, there are four related "satellite" projects, which, as they are extended, are expected also to be integrated with the overall project. The UNDP/Unesco program thus provides an umbrella for a range of anticipated technical assistance needs and helps to give some flexibility to the Blue Book planning. The overall project and its development strategy are approved in principle, but the satellite projects are subject to ongoing approval and refinement--with assistance from other sources substitutable where appropriate and available. It also gives Unesco a key role in BPP's planning.

BPP continued to develop its capacities to assist the Ministry with long-range planning and assessment/evaluation/experimentation, but the Ministry also looked to BPP for technical contributions to current implementation and operation functions. This diluted the attention and resources that could be given to longer-range planning and project development and also meant that BPP's work increasingly was limited to the areas in which the Ministry already was working or already had decided to develop programs. One of the most serious of these limitations was that educational programs, and thus educational expertise, were concentrated at the center. Though the expertise and self-knowledge available in Jakarta was increasingly good, the situation in the provinces was quite different.

A state university and an IKIP had been established in each of the 26 provinces, though many of them were of minimal quality. There was only indirect qualitative assistance, mainly through the reservation of places at the centers of excellence, which were expected to assist the newer and weaker institutions by osmosis. There were a number of assistance programs supplying faculty, library books and texts, and some fellowships, but there was little coordination and almost no assistance with planning.

In part this was a matter of other activities having successfully claimed priority, with those furthest from Jakarta being least competitive. However, it must also be kept in mind that for the first two decades Indonesia had struggled with the process of welding a republic from a vast archipelago, and though the government extended schools and educational opportunities as evidence of its intent to include the provinces at the center and to share overall development, it was very cautious with regard to any devolution of planning authority. It is not surprising then that assistance agencies were not encouraged to initiate major new programs of their own. This situation is found in other countries, though perhaps not so explosively, and much of the criticism that assistance agencies have concentrated programs at the center must be weighed against the centripetal policies the countries have themselves adopted.

In any case, Indonesia was again looking for ways to expand and improve education in the provinces, and, along with a cautious relaxing of some of the central control during the early 1970s, there began to be attempts to improve planning at the provincial level. There had been increasing interest on the part of assistance agencies in working at the provincial level, and agencies began exploring new programs considerably ahead of the time when the Ministry would have the staff time and administrative flexibility even to consider new programs under its aegis in the provinces. It seems too much to credit assistance agencies with having stimulated the provincial effort, as it is likely the Ministry would have developed its own program along similar lines, but it seems apparent that assistance agencies did accelerate the Ministry's plans. Some of the less obvious reasons for agency interest in provincial planning were as follows:

1. Assistance priorities were shifting away from higher education toward lower levels, and, in Indonesia, primary education funds were mainly provincial funds;

2. Policy shifts by most agencies had begun to emphasize the educationally deprived and the linking of educational planning to other social and economic development, and most of the youth not in school were concentrated in the outer provinces (this reasoning was particularly strong in the case of Unicef);

3. There was growing concern for the application of skills and capacities previously developed, and those agencies that had been assisting provincial IKIPs and regional universities were now looking for ways to involve those institutions in provincial development work--USAID and the Ford Foundation had been most supportive of postsecondary education and were also most concerned about the application of skills; and

4. Agencies were becoming sensitive to criticisms that they were too often simply reinforcing an elitist system dominated by the center. All agencies seemed sensitive to such criticisms, and some agencies seemed prepared to fund almost any project which would diffuse their effort. No clearly undesirable project seems to have resulted, but some projects seem inadequately designed and prematurely launched, partly due to the urgency of such essentially defensive programing.

Among the most important of the efforts to assist provincial educational development were the following:

Unicef assistance for provincial primary teacher training, 1969-72, supplying mainly equipment and materials, advisory assistance for provincial educational planning, and a demonstration project for rural educational broadcasting. All of these seem to have suffered from having been a bit premature and from having had inadequate links to an organization such as BPP to which inputs might be provided and projects demonstrated. Unicef's projects were, however, important first efforts from which later efforts took lessons.

Ford Foundation, partly following Unicef's start and partly extending from its work with the national assessment, assisted the development of planning units in the governors' offices in West Sumatra and East Java. Each unit, though part of BPP, draws its staff from the provincial IKIP, the university, and the governor's office, emphasizes noneducational expertise, and works as an advisory resource to the provincial education office. Assistance provides an adviser and initial operating funds, with the expectation that if these units prove their usefulness, they will be sustained and replicated by Indonesian funds.

Unesco assistance to the development school pilot projects. This is an attempt to experiment with an 8/4 system to replace the present 6/3/3 system. An interesting aspect of these pilot projects is that each is attempting to design according to local social, cultural, economic, and physical "ecosystems," requiring experimentation in content, materials, building design, and in the use of local supplementary staff. These projects are run by the IKIPs and seem to be an effective means of directly involving the IKIPs in both current and future reform. Assistance mainly provides specialists (to the IKIPs) and experimental classroom materials such as science kits.

Unesco/UNDP seminars, run during summer 1971 for provincial planning officials, by BCEOM/APT, were discussed above.

Some of the characteristics of these efforts to assist provincial educational development are listed below.

1. Assistance is generally provided through BPP (or another appropriate unit of the central ministries), but project administration and technical leadership is delegated to the provincial unit or institution. The central unit maintains coordinating and program leadership functions, but project implementation is kept as close as possible to the working level.

2. Considerable attention is given to involving local personnel and institutions in the provincial planning. This is considered both helpful in strengthening and giving relevant roles to the institutions and necessary to effective provincial planning and project development. External experts are usually limited to one or two per project and are used in advisory, not administrative, roles.

3. For assistance intended to effect change at the lower levels, advisory and technical assistance services are focused primarily on being useful to the provincial authorities, where planning and budget responsibilities lie. Policy coordination and administrative responsibilities are generally left to the Indonesian directors.

4. This assistance is needed because of the inadequate staff capacity at the provincial level. The projects seem to have had sensibly modest expectations for the initial phases and have concentrated on building planning teams and developing planning, data collection, and basic research capacities, rather than on moving quickly into actual planning and experimentation.

CHANGING EMPHASES, 1968-73

Though most of the assistance provided in the first programs renewed in 1967-68 continued the earlier emphasis on higher education, both the Indonesian Ministry and most of the donors in the succeeding years have sought ways to extend their efforts both outward to include more direct involvement in the provinces and downward to include more direct involvement with the planning and qualitative improvement of primary education and other forms of basic education. Some of the reasons for this shifting attention have been mentioned in earlier sections, and, particularly in tracing the evolution of planning mechanisms, one can see some of the ways in which assistance facilitated it. Though it is not the purpose here to discuss current programs in any comprehensive fashion, it seems likely that increasing amounts of assistance will be directed to work at the lower levels; thus it seems useful to trace some of the steps by which this program emphasis developed. Further, since many of the earlier assistance efforts have been a prologue to current programs, one can summarize some of the capacities that have been built and infer some of the work remaining to be done by examining some of the implementation problems.

The development of planning, and its extension to include work in the provinces, has already been discussed. However, it must be emphasized here that both the Ministry's effort to extend its planning purview and the shift of interest toward problems of mass education were part of the same process. As interest grew in the qualitative problems of the whole system, including those that limited the effectiveness of higher education, interest shifted toward the lower levels. As interest grew in working more directly with the primary education system and with those students not in school, interest shifted toward the provinces. As Indonesia moved through its five-year plan and began to be satisfied with its accomplishments in stabilizing and regenerating its economy and administrative systems, Indonesia's planners began to shift emphasis toward the extension of programs promising improved welfare, which included an emphasis on the extension of educational opportunity. At the same time, though for different reasons, most assistance agencies were beginning in the late 1960s and early 1970s to rethink their programs and to look aggressively for ways to popularize and improve the effectiveness of their assistance. Much of the advice they were getting concerned ways of becoming involved (1) at the primary level, (2) with the educational problems of those not in school, and (3) with planning problems at the local level, particularly in the context of efforts to integrate better all planning. What is most noteworthy about this set of dynamics is that each of several interest groups (those concerned with qualitative improvements, those concerned with more egalitarian distribution of educational opportunity, those concerned with more comprehensive planning, those concerned with more localized planning, those concerned with maximizing the effectiveness of external assistance, and those concerned with changing the public image of external assistance) found themselves arguing in the same direction--toward work directed at improving and extending education at the first educational level and toward work at the provincial and subprovincial administrative levels.

The first significant move away from the rather singular attention to higher education that had characterized earlier programs was the renewal of attention by the Ford Foundation to problems of English-language teaching and to the training of teachers who would use it. This support dates back to 1953 and is by far the largest and most sustained effort of its kind undertaken by the Foundation anywhere. In addition, it is the only one that tackled the problem comprehensively, dealing not only with the techniques of teaching English as a language but also with the need to train those who must use English as the medium of instruction. Parallel and indispensable to the success of both aspects were grants for Indonesian efforts to develop appropriate English-language teaching materials in various subjects. These were initiated in 1959, suspended in 1965, and resumed in 1968.

Initial grants concentrated on the development of indigenous teacher-trainers of English language for the IKIPs--through support for the colleges, graduate fellowships in the United States, and specialist expatriate advisers.

By 1962, enough Indonesian expertise had been built up in the teachers colleges to switch the emphasis of Foundation support from the training of language teachers to the training of the teacher-trainers of other secondary school subjects. This was done by assisting directly the teacher training colleges so they could train secondary-school teachers and also by establishing a Graduate English Language School at Airlangga University in Malang with the capacity to train initially to masters and eventually doctorate level language teachers for the other teacher training colleges. Most of this reinforcement of the basic ESL (English as a second language) program was for the training of subject teachers who use English as the medium of instruction.

Language problems had been a major problem for the entire system since Dutch was abandoned after Independence. The Ford Foundation effort is cited for two reasons: (1) it was the first large-scale effort to assist teacher training and thus, indirectly, secondary education; and (2) it is one of the first examples of assistance being directed to a problem area rather than a skill area. Though the program was disrupted with the other programs, the interest in the problems of language continued. A more important point is that the linguistic skills developed in the course of about ten years of concentration on the English language have proven valuable in the development of Bahasa Indonesian as the language of instruction. This has followed much the same pattern of basic linguistic work, curriculum development, materials development, training, and upgrading of teachers at the IKIPs. There have been a number of other programs assisting language training, including French, German, Japanese, and Dutch languages, but this was the largest effort and the only one that concentrated on the training of teacher-trainers rather than the training of teachers and that combined materials development in subject areas. The long-term impact of this work on English language has been to develop a capacity for language policy work and language training, which can now be applied to a variety of language and materials development problems.

Since 1967 there have been a number of additional assistance efforts at the IKIPs by Unesco, Unicef, United Kingdom, Canada, USAID, Australia, and New Zealand. The quality and capacity of the IKIPs, which have evolved from mainly training institutions toward resource bodies providing a general professional attention to qualitative problems at lower levels, are still very uneven, but the direction in which they are evolving seems clear. Prior to 1968, however, there had not been much direct assistance to levels below the IKIPs. There were some attempts to assist primary and secondary education more directly, from private sources such as religious bodies, and from bilateral sources such as the Netherlands, which provided capital assistance both directly to the Ministry and through the United Nations Fund for West Irian. The main restriction on other assistance was that the numbers at the lower levels made it difficult to use the expensive external personnel for direct support at those levels and the Indonesians preferred that external personnel be used at higher levels or in planning and advisory roles, which would not develop very quickly.

Direct efforts to assist lower levels began in 1968 with the contribution of materials in kind and with attempts to establish a materials production capacity, particularly for printed materials. The more important efforts are listed below.

1. A set of efforts by CARE, which provided food, vitamin pills, school equipment, tools, vegetable seeds, writing, and drawing equipment. Between 1968 and 1971, over $8 million was used in this way.

2. The provision by the Ford Foundation of equipment and eventually a building to establish a university press at the University of Indonesia. Though not related to materials production at the lower levels, it is part of the overall attempt to build a production capacity and is an example of the severe implementation problems, which result from inadequate attention to design and assessment of capacity.

3. A multifaceted Netherlands effort to develop the capacity of a printing industry. This included the provision of experts, equipment, fellowships, and a building for a Training Center for Graphic and Information Instruction, and capital assistance (building and printing equipment) for a School of Printing and Typography. They also provided small offset presses to five of the higher education institutions. These three projects amounted to about $3.8 million over five years.

4. A fourth effort was begun by USAID in 1967, when a survey team was sent to assess the book situation. In October 1968, a textbook development program began that combined (a) translation of foreign textbooks into Bahasa Indonesian, (b) courses for textbook writers, (c) self-enrichment for IKIPs and Pembina faculties, and (d) paper supply for the production of a TESL (teaching English as a second language) series. This program ran through 1970.

Of these approaches the third and fourth can be said to have had a lasting impact.

The first (CARE) effort filled an immediate need. However, there was little technical assistance, little provision for continuing supply or production, and, though the amounts were quite large, the numbers in the primary schools were even larger. There was little lasting impact from this program, though it was undoubtedly of immediate benefit to those schoolchildren.

The attempt by the Ford Foundation to supply the capital input to establish a university press seems to have erred on the opposite side from the CARE efforts. Although CARE filled an immediate need without much lasting effect, the Ford effort attempted to fill a long-term need without there being an effective immediate demand or an adequate materials development capacity. The initial grant sought to develop a publishing house with its own printing capacity. It got neither. The equipment was donated and turned out to be inappropriate for the purpose. The director of the press was not oriented to running a publishing house. After several difficult years, publishing was separated from the printing, and some progress began to occur on the publishing side, leaving the printing to job printers--which had improved, at least partly due to the Netherlands' assistance. By 1973, the university press had begun to publish enough to justify itself, largely by producing materials developed under the translation program assisted by USAID.

The Netherlands effort was more comprehensive, integrating capital equipment with training institutions for whatever publishing and printing industry might develop. Though it is difficult to evaluate the effort in terms of numbers of publications directly attributable to it, there is general agreement that the local printing industry is considerably improved. Large-scale efforts such as the Unicef/Canada and the current IDA/Canada assisted primary textbook programs are using Indonesian printers.

The USAID effort attacked the problem more directly, but also comprehensively. The supply of texts to IKIPs and other faculties was rather conventional, but several other aspects seem worth noting: translation program--helped with a problem of the system, rather than just supplying texts as material support; courses for textbook writers--not very ambitious, but again attempting to improve capacity; paper supply--set a precedent for the use of commodity aid paper in a technical assistance effort (Canada has since done the same with a Unicef project and is continuing to do so with the primary textbook project financed by the IDA credit); printing--this was left to commercial presses, as has been done in subsequent efforts (for example, Unicef/Canada, and the current IDA textbook project).

Though the USAID effort was preceded by a survey team, which seems to have been useful in identifying several critical tasks for text development, and the Netherlands effort seems to have been well planned, it is striking that there does not appear to have been any overall planning for either materials development or for the development of a materials development capacity. Each of these efforts (and several others that just supplied books) appears to have developed and implemented its own plans. It seems almost accidental that the pieces eventually fit together into a materials development pattern.

It may be more accurate to say only that a materials production capacity exists, which is not yet a materials development capacity.

These beginnings on materials development, though separate, were important for two large-scale efforts to provide primary-school texts. The first was a large-scale effort by Unicef in 1969-74 to provide books and equipment. It was coordinated with the Department of Education, though implemented by Unicef. This concentrated on the production and distribution of basic texts in four subjects: mathematics (Entebbe translations), grades one to six; Indonesian language, grades one to six; social studies, grades three to six; and science, grades four to six. This was intended to be a ten-year project (1969-79) with three objectives: (1) improve textbook content, (2) reduce unit costs through mass production, and (3) ensure that all primary students have textbooks. Approximately 60 million textbooks were produced and distributed by 1973. A further 138 million books were needed. In 1972 discussions were begun with IDA, and a credit was arranged in 1973 to finance the remainder. Canada provided the paper for the first 60 million and has agreed to continue this for the remainder.

The IDA credit is a larger effort than its Unicef/Canada predecessor and is combined with a number of related efforts using Unesco technical assistance for the upgrading and retraining of teachers and inspectors. The IDA project is intended to (1) develop arrangements for the preparation and texting of basic texts and related prototype teaching aids; (2) produce and distribute 138 million textbooks in four subjects (Bahasa Indonesian, mathematics, science, and social studies) for grades one to six; (3) in-service train 350,000 primary teachers in the use of the textbooks and teaching aids; and (4) upgrade 2,800 supervisory personnel. It proposes to do this by 1979, using local institutions, personnel, and printing capacity, with external inputs of funds, paper, 16 man-years of specialist assistance, and 8 man-years of fellowships (in mathematics).

It is arguable that materials production, curriculum revision, and teacher upgrading are the priorities for the primary level. However, this will be the largest development project of the system, and its priorities and work demands will influence the work plans of the rest. It is also the first credit of its type for IBRD/IDA, and lessons for the future application of loan assistance for primary education reform are likely to be drawn from it. Because it is likely to be influential both within Indonesia and with similar projects elsewhere, it seems useful to note both its objectives and those of its problems as could be anticipated at the beginning of the project.

The IDA project, though a continuation of the earlier Unicef work, clearly had benefited from this earlier experience on such aspects as the use of local printing and distribution capacities, the

need for more technical assistance on curriculum development and
text evaluation, and the need to include a major counterpart program
of teacher retraining and upgrading. However, several problems of
the earlier effort remained.

1. At the time the Unicef/Canada project started, there was
neither any agreement on what the curriculum should be nor was
there a curriculum development body. A project for the development of primary school curricula was started in 1969-70, with
Unesco help but with most of the work to be done by working groups
at the IKIPs. Thus, the production of materials and the development of new curricula started at about the same time and under
separate auspices. This situation continues in 1974, though the
problem is moderated somewhat by the curriculum developments
being further along.

2. The Unicef project focused mainly on the materials production problem and was not planned or implemented in the context of an
overall plan for primary school improvement. There has not yet
been a thorough evaluation of the Unicef textbook program, and the
implications for primary education of the national assessment efforts are still being debated. The textbooks are being prepared for
the existing six-year primary cycle, while the Ministry is beginning
to switch to an eight-year cycle (see point 1).

3. The mathematics and science materials were mainly translations of materials developed elsewhere and were put into classrooms with only perfunctory pretesting. The social science materials
are still being developed, and all the materials need revision and another pretesting or revision before being distributed. Many of the
first series must be replaced. BPP is charged with field testing and
evaluation of the materials, which will help ensure their quality and
appropriateness--equally importantly, it will give BPP a clearly defined role in implementation.

4. Distribution has been left to the printers (with payment
subject to the materials being delivered to the district offices).
This continues the Unicef approach which apparently has worked
well and seems remarkably inexpensive. The IDA credit allows
$.0015 a book for distribution. A weakness is that little help is be-
ing given to the administrative staff and inspectorate to enable them
to cope with the added burden.

5. There had been little prior attention to training or upgrading primary school teachers, and, though a separate Unicef project
attempted to help the primary teacher training schools, this was
only in a few provinces, was mainly help with materials and equipment, and was unable to provide much help with the immediate problems of those teachers already teaching and not knowing how to use

the new materials. The IDA credit has included a large and complex
in-service upgrading program, seminars and training for supervisory
personnel, and help with teacher manuals. This is clearly a needed
emphasis; however, it will be difficult to administer and implement
and will provide only a minimum number of contact hours at the level
where the materials will actually be used--that of the classroom
teacher. Further, there is a danger of the presently overloaded
training capacity and administrative structure of the IKIPs being
overloaded still more with new priority tasks. If there is a lesson
here, it is of the difficulty of mounting a frontal attack on an entire
sector with all reform elements having to proceed simultaneously.
Some elements will be out of phase and will delay or reduce the effectiveness of the overall effort.

The following observations suggest general lessons that might
be learned from the manner in which the IDA project has developed.
If some of them imply criticism, the criticism should be balanced
by the fact that IDA chose to break new ground and to move aggressively in this vital area.

1. The project was developed unusually quickly, moving from
preinvestment survey to signing of the loan in less than one year--
compared with a normal gestation period of about three years--and
it moved immediately into an implementation phase, unlike more conventional loans, such as the credit for technical education provided in
1970. Three general pressures combined to force the pace of project
development.

(a) Internally, IBRD/IDA was being pressed by its President to shift
    priorities rapidly toward the "lower 40 percent" and to develop
    loan projects that more clearly benefited the mass of people,
    rather than just contributing to the building of technocratic elites--
    as some of the Bank's critics had been charging. This policy shift
    began to be strongly articulated in the spring of 1972 (see Robert
    McNamara's UNCTAD speech in Santiago, Chile, May 1972),[3] and
    Mr. McNamara himself visited Indonesia that summer.
(b) Indonesia itself was shifting priorities toward the provinces and
    toward educational efforts, which brought tangible benefits to as
    many people as possible. A major expansion of primary school-
    ing was being considered, and there was concern that the prepara-
    tion of texts and materials and the training of teachers might not
    keep pace with the expansion program.
(c) The Ministry's planning had to be completed before the second
    five-year plan began in early 1974; and Unicef, which had begun
    the ten-year textbook development program in 1969, would be

finishing the first five-year phase in fiscal 1974. Thus, if IDA
were going to finance the second phase, it would have to complete
its loan preparations in 1973 and move into project implementation no later than the end of fiscal 1974.

Though these same pressures likely will not be duplicated elsewhere,
it would seem useful to develop some tools for checking the tendency
to force draft such projects in future. One approach would be to develop for a range of major projects likely to be undertaken in future
sets of project guidelines including reasonable preconditions (adequate materials production capacity, progress on materials development and curriculum reform efforts, and completion of a sector review at least to a stage where there is consensus on the areas and
directions for reform and the presence of adequate administrative
and project implementation capacity); estimates of minimum amounts
of time required for the development of each component (How much
time is required with adequate provision for pretesting and revision
for the development of, for example, a new social studies text? How
quickly can a primary teaching force be retrained? How quickly can
materials be produced and distributed in orderly fashion?); and,
finally, how the various elements and stages should be phased (What
degrees of overlap are possible? How should PERT*-type techniques be applied? What costs and dangers are involved in accelerating or short-circuiting these phases, and what are the comparable
benefits?). It should be possible to estimate minimum development
schedules--which could be extended but not contracted.
      2. The observations above are irrespective of the type or
amount of financing.

(a) Most of the costs for this project are in local currency. The
    major foreign exchange cost is for paper, provided by Canada.
    Only a few percent will be used for technical assistance and equip-
    ment. Counterpart funds in other countries might be used in this
    way were technical assistance available.
(b) As a loan-financed project, the entire project is financed from the
    beginning and evaluated with rate-of-return and present-value cal-
    culations. The loan is Indonesia's money, and there is an interest
    in reducing the period during which the Bank is directly and visibly
    involved in the project implementation to a minimum. These fac-
    tors encourage a project design which frontloads as many of the
    project implementation tasks in the early years as is possible.
    With a project as large and complex as this one (and this is the

---

*Program Evaluation Review Technique.

largest Bank project of its kind to date), it is difficult to retain
optimum timing and staging for the different elements. In this
case, the major element is the production of primary textbooks.
Successful implementation of the textbook program requires retraining and upgrading of the teachers who will use the texts. Retraining and upgrading is a slower and more difficult task than the
production of textbooks, yet it will have to be accomplished within
the time limits set by the production schedule. Ideally, curriculum development would precede teacher retraining, and new materials would be put into use no sooner than the teachers began to
complete the retraining. It is useless to wish that earlier work
on curriculum development and teacher retraining had been further along before the textbook loan was considered. However,
large loan-financed programs might be broken into stages, with
two or three loans provided at consecutive stages within a longer-
term program of educational lending.

3. This IDA project illustrates the problem of the time horizon
for projects. The planning horizon for countries is rarely longer than
the next five-year plan, and few granting or lending agencies can foresee their financing capacities or priorities beyond five years. Though
the loan or credit may have a term of 50 years, project implementation rarely extends beyond about five years. This has been adequate
in the past for capital assistance, institutional support, and "turn-
key" projects. However, as loan funds are used for program support, staff development, and long-term reform such as the reform
of primary curricula, ways will have to be found to ensure technical
assistance support over a longer period. A possible solution may be
the combining of long-term financial assistance (for example, IDA
lending) with long-term technical assistance commitments coordinated
by Unesco/UNDP, including bilateral assistance. Though it may not
be possible for any one agency to commit itself beyond its own budget
and program horizon, it may be possible for potential donors as a
group to commit themselves in principle to the provision of needed
technical assistance in an agreed sector.

The program priority represented by this credit is a new emphasis for the IDA, and it should be watched carefully. These judg-
ments were formed in early 1974 when the project was just beginning.
It is to be hoped that this IDA project is working out its problems as
it goes along. As with any comparably large project, there are implementation problems that could not have been anticipated. The
question remains, however, whether there are lessons to be learned
from this project that could be useful elsewhere.

The same question may be asked of Indonesia's educational experience as a whole and of the assistance that has been applied in
Indonesia over the past 25 years. Indonesia's education system in
1974 is vastly enlarged and improved from that with which it began
in 1949, and, despite being greatly diversified, more complex, and
more ambitious in its social aims, it is also much better managed
and more orderly. These are not insignificant claims for the world's
fifth largest nation. They become remarkable when one considers
Indonesia's turbulent history over this period. Indonesia still has
problems, and there are still questions of what further external help
is needed. Increasingly, however, it is Indonesians who are asking
the questions and articulating the problems. There is much that the
rest of the world can learn from Indonesia's educational experience.

NOTES

1. Ruth Daroesman, Bulletin of Indonesian Economic Studies 7,
no. 3 (1972): 90.
2. H. W. Arndt, "Survey of Recent Developments," Bulletin
of Indonesian Economic Studies 7, no. 1 (1972): 28–29.
3. Robert McNamara, speech delivered to UNCTAD, Santiago,
Chile, May 1972.

PERSPECTIVES AND
CONCLUSIONS

12

FUNDAMENTAL CRITICISMS
OF EDUCATIONAL COOPERATION:
AN ASSESSMENT

In our first chapter on trends and the chapters that followed on the different educational levels, administrative and operational problems, and country studies, we discussed many criticisms of educational cooperation as it has grown up and works today. Recommendations were made at different points arising out of the criticisms discussed and are summarized in the Conclusions.

In the present chapter some of the more fundamental types of criticism are considered, which question the system itself and the motivations that inspire it, as well as its usefulness. They are partly the result of the political views held by the various critics as to the state of the world in general and what can be done about it, but a number of them also have their bases in positions taken as to the value of current types of education and whether it is in fact possible to make useful resource transfers in this sector. The debate in this area is not a particularly rational one since it is based on value positions taken by the participants on political issues and different approaches to the problems of world development.

The first form of criticism, on which we need not dwell long, is part of general political controversy between power groups. An example is that educational cooperation is predominantly at the donor end an activity of the Western European and North American countries. The centrally planned socialist countries, as seen in Chapter 4, take a relatively minor part in the total of educational cooperation and one linked mostly to commercial treaties. At one period, the USSR delegation to Unesco was critical of the "Western" effort, referring to the OECD of which the donor countries were members as a "neocolonialist" group. Later the delegation of the People's Republic of China appeared on the scene and used the same terms to describe the USSR effort.

The second form of criticism arises from the deficiencies of total cooperation for overall development on a world scale and has been voiced in many parts of the world and by a variety of statesmen from different social systems. It goes back to the latter half of the 1960s, when it became evident that there was no likelihood of official aid for development reaching the target of 0.7 percent of the national income of each of the advanced countries, set by the United Nations for the First Development Decade. Only a declining half of the percentage was being attained, and this trend continued into the 1970s (see Table 12.1).

Moreover, while there had been a welcome increase in the volume of educational cooperation and in the number of donors, and important contributions were now being made by countries such as the German Federal Republic and Canada, which had earlier played a minor role, aid from the United States (by far the largest donor) was falling off and that from the United Kingdom and France, the other traditionally large donors, was rising only slowly or in some years, it actually was stagnated or declined. That the aid of the largest donor was declining at a time when it was involved in costly military operations in Southeast Asia struck, as the Vietnam war itself, a serious blow to morale. The targets set in the United Nations Development Decade seemed illusory, and the largest donor was under heavy political criticism, together with its allies.

In addition, it was being found that the rate of population growth of the developing countries was counteracting the rise in living levels, and the limitations of the world's natural resources were becoming apparent.

The situation did not improve in the following years, except that relief from excessive population growth was not estimated to be on the horizon for the 1980s and 1990s. At the time of writing a decline in economic activity is taking place in the main donor countries and on a world scale, and the opportunity has been lost to utilize the great burst of prosperity of the 1960s to bring the aid effort up to the target level.

Further, some of the governments of the developing countries were not showing the same sympathy to the development needs of the less privileged sections of their populations that they were expecting the more advanced countries to show toward the less advanced. The impact of economic cooperation, it seemed, did not reach the masses but rather enriched the smaller more privileged groups.

On the side of the recipient countries, the position seemed quite different. The rich countries were becoming ever richer, and the gap between the developed and the developing countries was growing. Moreover, there seemed to be a lack of willingness to tackle major problems such as the terms of trade and the need for a

TABLE 12.1

Official Development Assistance Net in Relation to Gross National Product, 1963-73

(percentages)

Countries	1963	1964	1965	1966	1967	1968	1969	1970	1971	1972	1973
Australia	0.51	0.48	0.53	0.53	0.60	0.57	0.56	0.59	0.53	0.59	0.44
Austria	0.05	0.08	0.11	0.12	0.14	0.14	0.11	0.07	0.07	0.09	0.14
Belgium	0.57	0.46	0.60	0.42	0.45	0.42	0.50	0.46	0.50	0.55	0.51
Canada	0.15	0.17	0.19	0.33	0.32	0.26	0.33	0.42	0.42	0.47	0.43
Denmark	0.11	0.11	0.13	0.19	0.21	0.23	0.38	0.38	0.43	0.45	0.47
France	0.98	0.90	0.76	0.69	0.71	0.67	0.67	0.66	0.66	0.67	0.58
Germany	0.41	0.44	0.40	0.34	0.41	0.41	0.38	0.32	0.34	0.31	0.32
Italy	0.14	0.09	0.10	0.12	0.22	0.19	0.16	0.16	0.18	0.09	0.14
Japan	0.20	0.14	0.27	0.28	0.32	0.25	0.26	0.23	0.23	0.21	0.25
Netherlands	0.26	0.29	0.36	0.45	0.49	0.49	0.50	0.61	0.58	0.67	0.54
New Zealand	--	--	--	0.21	0.21	0.21	0.22	0.23	0.23	0.25	0.24
Norway	0.17	0.15	0.16	0.18	0.17	0.29	0.30	0.32	0.33	0.43	0.46
Portugal	1.46	1.48	0.59	0.54	0.54	0.54	1.29	0.67	1.42	1.79	0.59
Sweden	0.14	0.18	0.19	0.25	0.25	0.28	0.43	0.38	0.44	0.48	0.56
Switzerland	0.05	0.07	0.09	0.09	0.08	0.14	0.16	0.15	0.12	0.21	0.16
United Kingdom	0.48	0.53	0.47	0.45	0.44	0.40	0.39	0.37	0.41	0.39	0.35
United States	0.59	0.56	0.49	0.44	0.43	0.37	0.33	0.31	0.32	0.29	0.23
Total DAC countries	0.51	0.48	0.44	0.41	0.42	0.37	0.36	0.34	0.35	0.34	0.30

Source: "1974 Review of Development Cooperation" (Paris, OECD), p. 202.

considerable transfer of purchasing power, on which escape routes
from poverty for large sections of the world's population depended.
A number of left-wing economic writers produced articles and books
denouncing current aid practices as new forms of imperialism,
which further worsened the atmosphere.

This disillusionment extended to a questioning of the basic concepts underlying economic and social cooperation programs, which
had hitherto been principally two. The first was based on the growing gap in economic and social living levels. It was postulated that
by transferring capital and technology from the developed countries,
the newly developing nations could obtain the same kind of economic
progress the advanced countries had achieved. The second conception overlapped the first in that it aimed at the economic and social
development of the "third world" but it considered that the limited
economic prospects and the rapid population growth of most of the
developing countries meant that the gap would continue to grow. The
emphasis accordingly had to be placed less upon unattainable equality
of economic progress and more upon a world "social contract," which
meant that no population should remain below minimum levels of living and all should develop at their maximum capacity in conditions of
equity. The first concept had the most appeal to the governments of
the developing countries. The second appeared to be a notion of
charity or tutelage, and did not solve problems of dependency, but
might even prolong them.

The new criticism of both of these concepts, which began to
gain momentum, took the following lines. As regards the first conception of aid, it was a fundamental error to suppose that the addition of inputs of capital and advanced technology, the absence of
which is the main economic distinction between the rich and the poor
countries, could lift the poor countries into faster levels of development. Such measures could raise their per-capita income, though
the impact would only be little since the present volume of aid was
small, but they did not necessarily contribute to changing the structure and motivations of their societies, which are the real cause of
development. Sometimes aid in the form of capital and technology
would in fact encourage and support existing social rigidities. As
regards the second conception--that is, of progress toward a "world
welfare state"--the state of dissension in the world on major political issues threatening world peace did not offer much promise of
progress in the economic and social field.

Some of the same critics also felt that the political organization of a number of the developing countries was not a viable one.
They stated that although these have mixed economies (that is,
neither fully state controlled nor left largely to private enterprise),
based on the pattern of the welfare states of Western Europe, they

were often led by autocratic governments. The mixed economies offered the disadvantages of both of the types of economy they attempted
to mix, in that they had neither the dynamism of private enterprise
nor were they genuinely socialist, except in their heavy bureaucrati-
zation. Little was done to correct the great inequalities of wealth
and income that prevailed, since the methods of income redistribu-
tion used in Europe, mainly through the fiscal system, could not produce the necessary results in less developed societies. A total restructuring of investment and public expenditure, and perhaps of
society as a whole, was required to create the more equal income
distribution needed to raise the levels of living, which was the real
purpose of development.

The latter criticism undoubtedly has much economic truth attached to it in the sense that development has long been recognized
to involve structural changes, economic and social, in society as
well as growth, though there are examples of countries where structures have evolved pari passu with the rise in their per-capita income,
and which have been assisted in this by having received aid. The
underlying question, however, is whether it is possible (even if it
were politically justifiable not to respect the sovereign rights of
states to fix their own policy) to determine from outside what should
be the nature of each country's pace of political and economic reform
so as to gear aid to this purpose.

One approach to the difficulty would seem to be to have some
agreement on certain minimum social standards to which aid projects
should conform. Although it would be interventionist for an aid agency
to say "we won't help you unless you change your mixed economy to an
unmixed one," or the other way around, it could well say that one of
its criteria is to assist projects that have high rates of benefit per
head of population and to avoid those with low rates. It has hitherto
been rare when aid projects are being appraised for the question to
be posed of how many people, directly and indirectly, may be expected to benefit, though this practice is now being more widely
adopted.

This criterion has to be applied in a time context, since especially as concerns activities such as education, which are long-term
investments, reductions of present consumable benefits may be required to produce future gains. This is particularly true of expenditures on higher education, related to development, which though it
involves many years of earnings foregone and also only covers a
small section of the population brings major indirect benefits to the
population as a whole. If it can become standard practice for this and
similar social questions to be asked and answered in proposals for
granting assistance under cooperative programs and in subsequent
evaluation reports, the door will be opened to the use of social criteria
by donors without direct political interference.

The current trend is strongly against aid agencies employing interventionist policies (though there have been certain unfortunate individual cases). Indeed, the problem is rather that it is rare for cooperation for development to be an important political issue in most of the developed countries, or for aid needs to be adequately publicized. Too often the problem seems to be one of facing huge needs and uncontrollable population growth. *

As the 1970s have progressed, a new crisis has been engendered by the energy problem and the economic recession. This has led to increased criticism of the insufficiency of cooperative programs and, more particularly, to pressure to find solutions to the fundamental economic constraints arising from inequalities in physical resource endowment, on the one hand, and in the terms of trade on the other. These pressures have resulted in the demand for the establishment of a New Economic Order, as proclaimed in the United Nations Resolution quoted in Chapter 1.

Whether it will be possible to take practical steps toward a New Economic Order will become clearer as negotiations proceed on individual issues such as the prices of oil and raw materials, and the volume and direction of aid itself. If a new development model aimed at putting world economic relations on a more equitable basis is adopted, the external inputs will aim at the evolution of patterns of economic and social progress that reduce economic, social, political, and cultural dependency, both inside and outside frontiers, while also promoting world trade on equitable terms. This is no easy formula to incorporate in cooperation legislation or for administrations to apply, but education as a sector of cooperation clearly would have a valuable role to play in reducing inequalities in productivity and utilization of human resources.

---

*An example, affecting educational cooperation, is that, in assessing the prospects of universal primary education being attained on a world scale, emphasis is placed on current high growth rates of the school-age population, without enough attention to the estimated decline of the rate of population growth foreseen by the late 1980s onwards. A valuable step would be for more analysis and demonstration to be made in the developed countries of worldwide educational needs and possibilities of meeting them in order to influence the volume of cooperation funds. An overhaul is needed of educational statistics, which are usually three or four years out of date before they are published in the Unesco Statistical Yearbook, and a more adequate statistical basis than the present one ought to be found for analyzing and assessing global needs for educational cooperation.

As regards the educational sector, the most severe type of criticism that arose in the late 1960s and early 1970s was a questioning of the validity of external assistance for educational development. Doubt was cast by some critics on the whole process because of inherited and inherent difficulties of sharing educational resources beyond national frontiers and because of the malfunctionings for development purposes of the educational systems of the developing countries.

In his book From Aid to Recolonization,[1] Tibor Mende wrote in regard to educational cooperation, "By the very nature of cultural decolonization, foreign aid has virtually nothing positive to offer in this domain." The argument is clearly at variance with the fact that educational and cultural cooperation with their ex-colonial powers has continued to be sought and obtained by governments of developing countries, which have seen it as now something they can use on their own terms to their advantage. This alternative was preferred to withdrawing into a narrow nationalism. Tibor Mende is aware of this but considers the governments did not take sufficiently into account their people's real needs. He describes some of the participants in cooperation programs as "mercenaries of the status quo."

One of the clues to Tibor Mende's attitude may perhaps be found in his statement that "Innumerable children in Asia and Africa continue to study the geography, history, and literature of their former colonizing countries. They continue to be formed by a foreign culture and to leave their schools ignorant of the real problems of their own country."[2]

The question whether there are innumerable children in Asia and Africa being educated today in this way is best answered by objective studies of the actual curricula and syllabuses of Asia and Africa. The position as regards Asia can be seen from a three-volume study made in 1970, entitled Asian Study on Curriculum: Comparative Study of Curriculum Development at the Stage of Elementary Education in Asian Countries, undertaken by the Japanese National Institute for Educational Research in conjunction with Unesco and participants from all the Asian countries. This study shows that not only have their school curricula been changed by Asian countries since independence but also substantial changes arising from economic and social reasons have been introduced over recent years. The report states, in fact, that the main curricula changes have risen from economic and social rather than educational initiatives.

In the case of Africa, an account of the Africanization of the content of education around 1970 is contained in an article by Michael Kelly.[3] This study shows that substantial progress had been made by 1970 in the English-speaking African countries, but less in the French speaking. The reason ascribed for the relatively slower progress in the French-speaking countries was not a lack of intent (progress was intended, as was frequently expressed in the various Conferences of Ministers of Education of the francophone countries and by the French technical cooperation authorities themselves), but rather the greater variety of vernacular and local languages not adapted to modern thought and the use of more technical terms. Considerable time is needed if the French language is to be replaced or supplemented as the main bridge with the outside world, for the purpose of economic, social, and cultural progress. Charges that African children are taught about "our ancestors the Gauls" are today, fortunately, more legendary than real.

At the same time there is still the need for much more progress to be made in relating education to national and local conditions of life and work and for cooperation programs to be kept under constant review to prevent the continuance of educational dependencies of all kinds.

No educational system can change its direction quickly, and on attaining independence more developing countries had the alternative of envisaging a large hiatus in their educational growth or continuing on the existing lines. This, in turn, meant support from the previous colonial powers with whom, in the matter of language and type of education, they were most heavily linked. Further, as part of the continuing interest of the colonial power (whether for reasons of friendship and cooperation, for "conscience," or for commercial reasons), assistance to educational development remained available.

After an initial period of filling gaps in educational systems as they were, cooperation extended increasingly into assistance in teacher training and curriculum development, vocational training to meet occupational needs, science teaching, and educational planning.

Certainly it is a historical fact that, after independence, educational dependencies continued for many years, operating through the school curriculum, the examination system, and the supply of foreign teachers. This was also true of the universities.

The extent to which this was due to the cooperation agencies and educators of the ex-colonial powers wishing to maintain dependencies in educational matters or to the leading groups in the emergent countries having a bias toward the type of education they had themselves attained, or to the pace of educational expansion moving so fast that there was no time to pause to make changes, or to the general inertia to change from which all educational systems tend to suffer is difficult to determine.

The slowness of the process of disengagement has led to criticism from time to time from the trade unions. An example is the case of Morocco, where there are at present 6,040 French teachers serving under the cooperation agreement, of whom 350 are volunteers under the French system of service for development being an alternative to military service. The national union of teachers organized in 1973 a meeting on "decooperation," which asked, as they said, not for the hasty withdrawal (fuite) of the cooperating teachers but for a planned and orderly withdrawal. This has already taken place in Morocco in the general field of technical assistance, where French personnel have been reduced from about 20,000 provided in 1957 under the first cooperation agreement to about 400 at present. This illustrates the phenomenon, found also in the African states south of the Sahara, that governments faced with shortages of qualified personnel usually prefer that the supplementation from abroad takes place in the education system rather than elsewhere in the economy.

The present number of French teachers in Morocco is little different from at the time of Independence, and an actual increase to 7,000 is envisaged for the near future to respond to the expansion of the demand for education. There are 750 French teachers at present working on teacher training, and their number will be increased to enable the first cycle of the second level of education to become entirely Moroccan. Thirteen regional pedagogic centers are being established for this purpose. These measures are expected to bring about in two years time the first set of replacements and return flow of French teachers at that level.

The Commission on International Development set up by the World Bank Group under the chairmanship of Lester Pearson,[4] stated in their report, Partners in Development,

> On the whole, however, it must be said that aid from abroad has served mainly to buttress classical methods, applied by unquestioning teachers, both local and foreign, trained in a mold cast over a hundred years ago. These traditional methods, with heavy emphasis on the humanities, do not adequately meet today's needs in the developing world. Attempts to establish the kind of dialogue that could lead to a new education conceived by and for developing countries have been made, especially in the field of teacher training, but are still too rare. Some aid has been channeled in the direction of new media, particularly educational television, but such experiments have been too timid, or based on inadequate research, experimentation, and evaluation. Aid to education should concentrate on the adaptation of the organization and content of educational

systems in low-income countries to their economic needs and social conditions.

In the same vein, Edwin Martin, the DAC Chairman, writing
in the 1971 Review of assistance to the developing countries, stated,

> There is so much wrong with education that it is
> hard to know where to start. Partly because of
> scarcity of resources, partly based on the mis-
> guided notion that reproduction of our educa-
> tional system would reproduce our standard of
> living, and partly because many countries were
> largely dependent on donors for teachers and
> other educational personnel who had nothing else
> to offer but the present system, the present
> situation is most unsatisfactory despite the
> great expansion of educational systems in the
> sixties.

George C. Lodge, the American statesman, wrote in Foreign
Affairs, July 1969, "While our assistance may have caused a marginal improvement in the standard of life of some, it has also, equally importantly, provided a source of patronage and political strength
for the status quo."[5]

An example of how educational cooperation may foster the per-
petuation of rigidities in educational systems that might have re-
solved themselves by internal pressures if there had been no assistance from outside, is Tunisia, where there is a great shortage of
medical and other professional personnel in the rural areas, though
there is no lack in urban areas of such national personnel, who prefer not to move to the countryside.

Many of the professional posts that are vital to rural life and
thereby to the country's major sector of production are filled by cooperation personnel from France and the Eastern European countries.
Thus, unconsciously, since this is not the intention, the pressure on
the government to secure a more equitable long-term distribution of
the country's human resources for development purposes is relieved
by external aid. The rigidities persist.

Since many donor countries are involved in this case, it is not
possible to use aid resources as an instrument to ameliorate these
conditions. A schedule is in operation for the replacement of the aid
personnel over time, but each case is likely to be difficult to implement without damage so long as no general solution has been found to
the reluctance of national personnel to work in the rural areas.

In considering these criticisms it is easier to recognize their general validity, especially those of the Pearson Commission and Mr. Edward Martin at the time they were made, and to note that there has been some improvement since, than it is to know how cooperation agencies should proceed to help or stimulate fundamental educational reform. The first consideration is that it is for the developing countries themselves to determine whether or not they want fundamental educational reform, as this is a matter of high-level domestic policy. Few developing countries have taken this option. The second requirement is knowledge of or procedures to find out the right reforms to recommend or aid. It is one thing to send out technicians and build universities in countries with systems like one's own. It is quite another matter to know what is the best type of change to try to bring about and how best to cooperate in educational reform.

The charge that elitist education rather than popular education has been supported by cooperation agencies has to be seen in the light of the fact that the educational priority in the 1960s was in terms of development needs at the higher and secondary level, as was set out for instance in the Unesco Conferences of Ministers of Education and the Overall Planning Authorities for Africa. Moreover the very pace of expansion required from the existing system helped the organizational status quo and inefficiencies of structure and curricula to persist.

Commenting on the complexities of aiding educational reform in a publication of the IIEP, H. W. R. Hawes wrote in 1971,[6]

> In fact, in the hardest and cruellest analysis it has to be admitted that, despite the new syllabuses, the new books, the curriculum conferences, the curriculum centres, the international programmes, relatively little impact is actually being made on the primary school curriculum. Nor is there any reason to believe that rapid changes are likely to occur in the foreseeable future unless a totally new approach to curriculum planning is achieved.
>
> History bears out these lessons. If we take, as an example, the last fifty years in English-speaking Africa, we encounter a wealth of liberal approaches: the call for more relevant and more rural curricula in the reports of the Phelps Stokes Commissions in the early 1920's, and the splendid concise statement of their policy of "adaptation" in the 1925 Colonial Office Memorandum, "Education in Tropical Africa";

a plea by the great biologist, Sir Julian Huxley,
in 1931, for a complete reorientation of the
primary school curricula in East Africa ("which
still approximate to mere collections of subjects") round a "central organic core", the
study of man and his relationship to his rural
environment; . . . Nyerere's brilliant pamph-
let, "Education for Self-Reliance." Throughout
all these documents the demands for reform, always slightly conflicting, are present--more
relevant curricula, more rural curricula, more
stimulating teaching; and every report calls for
a revolution which has somehow not yet taken
place.

The failures then and the failures now are
due to the same factors: the difference in objectives between those who design curricula
and those for whom they are designed, the lack
of money and the lack of manpower to carry out
the changes planned, and finally, a basic underestimation of the difficulties and complexities
involved in achieving effective curriculum change.

The rate of progress in educational change was also influenced
in the 1960s (though this is less so today) by the fact that the leading
groups and the educational establishments in the newly independent
countries in Africa turned naturally to European sources for their
world of intellectual discourse. Further, certain countries became
ruled at independence or within a few years by elitist groups who did
little to produce the social change aspired to as part of independence.

The above types of criticism led to the argument that since the
educational systems of the developing countries were inefficient and
dysfunctional, it was useless to aid them. It is, however, difficult
to maintain that assistance should only be given to efficient educational systems. It can be argued that the more inefficient education
is in the developing countries, the more they need assistance to help
them to reorganize their systems and build up patterns suited to their
own conditions.

On this point Jean-Marie Domenach in "Our Moral Involvement
in Development," published by the United Nations as an Executive
Briefing Paper, writes, "All this suggests that whereas development
demands a sustained effort the reasons for giving aid are not sufficiently thought out. Does a father question his obligations towards
his son, when the son gets bad marks at school? . . . Soon, the ac-
cused turns into an accuser and criticizes the underdeveloped country

and former colony for not being able to make proper use of its independence."[7] The simile of father and son is likely to be rightly regarded as one of tutelage, and to be unacceptable to governments of developing countries, but the basic point is sound.

In Gunnar Myrdal's book The Challenge of World Poverty: A World Anti-Poverty Programme in Outline,[8] he writes,

> But undoubtedly, foreign assistance specifically
> aimed at education reforms would make it pos-
> sible for the aid giving organisations or coun-
> tries to exert pressure on underdeveloped coun-
> tries to proceed more courageously along cer-
> tain strategic lines in the educational field--
> provided aid-givers were enlightened enough to
> want to use such pressure in the right direction.

This statement goes rather far, since although Myrdal is strongly against political pressure in general, which he considers undesirable colonialistic intervention, he favors "courageous" pressures, provided they are in the right direction and produced by "enlightened" aid-givers.

An example of a similar approach is shown in a statement ascribed to Jan P. Pronk, Dutch Minister for Development Cooperation.[9]

> . . . if Indonesia did not fulfill three conditions,
> the Dutch Government--"as a socialist govern-
> ment"--would reduce or even stop its aid to
> Indonesia. The three conditions were that the
> Indonesians follow a less capitalistic strategy
> of development; that they help groups such as
> small farmers and city slum dwellers; and that
> there should be a relation between socio-
> economic and political development.
> . . . Pronk made it clear that he shared
> the students' concern about the motives of aid
> givers and the uses made of it by the Indo-
> nesian Government. He said that he had come
> to Indonesia with two doubts--he was not sure
> whether the technocrats (who, he considered,
> were promoting a responsible policy) were given
> the opportunity to carry out that policy; and he
> was not sure whether the Government could
> penetrate the layers of bureaucracy to imple-
> ment its plans for the rural areas. He admitted

that at the end of his visit he still had those
doubts.

Pronk also said that the Dutch Government
considered that potential aid recipients fall into
three categories: those countries where structural change is occurring (he cited Tanzania and
North Vietnam); secondly, those where a "process of change" is going on (Indonesia included);
and thirdly, countries like post-Allende Chile
where the situation is "static." Pronk said that
his government would give aid to countries falling into the first two categories but not to those
in the third.

A different statement of a cooperation policy related specifically to education and one less politically based is that by the Swedish
International Development Authority (SIDA):[10]

In drawing up its educational policy SIDA has
taken note particularly of the following priorities assigned by the UN for the Second Development Decade. . . . In the formulation of aid
agreements and commitments the priorities of
the recipient countries are given first place.
When scope exists for a broader Swedish participation in planning and choice of project,
SIDA should be guided by the following points
of view.

SIDA's contributions in the programme
countries should be based on an analysis of the
educational sector of each country and should
have the form of support for one or more subsectors, possibly for the entire educational
sector. The aim of education should be, on
the one hand, to attain a more even distribution of knowledge, proficiencies and resources
and to promote economic growth, on the other
to enable people to gain a livelihood and to have
an influence on their living conditions. Among
the goals of the educational system, SIDA places
especial importance on the following: to provide
vocational knowledge; to provide the foundations
for communication and cooperation; to contribute to the achievement of equality; and to
permit social changes.

SIDA recommends that education should be
so planned that each educational system is related to the physical, economic, social, cultural, and political structure of the community.
In most developing countries educational planning should be based on the fact that, for a long
period to come, agriculture will offer the majority of employment opportunities. In the present
situation priority should be given to the following subsectors: non-formal education, elementary education, vocational training and supplementary vocational training, including agricultural training and training of teachers and administrators within these fields. The second
priority will then be secondary education, especially in science, technology and agriculture,
training of secondary school teachers and administrators. The third priority will be tertiary education.

The two instances given, the Netherlands and Sweden, are of
relatively small countries outside of major power politics. Do these
instances also reflect the practices of the larger donors? Although
education itself is a politically influenced sector of national life,
does educational cooperation have also to be of a political nature,
or can it be neutral and purely technical?

Some indications of its independence or otherwise from politics can be obtained from examining its distribution. While there
are clear geographical flows between ex-colonial powers and the ex-
colonies, and between countries of a common language and culture,
there is little evidence of the existence of mobile resources of educational aid that are switched about in the service of Big Power
strategies. This would seem to apply also to the educational cooperation component of U.S. foreign assistance. The figures of its geographical distribution show four times as many U.S. educational personnel at a recent date in countries without any strategic significance
than in those where the United States traditionally has had strong
political interests, both strategic and commercial. *

---

*The U.S. Foreign Assistance Act of 1973 says in part, "bi-
lateral development assistance should give the highest priority to
undertakings submitted by host governments which directly improve
the lives of the poorest of their people and their capacity to participate in the development of their countries."

The educational aid of the other large donors also seems relatively free in its distribution of bias for strategic purposes, though
in the special case of France and the United Kingdom, it is not easy
to distinguish the various factors involved since the language and
cultural links are more intense than in the case of the other donors.

If one looks at trading as distinct from strategic interests,
little educational cooperation is specifically linked to commerce,
except that of the Soviet and Eastern European countries, which is
part of commercial treaties. There are, however, indirect links,
through for instance transnational business corportations or the
textbook industry.

There also arise from time to time specific examples where
educational cooperation has been used as a component in commercial bargaining, for example, as shown in the case of Peru in Chapter 10. It arises also from time to time that educational cooperation
figures in overall political agreements between countries. There
are cases where, on a change of regime as in the case of Chile, educational cooperation becomes discontinued as part of a cessation of
overall cooperation. Nevertheless these cases are not typical of the
general run of educational cooperation.

The United Kingdom has strong commercial interests in South
Asia, yet the number of educational personnel from the United Kingdom giving assistance there is relatively small and exceeded by that
of the Federal Republic of Germany as well as the United States.
Similarly, U.S. commercial relations are much closer with Latin
America than with Africa, yet educational aid goes predominantly to
Africa. The picture as regards trainees is a similar one, as is also
the case with the supply of teachers, except in higher education,
where there is a counterbalancing effect of the larger number of educational institutions in Asia and Latin America than in Africa.

This may or may not be a matter of virtue. It simply may be
that education takes too long to operate as an ideological or political
instrument in terms of the pace of modern change. It might also be
in the British case that their system of education is, in any case,
firmly entrenched in Asia. Motivation is not a fruitful field of discussion, since the ultimate test is whether the results serve to improve education and development with due regard to other aspects of
living levels.

Another possible test would be to look at the supply of educational administrators and educational advisers, since they have more
opportunity of controling policy than teachers or expert personnel
working on particular subjects. Here again, little relation can be
found. In the case of Asia, the number of advisers in Southern Asia
for the United States was more than twice as many as in the Far East,
where the main strategic interest has been, while the bulk were in
African countries.

Equally, the growth of the number of students in third countries (that is, not the donor or the recipient country, though financed
by the donor) has been growing, which is also a sign of disinterested-
ness from the political standpoint.

It could, of course, be maintained that although the distribution
does not reflect political factors, the actual activities and content of
the advice or teaching given does. It is, however, difficult to find
any but sporadic evidence of this, though undoubtedly, the presence
of systems of education imported from other countries does have a
number of indirect effects (some good, some bad) on the policies and
cultures of the developing countries. The direct effect can be seen
if we try to answer the question, what happened to the estimated $20
to $25 billion worth of educational assistance of the last 20 to 25 years?

At the level of higher education there are in the developing countries several hundred universities, institutes of technology, research
and training centers, and so on that owed their existence at the time
they were created to support from external sources. Without such
support their establishment would have been delayed, and the supply
of higher-level cadres for political, public administrative, and economic activities, and for the process of building new nations would
have been held up. At the level of study abroad, as many as a million people over the period had the valuable opportunity to compare
traditions, experience, and knowledge in their country with others.

At the first level of education--although, except in the earlier
period, there was little direct aid--funds were released to help the
primary school through assistance given at the other levels. Large
numbers of children received an education, however, imperfect, as
a result of educational assistance. At the second and technical levels,
which were taken as the priorities for the 1960s, enrollments were
increased, schools built and equipped, and curricula changed in the
direction of development objectives as a result of educational aid.

In terms of educational objectives and results, the aid scene
is thus a very varied picture, which is not surprising since the views
both of governments and of educators are themselves varied. If, for
instance, some assistance favored higher education and second-level
education to the detriment of popular education, some also did the
opposite. Belgian policy of giving priority to universal primary education, for instance, has helped to achieve the relatively high first-
level enrollment ratios in Zaire and Rwanda, which are well above
those of comparable countries.

Similarly, the impact has been varied in terms of volume.
While the amount of educational cooperation as a whole has been
running at up to 17 percent of the public expenditure on education of
the developing countries as a whole, the differences between countries are very large. In some, the educational aid contribution was

costed at 40 percent or more from the donor standpoint of the educational budget of the recipient country. In terms of the recipient countries' actual budget, the contribution was less, because the cost was based on the standard remuneration of expatriate teachers and experts, which was much higher than that of nationals, and because the expatriates sent home part of their pay and there was a return flow to the donor of interest and capital repayments on loans. Thus the annual sum of $2,350 million spent on educational aid is best referred to as costs of cooperation to the donor agencies rather than in terms of equivalent value to recipient countries.

Although aid programs are not necessarily responsible for the phenomenon, "brain drain" is also a loss to the developing countries, though most of it results from private study abroad or that sponsored by the student's own country.* On the other hand, a "hidden" subsidy accrues to nationals when they study abroad, in the form of their participation in the social security system and in welfare and educational services of a general character outside the direct grants given to them; further, students who stay to work abroad after finishing their studies often send remittances to their families. Nevertheless, as an ILO report remarks in connection with the problem, "Many significant losses are just in the fields of medicine and engineering in particular--where expansion on the lines we propose will make great demands. In this respect the loss of high level manpower means a diminution of a key resource for the strategy."[11]

An analysis of the flow into the United States of foreign students made in 1966 estimated the net cost to the United States of foreign students over the first part of the decade at $45 million annually.[12] However, when the value of the education absorbed by U.S. students abroad was added, the balance was reduced to $18 million. When the value of the nonreturning foreign students was added, the annual cost became a benefit to the United States of $16 million a year from the foreign student program.

The question of the motivation for aid giving is raised by some critics as a key point. Myrdal, for instance, states,

> It is my firm conviction, founded upon study
> and reflection, that only by appealing to
> peoples' moral feelings will it be possible to
> create the popular basis for increasing aid
> to underdeveloped countries as substantially

---

*Britain in 1969 for instance financed 6,250 students and trainees from abroad, but the total of foreign students in any year in the United Kingdom is 50,000.

> as is needed. To put it clearly and convincingly,
> the moral reason for aid has to be separated and
> cleansed from all the spurious reasons of na-
> tional interest that I have criticized in relation
> to United States aid policy. [13]

The more usual view is that it is the act and not the motivation
for it that counts, and among donors there are only a few, including
Myrdal's own country Sweden, that declare their motivation to be entirely humanitarian.

Some commentators believe that the role of variations of motivation is a minor one, and that the dominant force is usually the particular historical conjuncture. In a chapter on this subject in his
recent study The Politics of Foreign Aid, John White of the Institute
of Development Studies, University of Sussex, writes, [14]

> The argument of this chapter is that the actions
> of donors are determined primarily by the his-
> torical situation in which they happen to find
> themselves and that in any given situation dif-
> ferent motives will give rise to similar action.
> Motivation in other words is a minor factor,
> the analysis of which does not help us in ex-
> plaining what it is that donors do.

While this may be true at the operational level, it would seem
nevertheless that the volume and direction of aid is influenced at the
allocation level by the motivations of the public in donor countries
expressed in the governing legislation, and that for long-run solutions Myrdal is right. Worldwide development, like worldwide peace,
depends in the end on the motivations in the minds of men.

The UN resolutions on aid take common interest as a desirable
component of aid for development, and the Declaration for the Establishment of a New Economic Order uses the expression "based on
equity, sovereign equality, interdependence, common interest and
cooperation." The centrally planned socialist countries usually
make a specific point of stressing mutual interest, and this has been
done by the USSR and other Eastern European countries over the
years. It is interesting to note a recent statement on this point by
Oto Denes of the Yugoslav Federal Institute for International Cooperation in the Unesco quarterly Prospects. [15] He states, "This implies
that the developed part of the world should take a keener interest in
promoting the more rapid growth of the developing countries, since
the world market, as well as its own high production, point to the
need to do so."

He quotes with approval a statement by Edvard Kardelj, an eminent Yugoslav politician and theorist, who said in the Yugoslav Parliament in 1965,

> The true reason for the struggle to organize international aid for insufficiently developed countries, with a view to speeding up their economic growth, lies not so much in the political wisdom of governments or in human values--although moral and political factors are beginning to play a greater role in world affairs--as in the fact that the development of these countries is becoming, and will continue to become an increasingly essential condition for the further development of the productive forces in the industrialized countries. [16]

Oto Denes adds, "Finally, the cooperation and relations established by the developed countries cannot be dissociated from their foreign policy, which reflects their own structure and social system. "[17]

Certainly, appeals to interest as well as human considerations are frequently used also in the nonsocialist states. In the British House of Commons when aid legislation is discussed, it is common to hear in its defense that for every pound given to the International Development Association a larger amount returns to England in trade because of its long-standing commercial relations with previous ex-colonies, though this is not said of educational cooperation.

The centrally planned socialist economies give most of their educational assistance as part of commercial agreements or loans on easy terms, and it does not have the heavy grant component of Western aid. Within the centrally planned economies Chinese assistance, though it is also predominantly in the form of loans, is on particularly easy financial terms.

Thus, it would seem that, on the whole, the idea of common interest entering into the aid process is one that is well accepted, but much depends on the interpretation and the terms and conditions under which the factor of interest to the donor is introduced. The tying of aid is a case in point. The objection is not so much to the fact that the donor benefits as to the implications on the recipient side that contracts cannot be put out to the most economical source of supply and that rigidities and forms of long-term dependence tend to be involved.

The Development Assistance Committee has taken a stand against the tying of aid, but most if its Member States still follow this practice, though some progress has been made. The International Commission on the Development of Education also condemned it in the following terms:[18]

> The practice of tied aid should be gradually
> dropped, especially in the sense that donor
> countries should agree to their aid being used
> in other developing countries (for training in
> national or regional institutions, for equipment
> supplied by neighbouring countries, etc.). This
> is clearly a development which cannot come
> about, however, unless the countries concerned
> make a concerted stand.

The tying of aid is not a major problem for the educational sector in the sense of the restrictions on the purchase of supplies and equipment, since capital loans and grants and equipment supply are a relatively small part of educational aid. The World Bank Group is by far the largest single provider of finance, and its loans and credits are untied, as is the case with the UNDP, Unesco, and Unicef in the supply of equipment.

There is an important sense in which educational aid is tied in that the bilateral and nongovernmental donors normally send their own nationals as experts or teachers, unlike the multilateral agencies, which select from the many nationalities making up their memberships. It is, however, difficult to imagine one bilateral agency financing, as a matter of course, experts from another country, except under a multilateral system, though there have been isolated cases of this. It would seem hard to condemn bilateral donor agencies for providing, for example, professors of engineering of their own nationality to teach some specialty in a developing country and to say that they ought instead to have sent someone of another nationality even though experts often lead to exports. As long as it is recognized, as it has to be, that bilateral aid is in the nature of things and a valuable form of international cooperation, it has to be accepted that it is not unreasonable that they should send out their own teachers and experts.

In the case of the reverse movement, however, namely the provision of fellowships and grants for students from recipient countries to study abroad, the situation is different. Many donor countries are increasing the assistance they are giving to "third-country training" (that is, they provide the funds for students from developing countries to study in other developing or developed countries). There

is also an increase taking place in grants for scholarships within the
recipient country.

In the case of the supply of materials, the International Commission on the Development of Education stated, "We hope . . . that
international aid will be designed not to provide consumer goods, but
to create or develop production potential . . . not to furnish paper,
but to assist in establishing a national paper industry."[19] Obviously
this is good general economic development doctrine, but it has to be
applied realistically, and in particular immediate needs have to be
met. Paper industries cannot be designed and staffed overnight,
and, in any event, few developing countries have soft timber for
paper pulp enabling them to establish paper industries on an economic
basis. On the other hand, steps are being taken to use substitutes for
soft wood in paper production, which Unesco and education ministries
are following with interest.[20]

On this same line of criticism, the objection sometimes is
raised to the practice of the World Bank in making loans for education at rates near those of ordinary commercial loans, though it
also provides very long-term credits with substantial periods of
grace, which are in effect almost grants through the IDA. The argument in favor of giving hard loans for education to developing countries whose financial situation and balance-of-payments position may
warrant it is that it obviously is not possible to raise funds as the
World Bank does through the ordinary financial markets of the world
without paying rates of interest approaching market levels. Otherwise the funds would not be subscribed. The positive factor is the
steering of commercial funds at reasonable rates through the World
Bank into public expenditure on education as a sector, the link with
the country's development plan, and technical assistance to implement it, which the Bank operations, which are conducted in cooperation with Unesco, provide as part of the loan. The more negative
factor is that while the proportion of grants to loans has been increasing in bilateral cooperation, multilateral assistance shows the opposite trend due to lack of resources contributed by governments for
soft IDA credits. The position as of 1974 was that 60 percent of the
educational assistance from the World Bank Group consisted of hard
IBRD loans and 40 percent of soft IDA credits.

Moreover there is a problem of the fact that hard loans create
debts that mount over the years; and although the loans to education
have not yet reached a level to be a substantial burden to the developing countries, the situation has to be watched, since the loans are
repaid on interest provided from taxation and not from profits, as in
the case of commercial projects. The Pearson Report, Partners in
Development, suggested the subsidization of interest rates on some
of the lending by the World Bank from interest payments due to be

made by developing countries on loans given by bilateral donors and the extension of the practice, already in operation to some degree, of blending loans and long-term credits in a suitable mixture as part of a system of avoiding too much debt creation.

In today's world, such practical expedients as these must probably substitute for Myrdal's pure humanitarianism. The truth on this difficult matter is perhaps best expressed in the UN publication Our Moral Involvement in Development, in which Jean-Marie Domenach states, "Morality does not consist in eliminating base feelings and replacing them by lofty ones because the two kinds are too closely intermingled; it consists in harnessing the greatest possible amount of human resources for the service of the good."[21]

It is not very profitable, therefore, for the purpose of improving the educational aid process, to make overgeneralized criticisms, and it is more useful to deal with actual cases and with establishing satisfactory criteria for selecting, preparing, and operating programs and projects.

The rawer kind of political criticism and charges of neoimperialism, which are current in some of the literature, are unlikely to yield valuable results. They tend to be unconstructive as regards possible alternatives to the present system. Meantime children await education. The requirement is that aid should be redeployed rather than destroyed. For this purpose good will is needed on both sides of the cooperation process.

Educational cooperation is a subject on which there is little published literature in the form of case studies and progress reports available to the ordinary reader, though there is massive documentation, usually unorganized and forgotten, in the official files of the departments concerned. Few departments at either end of the cooperation network have memory systems that prevent them from repeating past errors or "meteorological" offices that warn them in time of changes in the educational weather. This, combined with the rate of turnover of staff, means they are constantly improvising. This can have its advantages if the administrative machine is a flexible one. Too often, however, it is not, and improvisation means, "Do what you did last time."

Criticism of educational cooperation is, moreover, bound to be somewhat haphazard since no one person or agency can be an insider to the mass of individual transactions between the great plurality of donors and recipients that makes up the annual $2,350 million flow of educational resources across frontiers. The more knowledgeable types of fundamental criticism come from heads of major agencies and delegations which are partners in the educational development process. This, as shown above, has been considerable.

There has not been, however, a comparable amount of criticism at the middle professional or working level in the departments concerned at both ends of the cooperation network, nor has fundamental criticism of the present system been expressed by a majority of delegations. The fact that educational cooperation continues to grow, largely unchanged, indicates that in the view of a "silent majority" it fulfills, even with its deficiencies, a real need with some degree of satisfaction to both ends of the cooperation process.

This satisfaction may be the result of complacency and a sign of failure to respond to new needs. Director General M'Bow takes this position when he states in his report on the activities of Unesco 1974, quoted in Chapter 3, that "The 'assistance' provided by the Organisation's experts and consultants seems too often ruled by its own dynamics, its own ideology, and to represent a conception of cooperation which is now outdated." He has set up working parties to study the situation and make recommendations, but the results are not yet available at the time of this writing. These candid criticisms by Unesco's present Director General and his predecessor are not unique to Unesco but reflect difficulties experienced by other agencies--difficulties that are seemingly endemic to the aid process as at present carried out.

Summarizing, it can be said that there is little evidence today of educational assistance being used directly as an instrument of power politics, even when the total aid policy of the donor is so oriented, though it has been an arm of cultural imperialism in many cases in the past. The recipient countries are increasingly effective in protecting themselves from undesirable cultural adulteration, while welcoming the opening of wider doors to the world educational community.

There are, however, indirect effects of educational cooperation that may be harmful in prolonging rigidities of structure, reducing self-reliance, and delaying reform. Both parties to the cooperation have to watch this aspect carefully.

There are also indirect effects that benefit the commerce and culture of the donor. Under the mutual-benefit concept of aid, followed by both socialist and nonsocialist donor countries, this is not to be discouraged except where the bargain in unjustly tilted to the interests of the stronger country.

Aid from international organizations is preferable in such cases, and the proportion of total educational aid given through such channels should be increased. The plurality of donors and the possibility of choosing the most equitable terms also assists recipient countries to avoid unjust cooperation agreements.

The charge that educational cooperation has benefited the elite rather than the masses is true, though it is also true that this was the form the demand for aid took from most of the developing countries engaged on the initial stages of nation-building and replacing the qualified manpower of the colonial powers. The tide, however, is now turning to rural development and basic education, and major donors like the United States, the World Bank, and the United Kingdom, for example, have adopted specific policy declarations aimed at funneling educational aid by preference toward the less privileged populations.

The large amount of self-criticism taking place within the educational aid process at the organizational and directive levels should sooner or later bring results in more sensitive choice of projects, greater efficiency in operations and their conduct in a true sense of cooperation, and the avoidance of tutelage.

More difficult than the solution of organizational and diplomatic problems is the question of substance. How is it possible for educational cooperation to be more fruitful for educational development? How is it that despite the criticisms and demand for change, the volume of assistance grows and educators at both ends of the network combine to continue largely as before?

The main reason is that education has been itself resistant to change, and educational cooperation cannot move much faster than the policies of the recipient countries themselves, the pace of which has been in fact slow, though it is now increasing. There are clearly two forces at work: a dynamic that makes education one of the most popular fields of cooperation and another that makes it resistant to change.

It follows that assistance, if it is to be helpful, has to have a large element devoted to the existing systems, but also a growing one devoted to increasing the countries' capacity to work out for themselves programs of educational change.

While agencies at the donor end of the cooperation network cannot intervene in national educational policy, they can legitimately influence educational development by making available certain types of aid rather than others, and by engaging in an intensified critical dialogue with the developing countries as between equal partners, using especially the findings of the international studies of new norms, possibilities, and prospects of educational development.

This would mean the adoption of a number of new approaches at both the donor and recipient end of the network. The next chapter, on reform, innovation, and redeployment discusses these matters in more detail.

NOTES

1. Tibor Mende, From Aid to Recolonization (Paris: Seuil, 1972), p. 130.

2. Ibid., p. 128.

3. "The Africanization of Syllabuses in Anglophone and Francophone Countries of West Africa," Teacher Education in New Countries 2, no. 3 (February 1971).

4. Lester Pearson, Partners in Development (New York: Praeger Publishers, 1969).

5. George C. Lodge, "U.S. Aid to Latin America: Funding Radical Change," Foreign Affairs, July 1969.

6. Planning the Primary School Curriculum in Developing Countries (Paris: Unesco/IIEP, 1972).

7. Jean-Marie Domenach, "Our Moral Involvement in Development" (New York: United Nations, 1970), p. 7.

8. Gunnar Myrdal, The Challenge of World Poverty: A World Anti-Poverty Programme in Outline (Baltimore: Penguin Books, 1970), p. 209.

9. "Attaching Socialist Strings," Far Eastern Economic Review, June 1974.

10. "Aid and Education--Policy and Programme," SIDA (Stockholm), July 1972, p. 3.

11. "Towards Full Employment" (Geneva: ILO, 1971).

12. "Education, Manpower, and Welfare Policies," Journal of Human Resources 1, no. 2 (Fall 1966).

13. Myrdal, op. cit., p. 356.

14. John White, The Politics of Foreign Aid (London: Bodley Head, 1974), p. 34.

15. Oto Denes, in Prospects 4, no. 2 (Summer 1974).

16. Ibid.

17. Ibid.

18. Unesco, Learning to Be (London: Unesco-Harrap, 1972), p. 255.

19. Ibid., p. 260.

20. See Guide for Planning Pulp and Paper Enterprises (Rome: FAO, 1973).

21. Domenach, op. cit.

13

REDEPLOYMENT, REFORM, AND INNOVATION

At the recipient end of the cooperation network, change in the deployment of educational resources to be used among the different types and levels of education is an autonomous process under the control of each individual country. At the donor end it is dependent on the requests received from the range of countries with which it cooperates. A donor agency can always decide to specialize in a certain type of aid (for example, higher education, or science teaching), but obviously its impact will be greater if it is in a position to offer a range of assistance varying as needs change.

To be useful in educational cooperation programs, the donor agency has to have valuable resources or techniques it can contribute; otherwise the added value is limited to the psychological aspects of cooperation. Thus effective cooperation requires keeping abreast of changes in demand and being able to meet them by changes in supply.

Demand may be effective (that is, actually leading to change) or merely potential in the sense that it is expressed but for some reason does not alter what actually takes place. The situation in educational cooperation, as in education itself, is that there is a widely expressed demand for change that remains only potential.

The reasons for this may be of the following kinds:

1. Not enough developing countries sufficiently want major changes in the present system of educational cooperation for development;

2. They want major changes but these are resisted by donor agencies;

3. Donor agencies would themselves like and respond to suggestions for major changes if the recipient countries would propose them;

    4. Both want changes, major or minor, but are hamstrung by
inability to change at the required pace owing to built-in inertias; or
    5. There are not in reality substantial alternatives to the
present system, and what is required is not fundamental change but a
major improvement in its efficiency at the planning, administrative,
technical, diplomatic, operational, and motivational levels.

    The conclusion drawn from the present study and the consulta-
tion made at both ends of the cooperation network indicate that the
main cause of lack of change, despite exhortations from many quarters, is a combination of factors 4 and 5, and this involves examining the inertias.
    First there are the legal and legislative conditions governing
cooperation programs. Earlier it was mentioned that one large
donor had at one time 68 statutory requirements to meet when dis-
pensing assistance of any level and had a staff of 700 officials to see
that the regulations were followed. The multilateral agencies also
have a complex set of guidelines and bureaucratic procedures to take
into account. Both in national and international agencies, legislation
and delegates have a habit of introducing "pet" conditions into the
cooperation process, which overload criteria and reduce flexibility.
    International agencies have, on the whole, greater flexibility
as to criteria since their activities are not covered by formal legislation, and there is no system of day-to-day interpellation by members
of a legislature. Nevertheless it often takes longer for an international agency to complete an educational cooperation transaction than
it does a bilateral agency. Bilateral cooperation is often conducted
between two countries with a similar administrative and legal apparatus and supported by a more powerful diplomatic and administrative representation than international agencies normally are able to
provide. Nevertheless, in both bilateral and multilateral systems of
cooperation, there are many built-in delays to change arising from
unduly complex regulations that have to be applied.
    Secondly, there are financial constraints on redeployment. It
is easier to finance new types of programs from new funds rather
than to have to cut back on older types of programs to finance new
ones. But the volume of new money is not large and is not dissociable
from money used to continue existing types of projects. If annual
financial additions to the volume of educational cooperation could be
earmarked for innovation, a corresponding impetus could be given to
change. Cooperation budgets are not usually drawn up in this way but
generally consist of expansions of existing expenditure lines.
    Thirdly, a further constraint that delays redeployment is the
time taken to mobilize the new skills and forms of technical backstopping required to carry out new types of cooperation programs. Thus

a switch of assistance from higher education to basic education or
nonformal education means a switch in the type of expert to be used
and requires different information and equipment and different cooperative contacts both in the donor and recipient country. This is
likely to make some personnel redundant and others overworked.

Fourthly, redeployment requires a major effort of administrative will power and a good communication system in the aid agencies,
so that both headquarters and field staff can be convinced of the need
for new programs and actually carry them out. When priorities
change, the levels of responsibility and prestige of the different
administrative divisions change, not always in a way palatable to
those involved.

Fifthly, perhaps the biggest single constraint of all is the difficulty of bringing about educational reform itself. John Stuart Mill
in his inaugural address to the University of Saint Andrew in 1864
remarked that "reform even of government and churches is not so
slow as that of schools, for there is the great preliminary difficulty
of fashioning the instruments of teaching the teacher." Gunnar
Myrdal states in the Challenge of World Poverty, "A revolution of
the education system would assume that which is often mistakenly
said to be what these countries have been going through: a social
and economic revolution."[1]

Despite these constraints on change, the demand for new approaches to the structure and functioning of the existing educational
systems of the developing countries persist. Partial reforms of
various kinds are part of the year-to-year development of education,
but if by reform is meant radical change, it is slow and occurs infrequently.

Further, since far-reaching reform has a political connotation,
there is some preference for seeking new solutions under the more
palatable heading in some quarters of "innovations." The parallel is
made with other large-scale activities, such as industry or health
services, where new ideas or inventions are worked out and then applied to increase productivity. Education has not yet been an activity
where major discoveries that raise productivity have taken place.

To see the possibilities of cooperation assistance to innovation
and the forms of redeployment of aid resources involved, it is desirable to distinguish two kinds of innovation. The first is purely of an
organizational nature. The resources of educational development
are combined in new ways (fundamental changes are made in the
structure of the system, the streaming that takes place, the balance
between the different levels, and so on), or new educational objectives may be introduced changing the behavioral patterns in both
teaching and learning. The second type involves the use of "hard"
technology in the form of new types of teaching aids, electronic

equipment, and the use of the media of television and radio. This type of "hard" technology may be accompanied by organizational changes of the first kind of innovation but not necessarily.

The first type of innovation is less easy for agencies at the donor end of the cooperation network to assist since it usually involves political options and close knowledge of the local circumstances that govern the pace and type of change. Nevertheless this type of innovation is the one that is likely to be most fruitful, and cooperation agencies can contribute by bringing to bear expertise from different countries and collecting and evaluating examples of innovatory projects, as well as by assisting with the technical aspects of the planning of reform. The comparative advantage of the donor agencies is, however, strongest in the field where at present there is the lesser prospect of a decisive contribution, namely that of "hard" technology. Few developing countries have production capacity and expertise in electronics and the new media equal to that of the developed.

This obvious comparative advantage led to considerable emphasis at one time on aid for new "hard" educational technologies to raise educational productivity and reduce costs. Donor-financed projects were set up, in particular, in Niger, El Salvador, Western Samoa, and the Ivory Coast. Much attention was given also to the possibilities of utilizing satellites to beam televised teaching programs over wide areas of language homogeneity. Generally it can be said that the enthusiasm exceeded the practical possibilities and lessened when feasibility studies and cost benefit analyses were made. The International Commission on Educational Development stated in relation to the use of satellites,

> Certain countries facing serious educational
> difficulties may be tempted to put satellites
> into orbit for widespread diffusion of educa-
> tion programmes before precise objectives
> have been clearly defined and content carefully
> prepared. Outside the enormous expense of
> such projects this would mean taking the risk--
> calculated or not--of a failure that would so
> break the budget and so shake the faith that it
> would block any other possibility for large-
> scale technological innovation. At the present
> time, considering the fact that audio-visual
> means--particularly local television and radio
> networks--have not yet been sufficiently devel-
> oped and utilised, projects of this kind may
> well appear to be incompatible with the commonly

prevailing situation in which resources are
scarce and serious, balanced, educational
plans are necessary. [2]

The National Institute of Educational Research in Tokyo, which
studies educational problems in Asia in cooperation with Unesco and
its Member States in the region, held in 1971 a workshop on instructional materials including the new media. Commenting on the evolution of audiovisual instruction in the region, the report stated,

> The development of audio-visual instruction or
> the effective utilization of instructional technol-
> ogy in any country has to pass through four dis-
> tinct states. . . . These steps are the crossing
> of psychological barriers with regard to the
> utilization of audio-visual materials on the part
> of teachers and teacher educators, visible and
> effective practice of preparation and utilization
> of inexpensive materials in the teaching-learning
> process, development and production of com-
> mercially produced materials and finally the dis-
> tinct emergence, availability and popular utiliza-
> tion of audio-visual materials, equipment and
> hardware.
>   There is a wide and easily perceptible
> divergence of production, availability and utili-
> zation of audio-visual materials in the countries
> of Asia. Countries which have advanced eco-
> nomically have a fully developed audio-visual
> technology. Hardware like projectors, TV
> sets, tape recorders are easily available and
> their purposeful utilization is increasing.
> While there are some countries where even
> the teachers have yet to be fully trained to im-
> provise their own materials and to use the in-
> expensive aids. The gaps in the status of utili-
> zation of audio-visual materials in different
> countries are appalling.

During the same workshop cautionary remarks were made by
the Indonesian participants about the problems of the distribution of
material and the upkeep of the apparatus. The fact that the materials
would be, for some countries, almost entirely imported from abroad
also causes difficulties of continuity of supply. This indicates the
limitations of the educational use of the new media in countries where

there is not already an important consumer demand. Nevertheless, in some countries such as India, there has been a considerable production of audiovisual materials; and the issue becomes more clearly an organizational one of how to incorporate the media into the teaching methods and curriculum development, with consequent retraining of the teaching force.

Generally progress has been slow because of those reasons, and it does not seem feasible to anticipate any large-scale demand in the near future within the field of "hard" technology. There will, however, always be scope for experimentation since in the long run an increasing use of the new media together with the retraining of teachers is bound to become an ever increasing influence in educational development. Further, there are problems of supply for countries where the necessary organizational and other conditions exist, as shown by experimental projects, but where resources are lacking to spread the approved methods over a much wider area of the country. This applies not only to the new media but also to teaching machines and methods of programed instruction, which though not at present or in the future offering major contributions to educational development, have their uses in favorable conditions and in certain fields of education, including language teaching.

The largest single innovatory efforts that have relied heavily on educational assistance from abroad have been the Unesco/UNDP Experimental Work Oriented Literacy Program and the Ivory Coast Educational Television Project. The latter has been supported by a considerable number of major donors, bilateral and multilateral. The former received just over $11 million from the international contribution over the period 1967-72, which was matched by just over $16 million from domestic sources.

The literacy program begun in 1967 still remains an experimental program in the sense that it has not yet been accepted as a permanent continuing part of the Unesco/UNDP Program, nor have the developing countries themselves shown signs of taking it over on a large scale. Eleven countries have so far participated in the experimental program, and a little more than one million people were enrolled, though many dropped out.

The concept behind the UNDP/Unesco literacy program was that it had been demonstrated frequently that literacy was best acquired when associated with conditions and motivations that could lead to the self-advancement of the learner in concrete economic terms. It was also clear that literacy linked to work qualifications could be an important factor in raising the productivity of the labor force in countries where illiteracy was rife.

Difficulties that arose have been those of implementation, such as problems of the adequate selection of the sites of the projects.

Other causes of concern were the size of the dropout rate, which reduced the cost-benefit ratios, the cost for each enrolled participant being $17 while that for each who completed the course was $31. If research and development costs are included, as they must be as these were handmade projects, the foregoing costs per head rise to $26 and $50, respectively. Another problem encountered was the varying degrees of commitment of governments to literacy as a national objective.

Further difficulties arose from problems of obtaining sufficiently skilled staff to run the projects, as the conception of the teaching of literacy to be used was different from that normally understood. Once staff were appointed, it was not always easy for them to break with their past experience and to adapt themselves to the new approach. Some projects had a tendency to be neither fish nor fowl in the sense that they provided neither adequate work training nor real literacy attainment. Fundamental to the whole success of such projects was the right degree of balance to be obtained between the literacy aspect and that related to orientation for employment.

Certainly much valuable experience has been obtained, new types of curricula have been developed, and many people have benefited from the program. A particularly successful project was that initiated in Iran, where the government undertook major commitments, not only to the experimental project itself but also to its wider extension in the country.

In one case the type of employment to which the teaching was oriented did not in fact call for literacy skills, and the experimental project had to be abandoned and is in the process of being redefined. In another case the government's commitment was to different approaches to illiteracy, and there was some division of intention, which caused confusion in its implementation.

At the level of the funding and administration of the experimental program as a whole, there has been some underestimation of the time required before such projects can be put into operation, since delays are often necessarily involved in the production of the necessary instructional materials, the training of teachers, and the links with the world of work to be established. Further, considerable time is required for the results of the teaching to be evaluated before the project is used as a model for duplication in other parts of the country. This led to some impatience on the part of the funding agency, which had been troubled by short-term problems of justifying the regular renewal of an experiment that was really of a longer-term nature and justified by broader concepts than those in use in many other projects that were being funded.

The cause of some of the difficulties and misunderstandings that arose was that which we saw was given prominence in the UNRISD study of assistance projects already cited, namely some lack of clarity in the original concept. It was never entirely clear whether it was an experiment or an actual program. The International Evaluation Committee, which has been appointed by the Director General of Unesco to report on the program, states in its interim report,

> Before experiments could be conducted in the application of the functional literacy method, it had to be devised and worked out in the individual projects. The preparatory EWLP documents and the operational plans had probably failed to draw a sufficiently clear distinction in this respect between innovation and experimentation, which accounts for the lengthy delays noted in the execution of almost all the projects. The fact is that in the educational sciences the purpose of experimentation is not to innovate, but merely to test innovations and measure their effectiveness. Thus innovation and experimentation are seen to be two complementary but separate processes, one based on pedagogical theory and practice, the other making use of the techniques of statistical analysis and experimental psychology.[3]

As regards the second of the large programs of innovation that have been assisted by cooperation funds, namely the Ivory Coast Television Program, this is being watched by many countries with great interest. Hopes that were widespread at one time as to large-scale use of electronics and the mass media to increase educational productivity have tended to become relegated to the more distant future, since these methods are expensive and do not economize in teachers (whose salaries make up four-fifths of educational budgets) but rather call for their retraining and even upgrading. Accordingly, a wait-and-see attitude prevails generally as regards large-scale programs. Certain programs, however, have been tried or are in progress in a limited number of countries, notably Niger, the Ivory Coast, Tunisia, El Salvador, and Western Samoa.

The Niger television project was scarcely a success owing to its high cost in relation to output. This was taken into account in the design of the nationwide program being carried out in the Ivory Coast as from 1971, after three years of preparation and considerable assistance from external sources (five donor countries, six international agencies, and one foundation). The program provides for televised education in the primary schools to become general by 1980 and embrace the whole primary school curriculum by 1985-86.

The material put out by the government reads as follows:[4]

> The introduction of educational television in the Ivory Coast is more than just the application of modern technical facilities to the teaching of children. The Ivory Coast education venture is an integrated programme based on experiments and achievements almost everywhere in the world: school broadcasts in European countries; the Italian telescuola; seven educational television channels in Japan; the pilot projects in El Salvador, Niger, and the American Samoas.

The Report of the International Commission on Educational Development comments as follows on the Ivory Coast Television Program,

> In the Ivory Coast, the introduction of television instruction in primary schools, with the accompanying necessary upgrading of teachers' qualification, increased the unit cost per student from $60 to $80 per year. But the increased efficiency expected from the revamped system aims at reducing the present expenditure (average fifteen school years) per student completing the primary cycle to eight years' expenditure. That is, cost per completed student, now 15 x $60 or $900, will drop to 8 x $80, or $640.[5]

Michel DeBeauvais writes more cautiously.[6] He states,

> . . . the introduction of this technological innovation (apart from its efficiency as a teaching tool, which the arguments for the project do nothing to prove) would be more likely to lead to an overall increase in expenditure rather than to a reduction, because: (1) the ban on repeating is not necessarily linked with the introduction of television, any more than it is with an improvement in educational efficiency. (2) Calculation of the "unit cost per certificated student" means that the total cost of all the years of education dispensed

to a whole batch of students is ascribed only to
those who finish the course, since that total includes the cost of the years spent by those who
have dropped out. The Report even goes so far
as to speak of "reducing the present expenditure
(average of fifteen school years) per student
completing the primary cycle to eight years'
expenditure."

This interpretation of an index of educational
efficiency as a concept of "the cost of wastage in
non-monetary terms" thus creates the illusion
that a saving could be made simply by putting a
ban on repeating. It would be better not to confuse the educational aspects of school wastage
with financial considerations.

Dealing only with these latter considerations,
it would seem more correct to say, according to
the data given in the Report, that in order to attain the growth target of 94 percent in enrollment
at public primary schools, and taking into account
the one-third increase in unit costs, expenditure
would increase (all other things being equal) by
150 percent, given constant prices, between 1969
and 1980.

Some other important factors to be borne in mind are, first,
that the cost of the teacher training and recycling required takes up
80 percent of the additional unit cost per pupil. It is not the television itself that accounts for the higher additional unit cost. Further,
from the government's standpoint a factor in the cost-benefit account
is the existence of the television network, which when completed will
be a unifying instrument in the country in terms of general communication and the cultural integration of the population as a whole.

A good beginning organizationally has been made in Asia with
the setting up of APEID (Asian Program for Educational Innovation
for Development) and INNOTECH and, at the world level, of the International Report Service on Innovation of the IBE, though it remains
to be seen how they will actually perform. There would seem to be
an organizational gap in that similar efforts are required in the other
regions, while at the world level a center or a branch of the IIEP may
be required to promote the interchange of expertise and support experiments. Such a center might operate as CERI does for the OECD
countries but also have access to "pump-priming" funds to assist research and development and experimentation. It should avoid duplication with other organizations and work to the maximum extent

possible through institutions in the developing countries themselves, which it could encourage and support.

An alternative favored by the International Commission for Educational Development was an international program of aid for innovation to be operated through present international institutions and programs. Little or no specific progress has been made on this recommendation, though agencies continue to seek cooperation in innovation in a world in which few countries have taken policy decisions to make substantial educational innovations.

The other type of case of assistance to stimulate and support innovation, in addition to the two large-scale programs described, has been the setting up of pilot projects in the hope that they will be imitated and extended over a wide area. Here, particularly as regards projects in rural areas, results have been poor, tending to cast doubt on the pilot project method.

In the report Attacking Rural Poverty: How Nonformal Education Can Help, prepared for the World Bank by the International Council for Educational Development, it is stated,

> Another common past practice has been to support "pilot projects" which hopefully would take root and multiply, using the country's own resources. Many of these pilots, however, have limped along and never spread, or have failed and disappeared altogether, basically because their long term viability was never seriously assessed in the first place.
>
> We suggest that it would be an instructive exercise for each agency to undertake an objective, critical review of a dozen or so of its own pilot projects launched several years ago to determine if possible the main factors that caused some to succeed--or at least to survive--and others to fail.
>
> Our own findings prompt us to caution strongly against the further proliferation of pilot projects. There will certainly be strong justification for some, but the criteria should be tightly drawn and their rationale clearly established. On the whole, however, we believe that available resources would be more usefully spent, not striking out in brand new directions of dubious viability but on imaginatively modifying, strengthening, and reorienting selected existing activities that already have a momentum, and indigenous coloration, and assurance of strong local support.[7]

The key words in the foregoing are "brand new directions of dubious viability." Most pilot projects suffer from not having been sufficiently investigated before the start in terms of their prospects of taking root and leading to their wider spread. We have already drawn attention to the findings of a survey made by the United Nations Research Institute for Social Development of the causes of failure in aid projects,[8] in which it was found that the largest proportion of mistakes were attributable to the project not having been thought out adequately at the start. Fifty-two percent of the sample of foreign experts consulted attributed major errors made to "mistakes in planning and conception." Fifty-nine percent of the national experts thought likewise.

The solution to these weaknesses often has been thought to be better briefing and training and better selection of the foreign experts involved. Basically, however, no amount of training and briefing, although it obviously can help, is a substitute for the knowledge of actual conditions the local people have and for the degree of commitment to the project that arises from its being the result of local rather than external impetus. Thus, the fundamental solution consists in the training and better briefing of the nationals of the country concerned rather than of the external aid experts. Fortunately, this is the new trend of thinking among many aid agencies, though it has yet to be implemented in terms of substantial programs.

At a less ambitious level, a number of innovations dealing with particular situations and not regarded as pilot projects have been set in motion under Unesco-operated programs or through action by bilateral and voluntary agencies. These usually have been the most successful where, as in the case of Unesco/Unicef projects and those of voluntary agencies, there is a large degree of local delegation of responsibility. Innovations of this kind, however, tend to be patchy, to depend on the personalities of particular individuals, and often not to last when they move on elsewhere from the project. The dilemma is how to mobilize the local cooperation to bring about innovation and at the same time to secure its institutionalization in order to enable it to have a considerable effect over a substantial period of time.

Cooperation programs, since they are expected to meet educational shortages, to fill occupational gaps, and also to innovate, have a particularly difficult task. The reason is that when there are shortages that do not respond to pressures of demand and supply and when education systems are not responsive to change, there are usually important socioeconomic, sociological, and cultural causes. Often cooperation agencies get involved in projects in such areas, which cannot be solved by educational means.

An example is related in the <u>Review of International Develop-</u><u>ment</u>[9] in an article by Csanad Toth. He comments on the Poder Project, a program for training rural people in Colombia, which was set up in 1967 and terminated after a short existence.

> . . . it was taken for granted that the Colombian system is flexible, robust and willing to accommodate popular participation. This view, of course, predetermined the major thrust of the project. Consequently, it was not intended to confront the Colombian system, but to confront its victims, the <u>campesinos</u>. Instead of focusing on challenging the conditions of dependency in Colombia, the project was launched against the campesinos' attitude of dependency as if this attitude alone, rather than the realities of dependency, was keeping the campesino out of the political and economic decision-making process.

He goes on to say, "Such training programs as this, tinkering with the attitudes of others, are exemplary of the ethnocentric and superior posture many of us in industrialized countries have and continue to adopt vis-a-vis the people of the Third World."

This project and the official report on it, together with Toth's comments, pointed out the importance of what is usually called the integrated (but could perhaps better be named a "coordinated") approach to rural problems. The numerous failures of attempts to spark rural development through education, which already have been discussed in other chapters, indicate that educational innovation has to be associated with the other factors, such as physical investment and shifts in the local power structure. These matters are usually outside the scope of particular assistance projects for educational innovation in rural areas. Caution is required in such ventures unless the other factors are present.

The main recent initiative to encourage innovatory action within the developing world itself has been the setting up of the Asian Program for Educational Innovation for Development.

The Unesco General Conference in 1972, following recommendations of its Conference of Asian Ministers of Education, decided to establish an APEID attached to the Unesco Regional Office for Education in Asia at Bangkok, which became operational at the beginning of 1973.

The program of APEID has as its main objective to increase each Member State's capacity to find new solutions, rather than to try to present "instant" remedies. Its institutional framework will

be a regional center for cooperation (ACEID) and associated centers
in Member States.

The functions of the regional center are (1) to provide consultative and technical services to participating cooperating associated
centers; (2) to coordinate and support pilot experiments, studies,
and programs of regional interest in the Member States, such as
those that are of direct relevance to the management of innovation;
(3) to encourage and facilitate exchange of persons and experiences
among the Member States; (4) to assemble and diffuse documentation
and information on new techniques and educational innovation; and
(5) to serve as the secretariat to the Regional Experts Committee
and to assemble data for periodic review and evaluation.

The functions of the Associated centers are (1) carrying out
problem-oriented action programs and research and development
work on new methods and techniques, in cooperation with ACEID and
other agents in Member States; (2) organizing regional or subregional
training courses and seminars to prepare key personnel in the Member
States in the development, adaptation, and use of innovative approaches
and products; (3) cooperating in the design, implementation, or evaluation of pilot experiments and innovative schemes and projects with
the regional center (ACEID) and institutions in other Member States;
and (4) facilitating dissemination and exchange of experience and information on new developments in its program area.

By mid-1974 there were 12 centers in eight Asian countries
associated with APEID. ACEID organized in 1974 a Regional Field
Operational Seminar on Educational Innovation. The 25 participants
from 16 countries visited, in teams averaging six members, 46 innovative institutions and projects and prepared short case studies
on them.

A further step in international collaboration to aid innovation
is the action taken by SEAMEO in setting up INNOTECH. In 1967
SEAMEO decided to establish a Regional Center for Educational Innovation and Technology (INNOTECH), first located in Singapore and
then in Saigon. The functions of the center are described by SEAMEO
as follows:

> The centre offers at present a three-month course
> three times a year for key educators from the re-
> gion who share with their fellow participants and
> the Centre staff the experience gained in their re-
> spective countries while at the same time acquir-
> ing the latest skills and knowledge necessary for
> educational planning, decision-making and appli-
> cation of realistic change strategies.

In the field of research and development,
INNOTECH is engaged in two of the four projects
of the SEAMEO Educational Development Pro-
grammes for the 1970s, namely: (1) Develop-
ment of Instructional Objectives by SEAMEO
Member Countries; and (2) Development of an
Effective and Economical Delivery System for
Mass Primary Education.

The International Commission on the Development of Education,
when it studied the question of innovation, fell into a duality of view.
Some members felt that it was

> . . . not necessary to create new programmes,
> centres, or special funds in order to introduce
> innovations--the importance of which we recog-
> nize and welcome--into education. Those in
> question believe that a reasonable balance must
> be reached between innovation in education and
> the tried and tested present-day educational
> models, and that this requires proposals aimed
> at reorganizing and redistributing programmes,
> centres, and existing means in a new way. . . .
> Others among us have devised a method which
> would appear to deserve attention. It would in-
> volve launching an international programme
> aimed solely at providing scientific, technical
> and financial aid for States wishing to explore
> new educational paths. . . .[10]

The Report goes on to state,

> "International Programme" should be under-
> stood to mean here an organism attached to an
> existing international institution. Its mission
> would be to mobilize funds from various sources
> for specific and limited goals, and to assist
> countries at their request for specific activities
> engaging both governmental and nongovernmen-
> tal sectors. The World Food Programme is a
> precedent demonstrating the validity of this
> type of action.

No decision has as yet been taken on this question by Unesco.

Expenditures by governments on the necessary study of such reforms and the undertaking of experimental projects is not easy to provide, and much educational reform involves some conflict with parents' views or with those parts of the educational establishments that have vested interests in the status quo.

Practically the whole of the educational budgets are taken up by teachers' salaries and the actual working of the present systems, and it is difficult to secure the allocation of resources devoted to the study and implementation of change. Here, therefore, is an area where there is a major need for assistance. This can usefully take the form of increasing the capacity of developing countries for research and development in education, with the necessary support for institution-building and staff training that may be required. A further field for cooperation is the actual funding of risk-taking ventures and experiments, which the regular budgets of the developing countries may be reluctant to finance.

Redeployment measures among cooperation agencies, therefore, should contain a bias in favor of becoming ready to assist countries to increase their capacity for education change. The setting up at the IBE of the International Reporting Service on innovatory projects through the world, which is receiving financial support from a group of bilateral and multilateral donor agencies associated with the Bellagio Conference organized by the Rockefeller and Ford Foundations, is an interesting step in this direction.

This leads to the conclusion that the main measures of redeployment that the suppliers of aid could best take would be those linked with reforms and innovations that are already in movement in the developing countries, or, alternatively, they should aim at assisting developing countries to increase their capacity for reform by cooperation in research and development and experimentation. The suppliers of aid, while not intervening in national policy, can influence the trend of cooperation by action by earmarking resources for use in certain ways. An example would be the additional provision of scholarships for use in the developing countries themselves, or in third countries, rather than as traditionally in the donor countries.

There follows a schematic presentation of suggested shifts of emphasis and measures of redeployment. These reflect both actual trends and views expressed at both ends of the cooperation process, and also the results of international assessments of educational needs, such as that made by the International Commission on the Development of Education already cited. There is also a listing of the obstacles to the redeployment of resources in those directions. The applicability of the list of suggestions and obstacles will naturally be different in respect of different developing countries and cooperation

agencies and will vary according to changes in circumstances.
Further, the actual demand for such shifts of emphasis would have
to originate from the developing country itself in each particular
case, and would best be channeled through country programing procedures.

The schematic presentation is purely indicative and intended to
be no more than a framework around which agencies at both ends of
the cooperation network can review redeployment needs for cooperation resources. The necessity for such a review is that, as indicated
earlier, the process of redeployment, which involves new types of
expertise and backstopping and often changes not only in resources
but also in methods for their use, is necessarily a process spread
over a considerable time period. Unless such reviews are made,
there is the danger of cooperation methods and resources remaining
as before, owing to the natural forces of inertia in all such large-
scale administrative processes.

| | Study Abroad | | |
Shifting of Emphasis Required	Redeployment Measures	Obstacles to Redeployment	Additional Approaches or New Directions
1. Large shifts would seem in- dicated, on an overall basis; but position varies consid- erably between donors. The shifts would be partly from study abroad programs to other activities, and partly within study abroad (for example, more use of the group fellow- ship system).	1. Distinguish between the more purely cultural and political and the more strictly devel- opment objec- tives, and finance them under different budget headings. 2. For devel- opment pur- poses limit study abroad in the donor country to those cate- gories of study	Recipient's side 1. Failure to define and plan study abroad in educational planning. 2. Lack of re- sources for creating facili- ties to substi- tute study abroad. 3. Antago- nisms between neighboring countries, and national com- petition for lo- cations of	Recipient's side 1. Strengthen the links be- tween the ad- ministration and planning of study abroad and overall educational planning. 2. Use interna- tional aid to ex- amine domestic substitution as well as third- country and subregional possibilities.

Shifting of Emphasis Required	Redeployment Measures	Obstacles to Redeployment	Additional Approaches or New Directions
	for which facilities are not available in the recipient country.	regional centers of excellence.	3. Evaluate existing programs better and more regularly, and use results in overall requests for educational aid.
	3. Build up the necessary substitute facilities in recipient countries except where application of cost-benefit analysis gives a negative indication.	4. Amenities of study in the donor countries, and the prestige of study abroad.	
		5. Ruling groups with foreign diplomas protect their own status; nepotism.	4. Divert unavoidable nepotism into the cultural studies.
			Donor's side
	4. Assist study abroad in neighboring countries (third countries) and aid the setting up or growth of regional centers of excellence.	6. Lack of coordination of requests for aid. 7. Lack of familiarity with cost-benefit analysis, shortage of data.	1. Separate out quotas of expenditure on fellowships according to location in donor or recipient countries.
		Donor's side	2. Reduce allotments under first heading and increase them under the second. Give special attention to scholarships to the disadvantaged classes so as to aid social mobility.
	5. Apply more funds to internal scholarships in recipient countries to aid socially disadvantaged students.	1. Confusion between developmental and more purely cultural or political objectives.	
		2. This leads to insufficient attention	3. Give aid for the better
	6. Denepotize the selection		

Shifting of Emphasis Required	Redeployment Measures	Obstacles to Redeployment	Additional Approaches or New Directions
	process and establish incentives or penalties to ensure the knowledge obtained is applied to the development of the recipient country.	given to cost, for example, of "hidden subsidies" involved in participation of foreign students in social insurance, general student facilities, and such, and of student places foregone that could be used by nationals (for example, half of the Graduate School of the London School of Economics consists of foreign students.) 3. Lack of data for and practice in cost-benefit studies. 4. Lack of regular process of evaluation and comparison with other alternatives. 5. Forces of habit in administrations and	planning of study abroad in recipient countries and assist them in cost-benefit and substitution studies. 4. Evaluate impact of study abroad programs as effective instruments of aid and publicize the results. 5. Coordinate more effectively with the overall planning and execution of educational aid.

Shifting of Emphasis Required	Redeployment Measures	Obstacles to Redeployment	Additional Approaches or New Directions
		weaknesses of coordination and planning.	
		6. Exaggerated belief that returning students will substantially influence the direction of commerce.	
		7. Absence of standing administrative machinery that studies alternatives.	

Shifting of Emphasis and Redeployment Measures Required	Investment Obstacles Affecting Redeployment	Additional Approaches or New Directions
A lesser proportion of aid to straight building programs for general secondary and higher.

More help to "centers of excellence," especially in applied science and technology, and less to ordinary technical education and vocational training institutes. | Attractiveness to transient Ministers of loans.

Conservatism within the profession. Administrative immobilities and conservatism in Agencies.

Difficulty of controling what goes on in the buildings financed. | Strengthen the expertise and data collection required for the shifts of emphasis.

Issue new instructions to identification and preparation missions. Examine social equity as well as economic factors and nonformal as well as formal education possibilities involving industry and the communications services in the community. |

Shifting of Emphasis and Redeployment Measures Required	Obstacles Affecting Redeployment	Additional Approaches or New Directions
Ensure industry is involved in aid given for technical and vocational training.	Shortages of expertise and data for innovatory approaches.	Link aid to integrated curriculum development (creation of local teaching and learning situations in which subject matter, teacher training, and equipment are planned as a whole).
Link capital investment in education more closely to physical investment.	Difficulties of obtaining the necessary interdisciplinary breadth in project diagnosis, and shortage of data for the purpose. This applies both to Agencies and recipients.	
A greater proportion of investment in (1) basic education (formal and nonformal), and (2) education oriented to local development possibilities, especially for the poorer part of the population; and (3) employment-generating projects for youth.		Give capital aid for research and development for new educational patterns and risk taking. Create necessary administration and technical link with other capital investment.
Greater emphasis on pretechnical preparation, especially of youth who dropped out prematurely.		Establish special units for this purpose in donor and recipient agencies to foresee and influence educational component of future employment situation.
Readjust the time perspective, for example, stress the short term by giving more aid to adult education, functional literacy, family		Search out, through the country's development plan and by employment analysis, the areas where the labor force is not ready for modernization, but industry will grow. Create pre-employment centers.

Shifting of Emphasis and Redeployment Measures Required	Obstacles Affecting Redeployment	Additional Approaches or New Directions
planning, and nonformal education generally, including "first aid" projects.		Encourage and even subsidize more takeover by employers of technical and vocational training.
Aim to make an impact on the educational level (workwise and citizenwise) of the mean of the population within 10 years.		
Invest in the new media but less related to the formal system and more as a means of using all the community's educational influences, including parents, trade unions, cooperatives, and local government services.		

Teacher Supply and Training

Shifting of Emphasis and Redeployment Measures Required	Obstacles Affecting Redeployment	Additional Approaches or New Directions
The proportion of aid going to the supply of expatriate teachers is, to some extent, declining and being redirected to aid to teacher training and educational planning and administration.	The momentum of the existing recruitment system, contract renewals, and such, perpetuates present type of teacher supply.	Reduce progressively the supply of expatriate teachers. Increase aid to domestic teacher training and to the training of trainers of teachers.

Shifting of Emphasis and Redeployment Measures Required	Obstacles Affecting Redeployment	Additional Approaches or New Directions
This process needs acceleration since the expatriates, while playing an important role, occupy jobs which nationals ought to fill and tend to maintain artificial salary structures inherited from the colonial era. Teacher supply and training tends to be concentrated too exclusively on the pedagogic or academic aspects of education, on the one hand, or on technical training on the other. In the formal systems poor teaching methods (such as use of rote learning) should be replaced by more modern ones involving public participation and use of the new media. More effort should be devoted to increasing teacher supply and training in basic education for children and adults also, including functional	On the other hand, educational expansion in donor countries is reducing the number available for overseas. Supply is also diminishing by a disillusionment with the aid program owing to current criticism. The pace of teacher training in recipient countries is limited by domestic financial problems and bottlenecks in the number of teacher-trainers, in the quality of curricula, and physical facilities, and lack of pilot schools for experimenting and opportunities for in-service training. The gap between new theories and instructions and their practical implementation is difficult to bridge owing to conservatism of the profession and the isolation of many of the individual teachers.	No aid to teacher training without relation to curriculum development. Encourage movement of teachers between developing countries with same language to help meet shortages. Diffuse throughout teacher training improved teaching methods based on participation and creation of teaching situations rather than on instructional techniques and rote. Increase inspection of training. Ensure that old methods are not used to train teachers in new methods and so destroy credibility. Sponsor seminars for headmasters and local educational officials. Aid the setting up of more pilot schools, in which teachers can try out new methods. Concentrate on in-service training in first place, since the returns are highest.

Shifting of Emphasis and Redeployment Measures Required	Obstacles Affecting Redeployment	Additional Approaches or New Directions
literacy, "first aid," and recuperative types of education, and instructions in health, nutrition, and family planning. The gap between education and work life should be diminished through training teachers to impart knowledge of the work environment, and to promote the idea of recurrent education. Teacher training should be integrally linked with curriculum development. An increase of technical assistance is needed, but it should consist mostly of expertise that will aid educational regeneration and innovation. The need to concentrate on quality and relevance of education and to improve cost efficiency means that technical assistance could take an increasing	Salary insufficiencies and poor general education of teachers on which further training has to be built. Lack of facilities for nonformal education. The amount of expertise available for educational innovation is not large. There are few tried and tested models that the technical assistance expert can carry with him to new environments. The obstacles to innovation in education in the recipient countries have their counterpart in similar conservatism in the educational provision in the donor countries. Reliance on the normal channels will not necessarily produce new solutions.	Use both material and psychological incentives to encourage teacher productivity. Ensure teacher training includes link with nonformal education and propagates an understanding of work needs and the need for recurrent education. Assist training of teachers for functional literacy, and preemployment centers of education, especially for youth who missed formal schooling. Help to attract into nonformal education parents, community workers, social service officials, and so on, as teachers and provide centers for discussion and experimentation. Equipment and experts should be provided for resource centers and data banks necessary for evaluating and reshaping educational output.

Shifting of Emphasis and Redeployment Measures Required	Obstacles Affecting Redeployment	Additional Approaches or New Directions
proportion of aid funds at the expense, if necessary, of quantitative expansion.	Technical assistance is too often a hit-and-run affair, and it is difficult to leave lasting results unless there are adequate commitments and counterpart staff provided by the recipient government.	Technical assistance should be regarded as the main point of entry of educational reform and should be oriented to integrated curriculum development.
	High turnover both of Ministers and of staff, which creates breaks on continuity and ambiguities as to commitments.	Less reliance should be placed on individual experts and more on educational institutions in both recipient and donor countries. This would give more prestige and continuity to the operations and would safeguard quality, though high-level experts with specialized knowledge should continue to be used.
	Local costs are found to be a burden by recipient countries.	
	The level of the technical assistance from abroad can fall below the available level of domestic experts unless careful regard is paid to the quality of the expert and his "intellectual backstopping" and briefing.	This would mean some administrative shifts under which recruitment becomes less a function of general administrators and more a task falling on those responsible for the "intellectual backstopping."
		In order to improve continuity, career services should be provided, both in donor and recipient countries, for individuals

Shifting of Emphasis and Redeployment Measures Required	Obstacles Affecting Redeployment	Additional Approaches or New Directions
	Technical assistance has to be supported by linkages with other types of aid, such as provision of equipment and sometimes capital, in order for its full impact to be obtained. This link is not always made.	of proven competence. Incentives should be created to enable them to stay with the job as long as possible. The "intellectual backstopping" services should be of a flexible nature and kept constantly under review in order to foresee and later implement new priorities.

Institution Building

Shifting of Emphasis and Redeployment Measures Required	Obstacles Affecting Redeployment	Additional Approaches or New Directions
Less aid to general second and higher-level studies. Help build new types of institutions to meet new needs. More aid to centers of excellence (especially in technology and the natural sciences) and to basic education. More to nonformal institutions, such as functional literacy	Pressures from politically powerful sections of the population to expand second and higher education. Lack of information as to cost-benefits of different types of institutions. Prestige value of diplomas, and grandiose projects.	Better project diagnosis and identification in relation to development needs. More coordination among donors and greater selectivity in choice of projects. Encourage university-to-university aid, but increase the communication of new policies down the line.

Shifting of Emphasis and Redeployment Measures Required	Obstacles Affecting Redeployment	Additional Approaches or New Directions
centers, community schools, pre-employment centers.	Competition among donors.	Consult with other departments as well as educational authorities.
More to educational institutes and research and development centers.	Stability of existing system of expectation of parents.	Sponsor cost-benefit studies; take care not to perpetuate inefficiencies by "tinkering," except for clearly urgent short-term needs.
Reduce tinkering and go for deeper reforms.	Examination system and expectation of employers and pupils.	
Modernize curricula by relating them more to the actual local needs of the majority of school-leavers but also provide adequate streams to meet national needs and the promotion of excellence.	Insufficient incentives for the study and formulation of curriculum reform programs.	Consultations at all levels to discuss expectations and realities and diminish prejudices. Take more integrated approach including review of examination system.
	Lack of enthusiasm for integration among the activities, which should be linked with curriculum development.	Better data collection and evaluation of results of old and new curricula and methods.
Curriculum changes to be accompanied by changes across the board (teacher training, textbooks, design of school buildings and equipment, scholarship ladders, structural changes in the cycles).	Differences of prestige between the various educational streams.	Financing of experimental projects, including certain recurrent costs.
Try out new organizational patterns of	Shortage of good tested models for basic education and experience of applying them.	Aid setting up of new economical types of school, particularly suited to local needs, with bridges and ladders to the national system.

Shifting of Emphasis and Redeployment Measures Required	Obstacles Affecting Redeployment	Additional Approaches or New Directions
education and improve learning capacity of pupils.	Preference of both donors and recipients for visible shorter-term results.	Exchange of information on innovations to be organized on international basis.
More resources to go into educational research and development.	Shortages of research staff and data.	Allocate funds for research and development on an independent basis so that they do not compete with short-term needs.
Within existing research more emphasis to be placed on studying ways and means to promote educational renovation and innovation, and use of new media.	Failures to define problems adequately in formulating research.	
	Pressure of certain expenditure on budgets leading to research costs being squeezed out.	Consider establishing an international center for educational research and development for the developing countries financed from ex-budgetary sources.
Research to be integrally linked with curriculum development and teacher training.	Overelaborate nature and clumsiness of many research methods.	Aid universities to increase resources devoted to educational studies.
Situation of the community seen as a whole, including other means as well as the schools.	Difficulties of comparison with the past statistics.	Set up a five-year technical assistance project to recast basis of educational statistics including aid.
Recasting of present form of educational statistics.	Soothing effort of present form of presentation of statistics.	Publish unenrollment statistics like the unemployment figures, and not only enroll-
Improvement of the statistics of educational aid.	Shortages of data and appropriate methods of analysis.	ment.

Shifting of Emphasis and Redeployment Measures Required	Obstacles Affecting Redeployment	Additional Approaches or New Directions
Extend planning to take in noneducational factors, which have a vital impact on educational performance.	Lack of time and staff.	Train more research staff and work out simpler research methods.
Give greater depth to project diagnosis.		Provide experimental schools and equipment. Contribute to local costs.
		More methodological studies and case investigations.
		Strengthen analysis teams on both donor and recipient ends.

NOTES

1. Gunnar Myrdal, Challenge of World Poverty: A World Anti-Poverty Programme in Outline (Baltimore: Penguin Books, 1970), p. 180.

2. Unesco, Learning to Be (Paris, London: Harrap, 1972), p. 123.

3. "The Experimental World Literacy Programme and Its Global Evaluation," Unesco 18 C/68 of 28 October 1974, p. 7.

4. Television in the Modernization of Education in the Ivory Coast (Ivory Coast: Secretary of State for Primary Education and Educational Television, 1969), p. 35.

5. Unesco, Learning to Be, op. cit.

6. Michel DeBeauvais, "Problems of Costs and Opportunities," Prospects 3, no. 3 (1973).

7. Philip H. Coombs, with Manzoor Ahmed, Attacking Rural Poverty: How Nonformal Education Can Help (Baltimore: Johns Hopkins Press, 1974), p. 252.

        8. Herbert H. Hyman, Gene N. Levine, and Charles R.
Wright, Inducing Social Change in Developing Countries (UN 67.
IV. 3), p. 152.
        9. Csanad Toth, "The Poder Project," Review of International
Development, no. 4 (1971): 19.
        10. Unesco, Learning to Be, op. cit., p. 261.

14

Cooperation for development is in a critical position. The opportunity was lost in the rising income levels in the 1960s to transfer to the developing countries a share of the world resources, which would have raised their living levels, reduced population growth, and laid the basis for a future world society based on considerations of equity of opportunity and human welfare rather than purely economic competition between countries in which the developing countries were at a disadvantage.

It is true that educational cooperation, which is our concern, grew, while overall aid lagged or declined and had often more appeal and gave more satisfaction than other sectors. Around 1973 it was running at an estimated $2,350 million a year, valued at standard costs to the contributors, which is not necessarily the value to the recipients. This sum equals about 17 percent of the total educational budget of the developing countries. Yet educational cooperation has not been nor is it wholly successful. There is much self-criticism and some disarray in the cooperation process. This is partly because of the unsatisfactory features of the general state of education in both the developed and the developing countries, and also because, inevitably, it becomes involved in the unsolved problems of overall cooperation.

Educational cooperation, while needing to be integrated at the planning and operational levels with each country's development plan, should maintain its own dynamic in the sense of continuing to grow even if there are setbacks in overall cooperation for development. It is more closely geared to human aspirations than some other forms of aid, especially in societies where it is desperately lacking. It contains within it the seeds of new forms of collaboration between countries for social as well as economic progress, and it

is one of the keys to the reduction of the excessive growth of the
world's population.

Nevertheless, finance for educational cooperation today has to
compete with claims for the relief of hunger and unemployment and
of shortages of energy, for the improvement of health, and for investment in the physical means of production. Care must be taken
through country programing to avoid distortion of priorities.

Earlier optimistic beliefs in education as a strong civilizing
force and promoter of social justice and movement between the
classes and understanding among nations are not being fulfilled.
Nor has the educational planning undertaken in the 1960s corrected
the imbalance between the educational levels, which restrains its
contribution to economic and social development. The number of
unenrolled children and illiterate adults is increasing. However,
the evidence is overwhelming that education can and should be further extended and democratized in order to contribute more than at
present to economic growth, to population planning, to expanding the
opportunities of individuals, to raising living levels, and to national
and individual development.

The educational message to be derived from the United Nations
Declaration regarding a New Economic Order is that greater economic equality between populations is not possible without the reduction of the massive illiteracy in the developing countries and the provision of basic education for the hundreds of millions of children and
youth growing up without it.

Reducing educational poverty and increasing the productivity of
countries' basic human resources has to be accompanied by building
up a better infrastructure of technologists, scientists, and managers
to fill gaps or take up emergent opportunities.

Cooperation plans to extend basic educational services to meet
the elementary needs of all but a small percentage of the world's
children and adults under 45 could be made at once and carried out
over the next 20 years. The task of foreseeing and providing for the
qualified manpower requirements of a hypothetical new economic
order is also vital but much more difficult. Specifically this task
would have to be geared to actual country situations resulting from
economic plans for a better use and distribution of the world's resources and opportunities. But generally it would call for shifts in
the patterns and structure of the capacity of educational systems,
many of which are required in any case to meet current economic
and social demands. These also could be designed now.

There is cause for optimism in the educational reforms, already taking place on a limited scale in most countries and fundamentally in a few. A good deal of rethinking of education is taking
place at both ends of the cooperation network, though there is still
little implementation of new ideas.

From a human-development standpoint, the priority would be
to concentrate on cooperation designed to eliminate mass educational
poverty as one of the initial bases of a world where no one falls below at least minimum levels of living, and where all countries and
individuals develop at their maximum capacity. Educational cooperation, however, consists of a mass of two-party transactions. These
tend to have a life of their own outside the complexities of carefully
framed aid policies.* There is likely to be a continuing flow of resources, negotiated case by case, which will go to educational levels
and assistance projects to meet individual country priorities. Indeed this is the essence of the country programing procedures.

It is unlikely, however, that certain global issues, such as reducing illiteracy in order to help to prevent another population explosion, or foreseeing the educational implications of a new economic
order, could be solved by concentrating only on purely national
priorities, which are often short term. Supplementary initiatives
have to be taken through worldwide organizations such as the United
Nations and Unesco.

Educational cooperation agencies can influence events (for
example, the World Bank's decision and that of other cooperating
agencies to increase the proportion of resources available for basic
education). Educational cooperation has to be seen as one of the
growing links between country needs and the wider needs and possibilities of development on a world scale.

There have been some striking changes in the sources of official educational assistance over the last ten years. For instance
in the bilateral area, the annual commitments for educational cooperation of the German Federal Republic rose from $48.3 million
in 1966 to $149.7 million in 1973, while over the same period that
of the United States fell from $182 million to $95 million. Canadian
and Swedish educational aid have also grown rapidly. In the multilateral area there have been great increases in the educational activities of the World Bank, Unicef, and Unesco.

Aid for educational cooperation is not an act of charity, though
it is a moral act. It is an act that is political in the best sense of
the term. Polemics as to "neocolonialism" are mostly out of date
and not factually based so far as educational cooperation is concerned, whatever may be the position in the other sectors. The
more useful approach lies in alerting world opinion to the dangers

---

*See the concluding sentence of the study by John White, The
Politics of Foreign Aid (London: Institute of Development Studies of
the University of Sussex, Bodley Head, 1974), which reads, "The
making of an aid policy lies in the hands of those who actually administer it."

of the present widespread educational deprivation of hundreds of
millions of people and to the need to renovate and strengthen at all
levels the capacity of educational systems to contribute to development. This would point to increasing the resource flow and giving
badly needed additional strength to the financial, technical, and administrative forces concerned in educational cooperation. Some of
the main requirements that appear to exist at the present time may
be set out as follows.

DEVELOPING COUNTRIES

1. Developing countries should review their use of educational
cooperation in order to ensure that the assistance given fits into
their national educational plans, safeguards their independence, and
does not create future educational dependencies that are unacceptable. They should exchange experiences among themselves of cooperation with developed countries and, in addition, seek additional
forms of cooperation among themselves. Some kind of standing organization seems necessary for this purpose similar to that (for instance) of the Development Assistance Committee of the OECD on
the donor side of the cooperation process.

2. As part of this review they should sharpen their participation in the dialogue preceding educational cooperation transactions.
Too much is at present left in the identification and preparation of
projects to the donor side. Institutions and experts in the developing
countries themselves should be assisted to increase their participation in both the diagnosis of aid needs and the preparation and evaluation of projects.

3. Counterpart staff should also be more carefully selected
with the necessary career arrangements to ensure a certain continuity in the cooperation process on the recipient side.

4. Needs for cooperation should be formulated at the same
time that development plans are drawn up, and time schedules be
placed on them. The role of external assistance should be seen as
either to fill immediate and urgent gaps, or to serve as bridging operations, or to help long-term reforms. Reform, though long term,
often needs short-term help to meet the temporary costs of the dis-
location caused by innovation or the movement from linear to non-
linear expansion of the system as a whole.

5. When needs are being formulated, particular regard should
be paid to exercises designed to increase experiments and promote
educational research and development capacity. The latter could
well be regarded as a particular field for the extra funds from outside assistance, since there are often resistances to such types of

expenditure investments among local sources of finance. This type of assistance, while leaving the policy initiatives entirely with the home government, provides the opportunity for a worldwide cooperative use of experience, expertise, and funds, and for assistance in institution building.

6. When preparing educational projects and programs for external assistance, developing countries should avoid transfering to donor agencies the difficulties they themselves experience of trying to solve by purely educational measures what are really social problems.

7. For instance, obdurate gaps in the supply of middle-level technicians require economic and social as well as educational action, since they are a reflection of employment conditions, pay structures, and prevailing public attitudes to different types of educational opportunity. External agencies are unable to influence these problems, but have too often been asked to sponsor projects that presupposed their solution.

8. Similarly, the emphasis in the past upon "breeder" or catalytic pilot projects should be viewed with some caution, since experience of attempts to work out pilot projects capable of wide extension later elsewhere has not been very favorable.

9. Educational development, especially if structural change and reform is considerable, involves an increase of planning, implementation, and management skills at the district and local levels as well as centrally. While aid for planning is often sought, the problem of educational management is usually regarded as domestic. Nevertheless more cooperation from abroad and exchanges of experience in the key field of management should be encouraged.

DEVELOPED COUNTRIES AND
MULTILATERAL AGENCIES

1. Cooperating agencies at the supply end of the network have to be ready to meet changing needs. The previous demand for large quantitative transfers of educational resources in the form of teachers and simpler forms of expertise in educational management and technology is to a considerable extent being replaced by a more selective need for assistance for quality renovation and reorganization of education. There are still specific quantitative needs, such as creating more centers of excellence at the higher level, especially in science and technology and administration and management. In these fields there will be for a long time ahead vital requirements both as to quantity and quality. This is likely to be the case also for middle-level technicians.

2.   There remains too the large quantitative demand at the level of basic education to which cooperation has so far little applied itself. Aid for whole programs as distinct from assistance for individual projects may be needed to attack large-scale educational poverty at the level of basic needs.   The demand at the basic level is likely to call for resources in the form of finance and expertise rather than in the supply of foreign teachers.   There may be considerable demands for new building and the extension of premises, and for assistance to structural changes.   The establishment, for instance, of nuclear schools, which serve within districts as outlets for the more incomplete schools, and the provision of ladders, bridges, and buffer cycles to preserve educational opportunity at the same time that a minimum basic education is given, may mean seed money from abroad in the form of financial assistance to programs as a whole, rather than projects, to get such new programs launched.

3.   Cooperation agencies at the supply end should increase the quality of their expert personnel sent into the field in order to match the increased competence the developing countries themselves have acquired.   Where possible, educational cooperation should take place through institutions that have a continuing life and can evaluate and follow up projects, rather than through individual experts who come and go.   As far as possible institutions in the developing countries themselves should be used or linked to cooperating institutions in donor countries.   National experts in the recipient countries should be used in the role of designers and activators of projects as well as that of counterparts.

4.   More assistance than hitherto needs to be allocated to educational research and experimentation, utilizing predominantly local institutions and experts for the purpose.   Cooperation funds should be used for training local personnel for this purpose as well as to create poles of attraction around local initiatives for educational regeneration and so increase the countries' capacity for change.

5.   Aid should also be given to support risk-taking and trial runs of new educational patterns suited to local conditions.   To spearhead such activities, an International Center for Educational Research and Innovation for the developing countries might be set up (or the International Institute for Educational Planning expanded for the purpose).   The spirit of renovation should also pervade all existing programs and centers.

TYPES AND FIELDS OF COOPERATION

1.   Special priority should be given to cooperation to assist countries to extend the human right of basic education to all their

citizens; to forms of instruction to improve the employment possibilities and living conditions of unemployed youth; and cooperation in nonformal education should be stepped up wherever good projects can be found.

2. Cooperation for rural education is of first-order importance because of its impact on food production and restraint on population growth. It should be designed in the light of local possibilities and in forms that have local support.

3. Cooperation for education for modernization through science and technology is also of first-order priority; there should however be a review of the aid given to technical and vocational schools in the formal education system as this area of aid activity has encountered special difficulties.

4. Study-abroad programs should be evaluated and compared with action to support local institutions, third-country training, or scholarships within recipient countries.

5. The technology of education and the improvement of the communication of knowledge and ideas is a field in which cooperation can be particularly helpful to increase educational productivity.

6. The education of women and girls, important for raising productivity and living levels and for population control, as well as for equity reasons, is a particularly desirable area of assistance.

ORGANIZATIONAL MATTERS

1. Unesco, in concert with cooperation agencies, should issue a publication detailing sources and conditions of cooperation--multilateral, bilateral, and nongovernmental--in education. Also, in concert with developing countries, a manual should be published on methods that have been found successful to identify, prepare, and assess cooperation projects in education. Also, examples, actual and hypothetical, of models of educational reform in typical developing countries should be prepared, costed, and set beside existing models; they should phase the breaks in the linear progression of existing models so as to reduce gaps and indicate the quantities and types of cooperation needed.

2. Procedures should be streamlined to reduce bureaucratic aspects and instead give more attention to project design and implementation. Seminars and training courses, at which officials from both aid-providing and recipient countries could meet to discuss the technical problems of educational cooperation, should be encouraged. Perhaps the IIEP could play an important role in such an effort.

3. The briefing of experts and institutions entering the cooperation field for the first time should be improved, utilizing modern

briefing methods (audiovisual, study of actual situations, and so on) instead of purely verbal media.

4. There should be increased evaluation of educational co-operation projects and improved statistics both of individual cooperation programs and of the overall trend of assistance.

5. Cooperation agencies at both ends of the network should improve project selection procedures, further develop the statistical and other data they use for assessing trends and needs, and work more through local institutions that can monitor and evaluate projects over time rather than individual experts who come and go.

6. A set of guidelines based on past successes and failures in basic education, especially in rural areas, and showing techniques of diagnosis of local learning needs is needed. It could well form part of an overall "manual" on methods of basic education in different types of environment.

7. Foreign industry, particularly the multinational corporations, could well make voluntary contributions to educational assistance to be carried out by Unesco through its Funds-in-Trust system.

8. The possibility of official aid for nongovernmental and commercial educational and training institutions, with guarantees in suitable cases, should be studied.

9. All concerned should make a greater effort to improve both the reality and the image of the cooperation process at the aid-supplying, aid-receiving, and the intermediary levels; school textbooks in the developed countries and educational material dealing with developing countries should be reviewed to ensure they adequately reflect cooperation needs and the "philosophy" of international cooperation underlying the Second Development Decade.

10. More attention should be given, especially in the least educationally developed countries, to the macroeducational level and to cooperation with total programs of reform rather than overconcentration on individual projects.

11. Each cooperation agency should set up a small "ideas" group of experts with experience in field work, but free of administrative responsibilities, to monitor the development of its present program and to consider future measures of improvement and redeployment of educational aid resources. Both sides in the cooperation should also develop memory systems and adequate evaluation and "trouble shooting" procedures to revise bad projects before they have gone too far and to prevent their reoccurrence, and to learn from experience.

12. A greater proportion of cooperation resources should be channeled through the United Nations system, especially the programs operated in cooperation with Unesco by the UNDP, Unicef and the World Bank Group/IDA, and through Unesco itself, either

directly or under the Funds-in-Trust procedures. The organizational problems inside the UN system in regard to educational cooperation and the methods of implementation should be the subject
of a special review, as proposed by Unesco's Director General.

REDEPLOYMENT OF COOPERATION RESOURCES

1. At the aid-supplying end of the cooperation network there
are special problems of redeployment in the sense that when the
recipient country declares its needs the donor agency's cooperation
depends on whether it has the types of resources and skills required
to meet those needs. It is easier to declare and define needs than to
be in a position to meet them. Donors are usually equipped to fulfill
needs that have become current over the last few years rather than
new needs, and major switches in requirements involve redeployment of their resources and often retooling. If, for instance, the
need for help in higher education falls off, and there is a switch to
basic education, the resources required, the type of expertise, and
the backstopping are different.

2. Redeployment is difficult since there are obstacles, some
real, some due to inertia, to be overcome. Each aid agency will
have its own special problems, and each recipient country its own
needs. To give an indication of the changes in demand that are current, or appear to be in view or desirable, and of the redeployment
problems involved, the following schema summarizes a number of
the major factors.

SWITCHES OF RESOURCES REQUIRED

1. While educational requirements flow from given situations,
some of the most important redeployment needs may be listed as follows. This list is based on the recommendations of the main governmental and expert meetings of the last few years. The "less" and
"more" in the list do not necessarily relate to any individual country
and are, of course, no substitute for diagnosis on the spot. They
refer to the needs of the Second Development Decade seen in bulk.

2. The utility of trying to see the needs in bulk is the guidance
this should provide to the overall planning of cooperation programs
and their administration, especially as regards changes in the channels and methods of cooperation and the type of "backstopping" and
"expertise" to be accumulated.

Less Emphasis on	More Emphasis on
Grants for study and training in the donor country	Grants for study and training in the recipient or in "third" developing countries
Supply of teachers	Teacher training
Supply of experts in administration and operation of traditional systems	Supply of experts in methods of educational change, innovation, and nonformal education; use of institutions both in developed and developing countries to increase capacity to design and carry out reforms
Overall literacy campaigns	Functional literacy related to work environment
Vocational training inside the formal educational systems	Arrangements for participation of employers in mixed formal and nonformal projects
Expansion of enrollment without sufficient regard to the internal efficiency of the system	Reduction of dropout and repetition; nonformal education to meet local needs
Limited manpower view of external efficiency of system	Unified economic and social criteria of external efficiency
Support of existing structure of educational system (cycles and pupil streams)	Restructuring to adapt better to economic and social needs of environment; basic education for all
Standard types of curriculum development and reform	Integrated curriculum development (that is, combining reforms in teacher training with changes in streaming of pupils, creation of new learning situations, use of new media, combined with review of syllabus)

Less Emphasis on	More Emphasis on
Aid to educational systems as wholes regardless of the social distribution of access to education, and of "democratization" needs	Special attention to educational deprivation--for example, for reasons of difference of language and in shanty towns and rural areas, education of females, and scholarship grants to aid social mobility
Support of ongoing foreign or standard national types of education without careful evaluation	Intensive dialogue with government and national experts, and through them with parents and teachers and local authorities
Unstudied acceptance of national education plans and prevailing priorities	Selective aid, consistent with development plans, but favoring only progressive objectives
"Hard" loans for educational development	"Soft" loans and credits
Independence of educational aid from total aid	Greater links with physical employment-creating aid
"Prefabricated" projects emerging from aid agencies	Country programing and local initiatives
Competition among aid agencies	Coordination (informal or formal) and use of UNDP country programing facilities
Documentation and expertise mainly from developed country sources	Creation of intellectual "backstopping" facilities in recipient countries or subregions
Experts from donor countries	Experts from recipient countries
Use of individual experts	Use of institutions in developing as well as developed countries
Traditional media and methods and academic approaches, sporadic and unscientific evaluation	New media, more scientific methods, and built-in evaluation and practical orientation

Less Emphasis on	More Emphasis on
Needlework and similar classes for young women	Training for employment, home economics, and family planning
Assessment of aid effort in monetary value as part of total aid flow	Use of cost-effectiveness studies
Separate collection of country data by each agency	Exchange of country analysis and information evaluating innovatory projects
Purely bilateral activities	Use of multilateral agencies, especially Unesco, directly or through Funds-in-Trust system

BIBLIOGRAPHIES, WORKING PAPERS, REPORTS
OF MEETINGS, AND SEMINARS

Borghese, Elena. "Recent Trends in Aid to Education." Presented
at the European Regional Conference of the Society for International Development on "The Educational Assistance to Developing Areas--Its Social and Economic Effects," May 4-6, 1970,
Cologne. Bonn: Deutsche Stiftung fur Entwicklungslander
(Doc. 28 II IT 7/70).

Capelle, J. Report on Education and Development. Strasbourg:
Council of Europe, 1971.

Colombo Plan. "International Assistance for Education for Development: The Colombo Plan Topic Report (1971) Considered by the
20th Consultative Meeting in Manila, February 1971."

Congres Flamand des Sciences Economiques. L'Aide au Developpement: Une Etude du Point de Vue des Pays Dont l'Aide Est
Sollicitee. Commission Report. University of Gand, 1967.

Deutsche Stiftung fur Entwicklungslander. Educational and Scientific
Aid Programme of the Federal Republic of Germany. Adopted
December 1971 by the Federal Government, Berlin.

Federal Republic of Germany, Ministry for Economic Cooperation.
"Technical Assistance of the Federal Government in the Field
of Vocational Promotion in Developing Countries." Presented
at the European Regional Conference of the Society for International Development on "The Educational Assistance to Developing
Areas--Its Social and Economic Effects," May 4-6, 1970,
Cologne. Bonn: Deutsche Stiftung fur Entwicklungslander (Doc.
15 II IT 7/70).

France. Secretariat d'Etat aux Affaires Etrangeres. La Coopera-
entre la France et les Etats Francophones d'Afrique Noire et
de l'Ocean Indien. Paris, 1972.

Gerin-Lajoie, Paul. Educational Innovation: New Perspectives for
Canada in International Development. Ottawa: Canadian International Development Agency, 1971.

El Hakim, Barbro, ed. Near East-South Asia Technical Assistance
    Program of US Non-Profit Organizations, Including Voluntary
    Agencies, Missions and Foundations. New York: Technical
    Assistance Information Clearing House of the American Council
    of Voluntary Agencies for Foreign Service, 1969.

Horn, Jackie, ed. Africa Technical Assistance Program of US Non-
    Profit Organizations. New York: Technical Assistance Informa-
    tion Clearing House of the American Council of Voluntary Agen-
    cies for Foreign Service, 1969.

Konrad-Adenauer-Stiftung. Institut fur Internationale Solidaritat.
    Genossenschaftsprobleme in Deutschland und Entwicklungslandern.
    Mainz: V. Hase und Kehler, 1969 (ITS Schriftenreihe, Bd. 2).

Lewis, A. J. "Guidelines for the Planning of External Aid Projects
    in Education." In Education and World Affairs (ITS Occasional
    Report no. 2). New York, 1967.

McNamara, Robert S. Address to the Board of Governors, World
    Bank Group. September 25, 1972, Washington, D.C.

_____. Address to the Board of Governors, Nairobi, Kenya, Sep-
    tember 24, 1973, Washington, D.C.

Masland, J. W. "Education Development in Africa. The Role of
    United States Assistance." In Education and World Affairs (ITS
    Occasional Report no. 4). New York, 1967.

Organization for Economic Cooperation and Development. Annual
    Reviews of the Chairman of the Development Assistance Com-
    mittee, Paris. (See especially for 1974.)

Ottawa University Institute for International Cooperation. Develop-
    ment Strategy at the Intermediate Level: Selective Bibliography.

Poignant, Raymond. "Developpement de l'Education dans les Pays
    en Voie de Developpement Pendant la Premiere Decennie du
    Developpement et Appreciation Critique des Experiences de
    l'Aide Internationale a l'Education." Presented to the European
    Conference of the Society for International Development on "The
    Educational Assistance to Developing Areas--Its Social and Eco-
    nomic Effects." May 1970, Cologne. Bonn: Deutsche Stiftung
    fur Entwicklungslander, 1970 (Document 1 II IT 7/70).

Rockefeller Foundation. The President's Review and Annual Report
1973. New York, 1973.

_____. The President's Review and Annual Report 1974: Financial
Information. New York, 1974.

Spencer, Richard E., and Awe, Ruth. International Educational Exchange: A Bibliography. New York: Institute of International
Education, 1968.

Technical Assistance Information Clearing House. Category Index
of Development Assistance Programs. Washington, D.C.: 1971.

_____. TAICH News (New York, various issues).

Thailand, Ministry of Education, Department of Secondary Education.
Final Report: Comprehensive School Project No. I, First
Canadian Advisory Team. Thailand, 1969.

_____. Final Report: Comprehensive School Project by Second
Canadian Advisory Team. Thailand, 1971.

Thompson, Kenneth W. "Higher Education for National Development:
One Model for Technical Assistance." New York: International
Council for Educational Development, Occasional Paper no. 5,
November 1972.

Unicef. Strategy for Children: A Study of Unicef Assistance Policies. Report of the Executive Board. New York: United
Nations.

UNITAR. The Brain Drain from 5 Developing Countries: Cameroon,
Colombia, Lebanon, the Philippines, Trinidad and Tobago. New
York: UNITAR Research Report no. 5, 1971.

United Kingdom, Foreign and Commonwealth Office, Overseas De-
velopment Administration Library. Select Bibliography of
British Aid to Developing Countries. London: Her Majesty's
Stationery Office, 1971.

United Kingdom, Ministry of Overseas Development. Education in
Developing Countries: A Review of Current Problems and of
British Aid. London: Her Majesty's Stationery Office, 1970.

United Nations. Assistance for Economic and Social Development Available from the United Nations System. New York: United Nations, 1969 (E/AC.5I/GR/21).

_____. Inducing Social Change in Developing Countries. Prepared by H. Hyman, G. Levine, and C. Wright (67/IV/3).

_____, Center for Economic and Social Information. International Development Strategy for the Second UN Development Decade. New York: United Nations, 1970.

_____, Department of Economic and Social Affairs. New Trends in Service by Youth. New York: United Nations, 1971.

_____. Towards Accelerated Development: Proposals for the Second Development Decade. New York: United Nations, 1970.

United States, Department of State, External Research Division. African Programs of US Organizations: A Selective Directory. Washington, D.C.: Government Printing Office, 1965.

Williams, P. Aid to Education--An Anglo-American Appraisal. Report of a Ditchley Foundation Conference held March 26-29, 1965, Ditchley Park. London: Overseas Development Institute, 1965.

World Bank. Sector Working Paper--Education. December 1974.

World Council of Churches. Development Education--Report of the Consultation Organized in Geneva in May 1969 by the Secretariat of Development Education. Geneva: the Council, 1969.

_____. Service Programme and List of Projects 1973. Geneva: Commission on Inter-Church Aid, Refugee and World Service in cooperation with the Commission on World Mission and Evangelism, 1973.

BOOKS AND MONOGRAPHS

Austruy, Jacques. Le Scandale du Developpement. Commentaries by G. Leduc and J. L. Lebret; analytical bibliography and critique by Guy Caire. Paris: M. Riviere, 1965.

Balogh, Thomas. The Economics of Poverty. London: Weidenfield
and Nicholson, 1966.

Brembeck, C. S., and J. W. Hanson, eds. Education and the Development of Nations. New York: Holt, Rinehart and Winston,
1966.

Butts, R. Freeman. American Education in International Development. New York: Harper and Row, 1963.

Carter, William D. Study Abroad and Educational Development.
New York: IIEP, 1973.

Centre for the Study of Education in Changing Societies. Symposium
on Educational Problems in Developing Countries, Amsterdam,
1968. The Hague, Groningen: Wolters-Noordhoff, 1969.

Cerych, Ladislav. L'Aide Exterieure et la Planification de
l'Education en Cote-d'Ivoire. Paris: Unesco/IIEP, 1967.

_____. The Integration of External Assistance with Educational
Planning in Nigeria. Paris: Unesco/IIEP, 1967.

_____. Problems of Aid to Education in Developing Countries.
New York: Praeger Publishers, 1965.

_____. Former des Hommes: L'Aide a l'Education dans le Tiers
Monde. Paris: Plon, 1965.

Coombs, Philip H. The Fourth Dimension of Foreign Policy: Educational and Cultural Affairs. New York: Council on Foreign
Relations, Harper and Row, 1964.

_____. The World Educational Crisis: A Systems Analysis. New
York: Oxford University Press, 1968.

_____ with Roy C. Prosser and Ahmed Manzoor. New Paths to
Learning for Rural Children and Youth. New York: International Council for Educational Development, 1973.

Crosby, Barbara, and S. J. Smyth, eds. US Non-Profit Organizations, Voluntary Agencies, Missions and Foundations Participating in Technical Assistance Abroad: A Directory. New York:
Technical Assistance Information Clearinghouse, 1971.

Dachoussof, V. Les Moissons et les Hommes: La Cooperation au
    Developpement Rural dans les Pays Non-Industrialises.
    Brussels: Editions de l'Institut de Sociologie, Universite
    Libre de Bruxelles, 1971.

Domergus, M. Le Role et les Methodes de l'Assistance Technique
    dans la Formation des Hommes, in Centre de Formation des
    Experts de la Cooperation Technique Internationale. Paris:
    Stage de Planification des Resources Humaines, 1966.

European Regional Conference of the Society for International Devel-
    opment, Cologne, 1970. Problemes de l'Aide a l'Education
    dans les Pays du Tiers-Monde. Paris: section francaise de
    l'A.D.I., 1970.

Gausi, R. De l'Eau aux Moulins des Pays en Voie de Developpement.
    Lausanne: Editions de l'Imprimerie Vaudoise, 1966.

Gollin, Albert E. Education for National Development: Effects of
    US Technical Training Programs. New York: Praeger Pub-
    lishers, 1969.

Grantin, Lowe J., and T. D. Williams. Seminar on Education and
    Nation-Building in the Third World. Edinburgh: Scottish
    Academy Press, 1971.

Hirschman, Albert O. Universities and Development Assistance
    Abroad. Washington, D.C.: American Council on Education,
    1967.

Inter-University Council for Higher Education Overseas. IUC and
    Related Services: A Guide. New York, 1972.

Klineberg, O. International Exchange in Education, Science and
    Culture: Suggestions for Research. Paris: Mouton, 1966.

Little, I. M. D. Aid to Africa: An Appraisal of UK Policy for Aid
    to Africa South of the Sahara. New York: Overseas Develop-
    ment Institute, Pergamon Press, 1964.

Makulu, H. F. Education, Development and Nation-Building in Inde-
    pendent Africa: A Study of the New Trends and Recent Philosophy
    of Education. London: SCM Press, 1971.

Mende, Tibor. De l'Aide a la Recolonisation: Les Lecons d'un
    Echec. Paris: Editions du Seuil, 1972.

Myrdal, Gunnar. The Challenge of World Poverty. London: Penguin
    Books.

Nasution Amir, H. Foreign Assistance Contribution in Adult Educa-
    tion in Nigeria. Nigeria: Ibadan University, Institute of African
    Education, 1971.

Organization for Economic Cooperation and Development. Aid to
    Education in Less Developed Countries: Note by the Secretariat.
    Paris: OECD, 1971.

_____. Enquete Pilote sur les Activites d'Assistance Technique
    Menees par l'Entreprise Privee. Annexe. Etude de Cas.
    Paris: OECD, 1969.

_____. Evaluating Development Assistance: Problems of Method
    and Organisation. Paris: OECD, 1972.

_____. Foreign Skills and Technical Assistance in Economic De-
    velopment. Paris: OECD, 1965.

_____. Technical Assistance Evaluation Studies: The Evaluation
    of Technical Assistance. Paris: OECD, 1969.

Pearson, Lester B. Partners in Development: Report of the Com-
    mission on International Development. New York: Praeger
    Publishers, 1969.

Phillips, H. M. Planning Educational Assistance for the Second De-
    velopment Decade. Paris: Unesco/IIEP, 1973.

Rossignol, Edouard. Le Developpement du Tiers-Monde: Aide en
    Matiere de Formation Professionnelle et Technique. Paris:
    Association Internationale d'Information Scolaire Universitaire
    et Professionnelle, 1973.

Sachs, Ignacy. La Decouverte du Tiers-Monde. Paris: Flammarion,
    1971.

_____, and Ester Bosrup, eds. Foreign Aid to Newly Independent
    Countries: Problems and Orientations. Paris: Mouton, 1971.

Shields, J. J., Jr. Education in Community Development: Its
    Function in Technical Assistance. New York: Praeger Pub-
    lishers, 1967.

Sinauer, Ernst M. The Role of Communication in International
    Training and Education: Overcoming Barriers to Understanding
    with the Developing Countries. New York: Praeger Publishers,
    1967.

Symonds, Richard, ed. International Targets for Development. New
    York: Harper Colophon Books, Harper and Row, 1970.

Thompson, Kenneth W. Foreign Assistance: A View from the
    Private Sector. London: University of Notre Dame Press,
    1972.

Unesco, International Commission on the Development of Education.
    Learning to Be: The World of Education Today and Tomorrow.
    Paris, London: United Nations, Harrap, 1972.

Unicef. Children, Youth, Women and Development Plans: The Lome
    Conference. Abidjan: Regional Office for West and Central
    Africa, 1972.

United Nations. Symposium on European Cooperation in Training
    Regional Planners from Developing Countries. Stockholm, 1971.
    New York: United Nations, 1972.

Wall, David. The Charity of Nations: The Political Economy of
    Foreign Aid. London: Macmillan, 1973.

White, John. The Politics of Foreign Aid. London: Bodley Head,
    1974.

Williams, P. Aid in Uganda Education. London: Overseas Develop-
    ment Institute, 1966.

World Congress of Comparative Education Societies. Role and
    Rationale for Educational Aid to Developing Countries. Pro-
    ceedings. Ottawa, 1970.

ARTICLES AND JOURNALS

Aubenas, Th. "L'Aide de la Grande-Bretagne au Tiers-Monde."
    Problemes economiques, no. 1 (July 1973): 331.

Cerych, L. "Vers une Strategie de l'Aide Exterieure a l'Education."
    International Review of Education (The Hague) 2, no. 1 (1965).

"Educazione e Assistenza Tecnica." Formazione e lavoro (Rome),
     January-February 1970.

Gant, G. F. "The Institution Building Project." Revue Internationale
     des Sciences Administratives (Brussels) 32, no. 3 (1966).

Myers, R. G. "International Education, Emigration and National
     Policy: A Longitudinal Case Study of Peruvians Trained in the
     USA." Comparative Education Review 17, no. 1 (February 1973).

Perkins, J. S. "Foreign Aid and the Brain Drain." Foreign Affairs
     (New York) 44, no. 4 (July 1966).

Phillips, H. M. "International Aid for Educational Development in
     the Form of Technical Assistance and Real Resources." In
     The Economics of Education, E. A. G. Robinson and J. E.
     Vaizey, eds. London: Macmillan, 1966.

Ripman, Hugh B. "International Financing of Educational Develop-
     ment." In The Economics of Education, E. A. G. Robinson and
     J. E. Vaizey, eds. London: Macmillan, 1966.

H. M. PHILLIPS has worked in the United Kingdom, with the international agencies, and in the developing countries on questions of education, manpower, and development. He was Assistant Secretary, Manpower Department of the Ministry of Labour, before joining the Foreign Office as Permanent Representative for Economic Affairs at the United Nations, and later became Director of Unesco's Analysis Office on the Role of Education and Science in Development, and Head of the Division of Applied Social Sciences.

He has undertaken consultancies and missions for the United Nations, ECLA, the OECD, the World Bank, the IIEP, and the Ford Foundation, as well as Unesco.

He holds an M. A. (Hons.) from the University of Oxford in Philosophy, Politics, and Economics. He is the author of Literacy and Development (Unesco, 1972) and Basic Education: A World Challenge (London: John Wiley, 1975).

FRANCIS J. METHOD is currently Associate Director of the Education Development Center, Newton, Massachusetts, concerned with new program development in the International Area. From 1970 to 1974 he was on the International Division staff of the Ford Foundation in New York. In that capacity he served as an evaluator of educational projects and an analyst of international assistance policy in the educational sector. He also assisted with the development of the Bellagio meetings on Education and Development.

Most of his writing has been internal staff papers. Two recently published examples are "Planning, Research and Development Capabilities in Education" in Education and Development Reconsidered, The Bellagio Conference Papers, F. Champion Ward, editor (New York: Praeger Publishers, 1974) and "Problems of Expanding Assistance to Education," Prospects 5, no. 1 (1975).

Mr. Method has worked and traveled extensively in Africa and other parts of the world. From 1964 to 1969 he worked in Nigeria with the U.S. Peace Corps. He earned his B.A. at the College of St. Thomas, in St. Paul, and his M.A. from the University of Wisconsin.

THE ECONOMICS OF NONFORMAL EDUCATION:
Resources, Costs, and Benefits
                    Manzoor Ahmed

EDUCATION AND DEVELOPMENT RECONSIDERED:
The Bellagio Conference Papers, Ford Foundation/
Rockefeller Foundation Report
                    edited by F. Champion Ward

EDUCATION, MANPOWER, AND DEVELOPMENT
IN SOUTH AND SOUTHEAST ASIA
                    Muhammad Shamsul Huq

EDUCATIONAL PLANNING AND EXPENDITURE
DECISIONS IN DEVELOPING COUNTRIES:
With a Malaysian Case Study
                    Robert W. McMeekin, Jr.

HIGHER EDUCATION IN DEVELOPING NATIONS:
A Selected Bibliography, 1969-1974
                    Philip G. Altbach and
                    David H. Kelly

THE MAOIST EDUCATIONAL REVOLUTION
                    Theodore Hsi-en Chen

391